G000093720

Digital Culture & Society

Vol. 3, Issue 2/2017

Anna Lisa Ramella, Asko Lehmuskallio,
Tristan Thielmann, Pablo Abend (eds.)
Mobile Digital Practices

The journal is edited by
Annika Richterich, Karin Wenz, Pablo Abend,
Mathias Fuchs, Ramón Reichert

Editorial Board
Maria Bakardjieva, Brian Beaton, David Berry, Jean Burgess,
Mark Coté, Colin Cremin, Sean Cubitt, Mark Deuze, José van
Dijck, Delia Dumitrica, Astrid Ensslin, Sonia Fizek, Federica
Frabetti, Richard A. Grusin, Orit Halpern, Irina Kaldrack,
Wendy Hui Kyong Chun, Denisa Kera, Lev Manovich, Janet H.
Murray, Jussi Parikka, Lisa Parks, Christiane Paul, Dominic
Pettman, Rita Raley, Richard Rogers, Julian Rohrhuber,
Marie-Laure Ryan, Mirko Tobias Schäfer, Jens Schröter, Trebor
Scholz, Tamar Sharon, Roberto Simanowski, Nathaniel Tkacz,
Nanna Verhoeff, Geoffrey Winthrop-Young, Sally Wyatt

[transcript]

This publicaton was produced by the DFG Research Training Group 1769 "Locating Media" at the University of Siegen with funding by the Deutsche Forschungsgemeinschaft (German Research Foundation).

Bibliographic information published by the Deutsche Nationalbibliothek
The Deutsche Nationalbibliothek lists this publication in the Deutsche National-bibliografie; detailed bibliographic data are available on the Internet at http:// dnb.d-nb.de

© 2017 transcript Verlag, Bielefeld

All rights reserved. No part of this book may be reprinted or reproduced or utilized in any form or by any electronic, mechanical, or other means, now known or hereafter invented, including photocopying and recording, or in any information storage or retrieval system, without permission in writing from the publisher.

Cover layout: Kordula Röckenhaus, Bielefeld
Typeset: Michael Rauscher, Bielefeld

ISSN 2364-2114
eISSN 2364-2122
Print-ISBN 978-3-8376-3821-9
PDF-ISBN 978-3-8394-3821-3

Content

Introduction
Mobile Digital Practices.
Situating People, Things, and Data

Anna Lisa Ramella, Asko Lehmuskallio, Tristan Thielmann,
and Pablo Abend

Mobile. Digital. Practices. Three concepts that need to be disentangled. Let us start with the last one, since the term 'practices' denotes the unit of analysis in this volume. According to Nick Couldry, who argues for practice-based media research, a focus on practices entails investigation of 'what people do with media' (Couldry 2004; 2010: 38). While this seems like a simple call to look at the actual handling of technology and interaction with it, the theoretical and methodological consequences are far-reaching. Media in this regard can no longer be thought of as a unit of analysis in the form of a closed device, product, or text unit. Hence, a practice-based approach shifts the centre of media research, moving it away from studying devices and media text to examining an 'open set of practices relating to, or oriented around, media' (Couldry 2004: 117). This instructive claim leads to diverse difficulties and uncertainties. What constitutes a practice? How do practices differ from actions? Where and when do practices begin, and when and where do they end? On what scales do practices operate, and are there hierarchies of practices?

This uncertainty and openness extends to the other two words from the title also, which were added in an attempt to narrow the scope of practices dealt with here; 'digital', referring to a specific set of media that is not 'analogue', but also not necessarily online, and 'mobile', seeking to draw out differentiations in the way these digitalities move and are moved by practices of media use as well as their affordances. The frequent use of ideas such as digital age, digitalisation, and digitality notwithstanding, it is by no means clear in every instance what makes a practice 'digital'. What are the specifics of a digital practice? From what point onward is a practice digital, and when does it cease to be digital? And then there is the general mobility of practices, which is of particular concern here. Does mobility put practices 'in motion', or is it rather more a condition for stabilising practices? What is it that mobilises practices in the first place? Are mobile practices different in some way from immobile practices, or can a practice ever be immobile? What is the relation between a mobile device, a mobile practice and the mobility of data itself?

The lowest common denominator for research into practices seems to be a reliance on empirical analysis, with a tight focus on the material studied. Method-

DOI 10.14361/dcs-2017-0202

ologically, particular interest is directed to *in situ* and *in actu* observations, mainly because of the public nature of the practices. The methodological claim is of observing and participating in real-world doings and sayings in the actual context and while they are executed. Therefore, the study of practices entails grounding theoretical statements in observations and following the actors and their work in the world. Couldry's call to study '[w]hat [...] people do with media' needs to be expanded if we wish to examine what people and media do together. Accordingly, we also have to take into account how humans and other humans, humans and non-humans, and non-humans and non-humans co-operate in various situations.

While the turn towards practices is relatively new for media studies, other disciplines have long focused on in-depth study of what people actually do with each other and with the artefacts, animals, and other – fictitious and spiritual – beings around them. Cultural anthropology, religious studies, science and technology studies, and the computer-supported co-operative work discipline are among the fields that have cultivated this kind of work, although often lacking explicit analytical use of concepts such as medium or media. Media studies again has turned its attention toward the role of media and mediations, especially with regard to how particular materialities and media infrastructures play a part in structuring what people do with, around, and through media.

While classical media theory (e. g., the work of Marshall McLuhan in Canada and Friedrich Kittler in Germany) is often cited in support of technological 'success stories' in which new technologies ultimately foster cognitive and social advances, or at times fail to do so (Schüttpelz 2018), social theories of media tend to see media mainly as a result of social interactions, taking supposedly unmediated face-to-face situations as a starting point. Placing focus on media practices is one way to take into account the roles played by technologies in situationally co-constructing social associations while allowing an emphasis on the importance of social circumstances in the formations of particular technologies. These technologies are often referred to as 'media', until, with time, they lose their 'medium-specificity'. Thus, practice-theoretical approaches invite one to consider the in-betweens of social and technological accounts. A key interest is in identifying, paying attention to, and describing what human and non-human actors do, then taking this as a basis for analysis (Schatzki 2001: 14). While some practice-theory scholars maintain that a focus on practices enables one to link these observations to larger social and cultural contexts, others posit that scale (i. e., 'micro', 'macro', 'local', or 'global') is created within practices and is not available for analysis outside them.

In light of the premise that practices can be made visible and are therefore to a certain extent public, practice-theoretical approaches make a strong epistemological claim suggesting to refrain from internalism (Swidler 2001: 83 f.) and focusing on observable changes through "bodily doings and sayings" (Schatzki 2002: 72) within practices instead. Although speech acts within practices are important, a core focus in practice-theoretical studies is on the ways in which bodies are connected to their surroundings – e. g., how human bodies and media technologies are used for participation in social situations. This entails focusing on skills and on tacit and embodied knowledge, which can be performed consistently until they become a routine and manifested in practice. Practice-theoretical approaches thus are concerned with the physical execution of practices in a material world. This emphasis on the materiality of encounters between actors is particularly visible in the influence of science and technology research on laboratories (Latour/Woolgar 1979), on the trading floor (Knorr Cetina/Preda 2004), and within the semiotic materialism of actor-network-theory (Latour 1991).

Being a 'field of practice' (Schatzki 2001: 11) itself, practice theory does not have a single set of clearly defined theoretical boundaries; rather, it is best understood as a bundle of theoretical positions with certain family resemblance (Reckwitz 2002: 244). Bourdieu's field theory, Goffman's interactionism, Garfinkel's ethnomethodology, and Latour's actor-network-theory all focus on practices, just as much as, for instance, Foucault's and Butler's work does. While all positions have their specific and distinct emphases, they do point towards a need to study 'how things get done'. One scholar with this in mind, Andrew Pickering, suggests: "All that one can do is register the visible and specific intertwinings of the human and the nonhuman. But this is enough; what more could one want or need?" (Pickering 2001: 176).

Practice theory initially was developed most strongly within social theory, which is why there is a certain emphasis on the (human) body and a tendency to privilege the doings and sayings of human actors even though its history could have encompassed greater focus on the 'doings and sayings' of specific technologies as well. Pickering, for instance, describes the laboratory equipment as a kind of counterpart imposing a "dialectic of resistance and accommodation" (Pickering 1995: 22) on human agency. In practice-theoretical studies it is usually the human subject who uses or utilises technical objects; an encounter that over time can shape practice. This overall focus on routines and ritual when one is examining interactions between humans and humans or humans and non-humans leaves aside much of the dynamics-rich landscape we particularly want to address in this volume. We wish to highlight practices' instability and the role of movement in possibly stabilising them, along with the assumption that practices are shaped first and foremost by the mutual movement of people, things, and data.

Practice-theoretical work on media has been developed in tandem with increasing focus on 'digital media'. While the computer has been posited to be a 'universal machine', or to constitute 'universal media', the difficulty of describing and delineating the boundaries of digitally networked computing has led various scholars to focus on how digital devices are constructed for and react to specific kinds of practices. Understood in this vein, digital devices are often only temporary media that need to be regularly updated and have limited life spans. Accordingly, the notion of a medium is more difficult to apply to forms of computing if one does not understand the practices within which a device, software, or a specific algorithm performs its mediation.

With our explicit focus on (mobile digital) practices, we do not want to give the reader *ab initio* definitions of the three words in the volume's title. Instead, we believe that each author's work contributes to the ongoing discussions and definition efforts surrounding mobile digital practices, and each article is a step towards answering some of the questions posed above. Rather than provide a full review of the existing literature and build our specific theoretical framework, which we as editors have expounded on elsewhere from our individual perspectives (e.g., Thielmann/Schüttpelz 2013; Lehmuskallio/Gómez Cruz 2016; Ramella 2017; Abend 2018), we wish to devote the space below to giving the reader an overview of how each article tackles the question of what constitutes mobile digital practices. Rather than offering mere summaries of the contributions, we try to carve out the specificities of the practices involved, and how they address the relation between digital and mobile practices. As the articles span across an intertwined spectrum of digitality, mobility and diverse actors of practices, rather than picking them apart in clusters, we have implemented a dramaturgy along those figures into the order of the content: starting with digital, offline data, moved primarily by the mobility of people, we pass via parallelised movements of people and online data towards data mobilities that move people. This way, the three main threads of this issue – digitality, mobility and practices – are made visible regarding their particular emphases as they transgress each article.

In 'Small Village, Big Data', Geoffrey Hobbis describes the sharing of digital media files in the Solomon Islands. Especially in rural areas, smartphones are not used primarily to go online at any time, anywhere. Internet connections' high cost and frequent unavailability have led to their use predominantly as mobile (offline) multimedia-players. Equipped with MicroSD cards, they are being used to store, transport, and consume films and photographs that, after being downloaded in urban areas, are brought to remote villages, mostly by temporary-labour migrants. The article traces how such files are downloaded on stationary devices or directly bought on MicroSDs in urban areas before the smartphone is used as a vehicle to transport them further. Thus, the mobility of the data depends on the physical movement of the workers as they transport the memory cards to the offline smartphone users in the isolated villages. Instead of being constantly online, the mobile phones' users 'bring the Internet to the village'. The author shows that the data thus transported can spark controversy, since, for example, data rendered on mobile-phone screens as foreign visual media get associated again with urban life; viewers connect the onscreen content with morally ambivalent lifestyles. Moreover, since mobile devices form a pathway to highly privatised forms of consumption and half of the islands' smartphones are owned by women, media consumption cannot be controlled by the male-dominated village elite any longer (p. 32). This situation challenges traditional gender hierarchies. Hobbis highlights the intertwining of physical movement with the mobility of data, which often goes less studied and explored. Instead of directly sharing digital content via a communications network, the islanders share files via a sequence of online and offline practices in and along movements of labourers. While digitality affords the transportation of large multimedia files and collections, the conveying of these files from urban to rural areas is dependent on the physical movement of the migrant workers travelling back and forth. Focusing on moral controversies, Hobbis provides insights into the impact of micro-level sharing practices on the larger social structure of the villages.

The paper 'In the Footsteps of Smartphone Users', by Anne Ganzert et al., examines the specific forms of spatio-temporal sociality brought about by practices of playing augmented-reality games such as Pokémon Go and Ingress. The authors are able to analyse these by referring to theoretical approaches based on the work of media-studies scholars such as Sybille Krämer (1998, 2007) on 'traces' and Michaela Ott (2015) on 'dividuation' to inform the model they develop of 'deferred communities'. Differences in emphasis between AR games in their central motivation with regard to the postulation 'I was here' serve as a guide throughout the paper: the authors employ analytical separation among 'I' (the player-subject), 'was' (the temporality of the traces and marks), and 'here' (the spatiality of the game). With the games, GPS tracking is used to open the door to a 'deferred community' where virtual traces of players both absent and present are combined with one's own physical path. This results in an understanding of digital mobility as something at the threshold of where human user, smartphone, and app used meet.

Donald Anderson's article 'Spatial Labour, Mobile Digital Platforms, and Soft Cabs' offers reflection on the development of e-hailing services as digital labour platforms, still in their infancy, and how the practices tied in with these transform mobile work through digital mediations between customers and workers. Anderson directs special attention to the conflict that arises from digital labour platforms interfering with social space, thereby underscoring the spatial character of the work that digital platforms are used to target. Here, mobility becomes visible as a constitutive aspect of the development and expansion of smartphone use, creating affordances for broadening the range of online services offered by digital labour platforms. By choosing to call these services 'soft cabs', Anderson takes into account the software-based meter that the workers use and differentiates these cabs from taxicabs, which took their name from the taximeter used to measure the cost of a trip. By characterising the digital labour platforms as mediators in a Latourian sense (Latour 2005) and not as intermediaries – because of the controlling qualities implemented and used by the platforms to mediate the information shared between customer and worker – he articulates how these platforms must be viewed as work of social reproduction in a digital context, made possible by the mobility of the smartphone.

By addressing Sinophone digital practices, Jamie Coates, with his piece 'So Hot Right Now: Reflections on Virality and Sociality from Transnational Digital China', reminds us that in researching any kind of media practices, we must always consider local contexts. His article deftly sheds light on how alterity becomes apparent when one looks more closely at the terms used to describe digital phenomena and how these limits are demarcated by specific mobilities between specific localities and socialities. Thereby, the article combines reflections on the digital and the mobile in a way that makes explicit how the digital is understood differently through the mobile: his interlocutors, already in a state of mobility by virtue of leading transnational lives as members of a Sinophone community in Japan, describe the virality of a digital phenomenon precisely by the way it moves – it is the circulation of a digital image via digital platforms that constitutes its virality, thereby bringing together digitality and mobility under a single term. It is important to point out at the same time, however, that the idea *re* or *huo*, translated as 'fever' or 'heat', does not proceed from description of digital phenomena; it must be seen rather as a 'digital amplification of a pre-existing social practice' (p. 82). Coates carefully analyses how phenomena emerging from digital and mobile practices are perceived in terms of 'sociothermic affects' (Chau 2008) in the Sinophone world, while in Anglo-European discourse they are translated with terms derived from biological processes, such as 'viral' or 'meme'. Yet, as Coates points out, both seem to transplant a notion of 'contagiousness' into understandings of media practices. He therefore recommends an etic distinction between the terms 'viral' and 'virality', the latter pointing to the importance of affective qualities for spreading of media content.

In the article by Samuel Collins, 'Twitter in Place: Examining Seoul's Gwanghwamun Plaza through Social Media Activism', practices of claiming urban space through mobile social-media practices, particularly via Twitter, are given the focus. In this case, digital mobile practices are involved in site-specific redefinition of the Gwanghwamun Plaza, framing this square in Seoul as a space of protest. Pointing to the connection between social-media practices and place, Collins shows how, even when geolocation is not enabled, tweets always are posted in a certain time and space. Drawing together data visualisation of Twitter traffic during the protests at the Gwanghwamun Plaza in 2016, he analyses how the particular practices involved as diverse participants tweeted at the plaza – protesters, conservative groups, tourists, merchants, commuters, and bots – together have shaped the many meaning of this public space. Creating what he calls a 'networked representation of Gwanghwamun Plaza' (p. 99), Collins renders the digitality and mobility of their social practice visible. Thereby, the article provides a thoughtful analysis of the relationship between social media and urban space.

In 'Screen Screen Tourism', Marion Schulze points out that a practice turn in media studies also corresponds to a changing perspective on analysis of the activities of fans of television series. In addition to well-researched online participatory practices such as blogging or writing fan fiction, her practice-based approach highlights how media content such as films and television series engenders and encourages actual physical mobilities. Discussed under the umbrella term 'media tourism' or 'screen tourism', this line of research shows that 'people who engaged heavily with media texts became highly mobile in visiting actual filming locations' (p. 124). But people also are growing increasingly mobile in browsing information online in order to find details about production sites and in virtually travelling to such locations on digital maps and virtual globes. Using the example of Korean drama series, Schulze reveals the complex ways in which digitally mediated mobilities intersect with physical travel to the sites of production. Moreover, Schulze shows how physical travel gets mediated again when fans use digital maps and globes to engage in practices of what she terms 'screen screen tourism'. Fans engage in onscreen travels to gain information on physical locations, which they then virtually navigate. The article makes clear that travels encouraged by media-related text transcend the boundary between 'physical' and 'virtual' mobility when online and offline navigation constantly inform each other. For the fans of Korean drama series, primary importance is accorded not to getting a glimpse of the physical set but to finding the place bearing the closest resemblance to the location shown in the series. The 'geographic familiarity' can be found either online or offline.

Maria Schreiber focuses on the socio-technological specifics of mobile photo-sharing practices in her article 'Audiences, Aesthetics and Affordances: Analysing Practices of Visual Communication on Social Media'. She analyses examples of networked visual communication of a group of female teenagers in Vienna, Austria. The teenagers use platforms such as Snapchat and Instagram as they develop an 'interpersonal, mediated practice of communication that always takes place in regard to specific audiences by means of aesthetics and is embedded in technical affordances of platforms' (p. 144). The paper shows how new mobile visual communication styles emerge from the interplay of expectations surrounding the targeted audience, aesthetic decisions on what to show and how to show it, and the affordances of the apps and platforms. Through these, the material agency of a particular platform influences the styles of visual communication. Schreiber gives examples of decisions about a photo's value and 'beauty' that are based on the social network targeted and the respective audience. Since most platforms afford circulation of the image data beyond a user's immediate circle of friends and family, public and interpersonal communication intertwine. In networked environments, contexts collapse, audiences get renegotiated, and the act of sharing has to be considered anew. Established boundaries between interpersonal and public communication, alongside traditional practices of social inclusion and exclusion, undergo transformations as visual communication starts to take place across diverse social media platforms. Schreiber illustrates how these novel practices of visual communication emerge in relation to the social settings of production, with regard to the intended audience and in negotiation with the affordances of the mobile phone and software used.

In 'Mobile Mediated Visualities: An Empirical Study of Visual Practices on Instagram', Elisa Serafinelli and Mikko Villi speak to the benefits of studying mobile visual communication from a practice-based perspective. By focusing on the mediation of practices and the role that visual communication plays in it, they discuss four elements that play a significant role in the lives of their study participants. Firstly, the mobility of mobile phones used for photo-sharing allows 'on-the-go' capturing of images, which enables creation of spheres of connection between the photographer and his or her broader social network. The apps used for sharing these photos, such as Instagram, provide a framework, and at times a reason, for taking and sharing photos in the first place. Secondly, motivations for photo-sharing give orientation to specific photographic actions. Taking and sharing pictures yields feelings of personal satisfaction, calls for reciprocal inter-actions, and provides an avenue to experiencing new kinds of images. Thirdly, the sharing is carefully orchestrated, providing rhythms of photographic expressions, which may be followed very strictly, as some participants reported doing. Finally, the use of the devices evolves over time, changing as people become more expe-rienced in taking pictures, learning what kinds of images are liked, and hence providing an opportunity to incorporate digital devices, with a particular fit, into day-to-day life.

Stefan Werning takes a tack different from this by focusing his discussion of social-media platforms on the uses of Facebook's official API and on IFTTT, a service for app 'remixes' via Facebook. Collecting 490 IFTTT applets and 378 mash-ups on ProgrammableWeb, Werning proceeded to analyse the kinds of applets created for automating tasks performed via social media, such as sending birthday greetings, sharing Instagram photos, making Periscope broadcasts over Facebook, or sharing a random Wikipedia article every Wednesday. These auto-mated tasks are highly relevant for mobile digital practices, because they momen-tarily stabilise uncertain situations by allowing repetition of specific kinds of actions. Both the mobility of particular data flows and their automation are part of co-construction and joint maintenance of social norms. As the examples above show, the tasks automated are relatively simple and usually harmless (though automated repetition of certain actions may have undesired social consequences). With APIs tending to limit the kinds of applets that are actually supported on social-media platforms, Werning shows convincingly that automation of mobile digital practices is very much directed in specific ways. Not all kinds of acts may be repeated.

Julia Hildebrand's paper 'Situating Hobby Drone Practices' calls into question the concept of cybermobilities with regard to the heterogeneous assemblage of human and non-human actors in motion. From this standpoint, recreational drone practice is described not only in terms of mobilities but also with regard to immo-bilities, especially the unstable speed of the drone flight and the complementary steadiness of the pilot's body on the other side of the picture. At the same time, these mobile digital practices are characterised by the recordings and 'screen outs', which recursively influence hobby drone practice itself. It is of particular significance that the article describes considerably different digital practice in offline vs. online environments. While drone hobbyists most often keep a 'low profile' in the physical space by adjusting their flight in respect for the presence of others or by manoeuvring the drone very carefully, pilots try to present a 'high profile' in the virtual sphere by sharing their images and demonstrating the visibility of their practical actions. Therefore, this mobile digital practice can be understood as a risk-and-return process that is characterised by greater 'social investment' within the online world.

Rashmi M. offers a conceptualisation of mobile phones as digital technologies rather than communication technologies, in his short article 'The Inchoate Field of Digital Offline: A Reflection on Studying Mobile Media Practices of Digital Subalterns in India'. While, as he points out, mobile phones have from their very beginnings been meant to be digital personal assistants rather than mere communication devices, they are appropriated in other ways. Here, he considers the offline digital practices of 'digital subalterns' in Bangalore, India. These 'low-end informal-sector urban working populations' (p. 221), often are unable to afford a mobile Internet connection and therefore use their mobile devices mostly offline for audio and video consumption. With large numbers of people there gaining access to digital technology through mobile-phone interfaces, Rashmi offers grounds for his argument that mobile phones may be better considered digital media complexes and infrastructure than communication devices. He uses his case study to introduce methodological considerations, which include the accountability of digital data not being a given, on account of the offline field. Much depends on offline data collection tied to inchoate yet patterned practices that are digitally invisible; unlike the structured practices afforded by such elements as social-media platforms, which media researchers in many other settings can benefit from.

Cherry Baylosis argues that the intersection of digital practices, mobility, and mad studies is useful for opening possibilities for research that delves into alternatives to asymmetrical accounts of experiences of madness. By focusing particularly on voice as the capacity to self-represent, she strives to question dominant power relations between those who are labelled 'mentally ill' and those who do the labelling. When one privileges expert voices, alternative readings of what counts as mad are not taken into account. For example, the Hearing Voices Network presents auditory hallucinations as meaningful forms of human experience, which the group argues do not need to be medicalised. The opportunity to create, publish, and share alternative voices digitally with ease allows a variety of actors, including those called mentally ill, to broaden our understandings of madness. In focusing on digital practices, Baylosis seeks to draw attention to the potential of voice by using relatively new technologies.

'Mobile Freelancers without a Stable Workplace', by Nadia Hakim Fernandez, is about a research project on mobile labour. Taking a reflexive methodological approach, the author uses her experience as a mobile academic freelancer as a starting point. Recalling her struggle to find an adequate workplace while travelling between cities and moving about within the same city, Fernandez reflects on the epistemological conditions of fieldwork in today's mobile and precarious work arrangements. Her auto-ethnographic account recounts the struggle of an academic to find the right workplace. The methodological framework is extended with digital geolocalised data gathered via the participant's mobile devices. The mixed-methods approach allows for thick and contextualised description of nomadic freelance labour 'through the lens of the labourer's experience' (p. 238). The approach is well in line with constructivist practice-based thinking, which builds on the premise that a field is not a given that can easily be discovered but a phenomenon constructed by the researcher. The piece highlights that the 'technological landscape' (p. 239) inhabited by researcher and participants alike is part of the construction. In this context, Fernandez highlights that the terms 'online' and 'offline' do not refer to separate locations within a field; they are articulations of work practices and affordances of locations. Mobile freelancers cross geographical and political boundaries and can be described by a shared set of practices deployed to make a new workplace daily.

The contributions to the special issue provide numerous insights into the reciprocal relations among mobility, the digital, and practices. The various papers show how inherently unstable interactions are situationally stabilised with a directionality provided by movement, with the momentary inscriptions and renderings created by digital means. A property specific to digital mobility is its relational correspondence to physical movement in space (see the papers of Anderson, Collins, Fernandez, Ganzert et al., Hildebrand, Hobbis, and Schulze in this issue). For mobile digital practices, this implies that we are not dealing simply with parallelism and interdependency between online and offline practices. Frequently, there is sequentiality of practices, which shift from a digital space into a non-digital space, and vice versa.

Hence, 1) digitality is a condition of possibility for contemporary mobile practices. At the same time, 2) mobility is a condition of possibility for the emergence and formation of a digital practice – e. g., as photo-sharing practices are shaped by affordances in motion, as shown in this issue by Schreiber and by Serafinelli and Villi. Lastly, 3) digitality is not something that is present or absent *per se*; it must be practically accomplished at individual level and also in co-operation, as is demonstrated in the paper by Fernandez. We find that a triangular relation of reciprocal contingency emerges that characterises mobile digital practices.

From this perspective, it is not surprising that the part played by the digital in the authors' contributions pulls in several directions. For example, Coates sees the digital as leading to reinforcement of pre-existing social practices, and Collins distinguishes among digital, spatial, and social practices, while Rashmi describes digital technologies as rendering patterned practices invisible.

On account of the heterogeneity of the phenomena described as mobile digital practices, a practice theory of digital media faces serious challenges. Couldry, for example, has listed various 'digital practices', connected to media in varying degrees. He starts with 1) 'acts aimed specifically at media', proceeds via 2) 'acts performed through media', and moves on to 3) 'acts whose preconditions are media' (Couldry 2012: 57). He includes among these basic digital practices 'searching and search-enabling', 'showing and being shown', 'presencing', and 'archiving' but also rather habitual practices of 'keeping up with the news', 'commentary', 'keeping all channels open', and 'screening out'. Even though these are rather general practices, they do show that particular media can condense and explicate practices. They are part of unifying and simplifying machinery, since media tend to transduce only certain elements of a complex and variation-rich practice – that is, they represent on one hand and transform on the other (see Kitchin/Dodge 2011: 71 ff.). Therefore, practices can never be conceived of without their supporting or enabling media, something that is increasingly discussed by means of the notion of infrastructure (Gillespie/Boczkowski/Foot 2014).

Many of the theoretical media practice deliberations are focused on certain digital technologies, such as those of various social-media sites, that appear to provide a basis for 'digital practices'. Such an approach does have the disadvantage of not being able to explain the emergence of new practices, dysfunctional practices, or workarounds. Therefore, scholarship focusing on digital practices must address the multitude of ways in which the digital is played out, as the contributions in this issue show. Thereby, analysis of mobile digital practices can add to our understanding of the emergence of significant technological changes unfolding through the history, development, and genealogy of digital media.

The special-issue contributions show that especially 'searching and search-enabling' (see Schulze) but also 'showing and being shown' (see Schreiber and Serafinelli/Villi) are significant for mobile digital practices. Both are practical actions characterisable by ambiguity between closed/private and broadcast/public communication. 'Presencing' (see Baylosis), 'archiving' (see Ganzert et al.), and 'screening out' (see Hobbis) also play a significant role. At the same time, some practices may no longer be questioned, since they seem to have become a given part and background condition of all mobile digital practices for some, as in the case of 'keeping all channels open'.

This leads us back to the more fundamental question of what a 'media practice theory' in the future may be, beyond the initial focus on media or digital technologies. One possible path forward has been laid with the ethnomethodology of Garfinkel. Considering his praxeological approach, one can argue that mobile digital practices unfold a permanent switch back and forth between documentary and procedural aspects as demonstrated in Schulze's paper, where media text offers reasoned accounts for imaginable journeys that need not have anything to do with mobile practices carried out *in vivo*. In their procedural form, media are much more resistant and addressed as a constituent 'embedded' detail of a spatial practice. As Garfinkel (1996) observed:

Under conditions of procedural description the map's [or, more generally, any mobile medium's] properties of order are unmediated, directly and immediately observed territorial objects. These territorial objects are observed in and as of a phenomenal field of ordered details of recurrence and generality – i.e. of structures.

The assortative properties of the media are linked chiastically and are inseparable from the spatial practices of a mobile human body. Hence, as many of the case studies here show, the production and distribution of media content takes place as a negotiation of the imagined addressee, specific aesthetics, and affordances, which all are in motion.

When we take a much more general view of media as practice, it can be argued that the future will see a need for analysing mobile digital practices such as 'searching and search-enabling', 'showing and being shown', 'presencing', 'archiving', and 'screening out' each in its specific documentary and procedural dimension. Future research based on the 'Lebenswelt Pair' of document + procedure might in this way bring a mobile digital praxeology into bloom.

References

Abend, Pablo (2018): "From map reading to geobrowsing: Methodological reconsiderations for Geomedia." In: Tilo Felgenhauer/Karsten Gabler (eds.), Geographies of Digital Culture, London/New York: Routledge, 97–111, (forthcoming).

Chau, Adam Yuet (2008): "The Sensorial Production of the Social." In: Ethnos: Journal of Anthropology 73, pp. 485–504.

Couldry, Nick (2010): "Theorising Media as Practice." In: Birgit Bräuchler/John Postill (eds.), Theorising Media and Practice, New York/Oxford: Berghahn Books, pp. 35–54.

Couldry, Nick (2012): Media, Society, World: Social Theory and Digital Media Practice, Malden: Polity.

Garfinkel, Harold (1996): Notes Comparing Two Analytic Formats of Occasion Maps and Way Finding Journeys: 'Documentary' and 'Essentially Procedural'. Unpublished manuscript. University of California at Los Angeles, 24 February.

Gillespie, Tarleton/Boczkowski, Pablo J./Foot, Kirsten A. (eds.) (2014): Media technologies. Essays on communication, materiality and society, Cambridge/London: The MIT Press.

Kitchin, Rob; Dodge, Martin (2011): Code/Space: Software and Everyday Life, Cambridge: MIT Press.

Knorr Cetina, Karin; Preda, Alex (eds.) (2004): The Sociology of Financial Markets, Oxford: Oxford University Press.

Krämer, Sybille (1998): "Das Medium als Spur und als Apparat." In: Sybille Krämer (ed.), Medien, Computer, Realität. Wirklichkeitsvorstellungen und Neue Medien, Frankfurt am Main: Suhrkamp, pp. 73–94.

Krämer, Sybille (2007): Was also ist eine Spur? Und worin besteht ihre epistemologische Rolle? Eine Bestandsaufnahme. In: Sybille Krämer/Werner Kogge/Gernot Grube (eds.), Spur. Spurenlesen als Orientierungstechnik und Wissenskunst, Frankfurt am Main: Suhrkamp, pp. 11–33.

Latour, Bruno (1991): "Technology Is Society Made Durable." In: John Law (ed.), A Sociology of Monsters: Essays on Power, Technology, and Domination, London/New York: Routledge, pp. 103–132.

Latour, Bruno (2005): Reassembling the Social: An Introduction to Actor-Network-Theory, New York: Oxford University Press.

Latour, Bruno/Woolgar, Steve (1979): Laboratory Life: The Construction of Scientific Facts, Beverly Hills, California: SAGE.

Lehmuskallio, Asko/Gómez Cruz, Edgar (2016): "Why Material Visual Practices?" In: Edgar Gómez Cruz/Asko Lehmuskallio (eds.), Digital Photography and Everyday Life: Empirical Studies on Material Visual Practices, London/New York: Routledge, pp. 1–16.

Ott, Michaela (2015): Dividuationen. Theorien der Teilhabe, Berlin: b.-books.

Pickering, Andrew (1995): The Mangle of Practice: Time, Agency, and Science, Chicago: University of Chicago Press.

Pickering, Andrew (2001): "Practice and Posthumanism: Social Theory and a History of Agency." In: Theodore R. Schatzki, Karin Knorr Cetina, Eike von Savigny (eds.), The Practice Turn in Contemporary Theory, London/New York: Routledge, pp. 172–183.

Ramella, Anna Lisa (2017): "Medienpraktiken 'on the road': Social Media im Kontext von Musikmarketing." In: Mark Dang-Anh, Simone Pfeifer, Clemens Reisner, Lisa Villioth, (eds.): Medienpraktiken: Situieren, erforschen, reflektieren. In: Navigationen: Zeitschrift für Medien- und Kulturwissenschaften, 17/1, pp. 37–54.

Reckwitz, Andreas (2002): "Toward a Theory of Social Practice: A Development in Culturalist Theorizing." In: European Journal of Social Theory 5/2, pp. 243–263.

Schatzki, Theodore R. (2001): "Introduction: Practice Theory." In: Theodore R. Schatzki/Karin Knorr Cetina/Eike von Savigny (eds.), The Practice Turn in Contemporary Theory, London/New York: Routledge, pp. 10–23.

Schatzki, Theodore R. (2002): The Site of the Social: A Philosophical Account of the Constitution of Social Life and Change, University Park, Pennsylvania: Pennsylvania State University Press.

Schüttpelz, Erhard (2018): "Epilogue: Media Theory before and after the Practice Turn." In: Ulrike Bergermann/Monika Dommann/Erhard Schüttpelz/Jeremy

Stolow/Nadine Taha (eds), Connect and Divide: The Practice Turn in Media Studies (proceedings of the 3rd DFG conference on media studies), Zürich/ Berlin: Diaphanes; Chicago: University of Chicago Press, (forthcoming).

Swidler, Ann (2010): "What Anchors Cultural Practices?" In: Birgit Bräuchler/John Postill (eds.), Theorising Media and Practice, New York/Oxford: Berghahn Books, pp. 83–101.

Thielmann, Tristan/Schüttpelz, Erhard (eds.) (2013): Akteur-Medien-Theorie, Bielefeld: transcript.

Field Research
and Case Studies

The MicroSDs of Solomon Islands

An Offline Remittance Economy of Digital Multi-Media

Geoffrey Hobbis

Abstract

Based on twelve months of multi-sited ethnographic fieldwork, this article investigates the offline circulation of digital media files in Solomon Islands. It explores how circular temporary labour migration drives the acquisition, movement and consumption of digital media, and how these media files contribute to moral controversies. Before the rapid proliferation of mobile phones in 2010, people living in rural environments had limited access to electronic media and the male village elite controlled access to this media, especially foreign movies. Mobile phones, on the other hand, are individually owned and encourage private consumption of media files. At the same time, migrants living in urban areas can easily obtain digital media files and have started integrating them into remittance networks. Access to electronic media in rural areas has exploded. Because foreign visual media are associated with urban, morally ambivalent lifestyles, this proliferation has also fuelled moral uncertainties among rural residents. This article suggests that to understand these moral controversies, and their significance in contemporary Solomon Islands, it is crucial to account for the mobility of digital media files offline and alongside the movements of temporary labourers.

Introduction

Located in the Lau Lagoon on the north eastern tip of Province of Malaita in Solomon Islands, a small islands developing state in the South Pacific, the village of Gwou'ulu is crossing the digital divide. In 2010 mobile phones started to trickle into the village, and by the time of my fieldwork (February 2014 to February 2015) they were nearly omnipresent in daily life. In 2014 Gwou'ulu was home to some 250 adults who owned approximately 100 mobile phones, at least seventy of which were Internet-enabled smartphones.[1] This sudden proliferation of digital information communication technologies (ICTs) can be linked to the arrival of a second

---

1   The number of functioning mobile phones in Gwou'ulu fluctuates significantly. They break relatively easily and repair options are limited to urban centers (cf.

DOI 10.14361/dcs-2017-0203

telecommunications company, Bmobile (since mid-2014, Bmobile/Vodafone), that ended the monopoly of the national telecommunication provider, OurTelekom. The cost of producing these and auxiliary technologies such as solar power units dropped at around the same time. This confluence of factors allowed for a variety of mobile phones to become more affordable and therefore more accessible, from basic handsets to the smartphones preferred by younger generations, with all phones sharing three core features: they allow for making phone calls, for texting, and for consuming and at times producing multi-media files (photographs, videos and music).

Mobile telephony has become integral for maintaining kinship networks, for coordinating shipping and travel between village and town, and for keeping the family informed of the welfare of family members living in both urban and rural settlements. But these activities cost money for minutes, texts and data, and Gwou'ulu residents have little access to the cash economy. Most families rely on self-provisioning activities. Men fish in and beyond the adjacent lagoon. Women grow root crops such as cassava and exchange the fish caught by men at regular "bush markets," often directly for food crops or for money that is then immediately spent on food sold at the market. To access more flexible cash, e.g., to pay for school fees or to buy mobile phone minutes, some villagers operate small canteens (selling rice, canned tuna and sugar). Others run small tobacco and betel nut stands, or sell baked goods. However, the most reliable source of cash is domestic remittances from urban relatives or temporary labour migration to town, plantations and canneries. Villagers often use remittances to purchase mobile phones but, as I explain in more detail below, they rarely cover usage costs. Thus villagers' access to calling, texting and online activities is limited, engendering what Jonathan Donner calls "a metered mindset" (2015: 123–126): mobile phone users actively calculate when to use their phones and for what purposes in view of the complex economics and cost structures that surround users' access to the cash economy including to mobile phones.

This "metered mindset" limits villagers' use of mobile phones *as* phones. Instead, mobile phones are, on an everyday basis, largely used as (free) multi-media devices. Women watch movies on mobile phones while taking a break from garden work or while waiting for the rice to boil. Men often watch movies in the evening when waiting to go night fishing, which is the most effective method to obtain enough fish to exchange at markets. Parents will entertain and distract children by playing movies on their smartphones, and so do babysitters. In fashion of a flâneur (cf. Coates 2017), especially adolescent boys stroll through the village, playing music on their phones, frequently to the discontent of (working) adults disapproving of this blatant display of leisure. In addition, villagers of all ages experiment with the camera functions of their phones. Teenagers and young

G. Hobbis 2017a: 158–173), but they are also popular gifts from urban visitors, or purchased anew whenever possible.

unmarried adults may pose on the white sand beach mimicking what they had seen on images or in videos produced abroad (e.g., in Rihanna's "If It's Lovin' That You Want"). Married adults with children most commonly take pictures and videos during family events such as baptisms, or during political events such as the 2014 National Election.

Local and international popular music and foreign movies abound on villagers' microSD cards, complemented (yet not dominated) by home pictures and videos. There are too many different movies, music videos and other media files on the 50 microSD cards that I surveyed. Yet, some general observations can be made: the vast majority of digital media are produced outside Solomon Islands (and Melanesia at large). This is especially true for movies. Movies produced in Asia were popular in town, but I did not encounter any on Gwou'ulu microSD cards. Instead, these cards were filled with Hollywood productions, mostly Westerns[2] (e.g., *3:10 to Yuma* [2007]) and action movies (e.g., *Blood Diamond* [2006], *the Expendables* [2010]) which dominated men's microSD cards but could also be found on those of women. Particularly popular on women's phones were cartoons such as *Tom and Jerry* (1940-) or *Finding Nemo* (2003).[3] Music files and music videos were often more diverse, including a wide mix of local and foreign artists, from ABBA's "The Winner Takes it All" to Chris Brown featuring Keri Hilson's "Super Human" to English-language gospel songs (e.g., "His Name is Wonderful") to songs from Malaitan artists, Gwou'ulu's own "White Sand Beach" as well as groups such as the Rainboy Boyz and the E. M. Children's Choir.

Most of these files – at least of those produced outside Solomon Islands – have been downloaded off of the Internet, but *not* in the Lau Lagoon itself. In 2014, Gwou'ulu was serviced by a spotty 2G network. I was able to read my emails on my smartphone, however, this was a costly affair which afforded a great deal of patience. No one I talked to in Gwou'ulu ever went online. In the words of Mark, a 30 year old subsistence gardener and fisherman, who regularly travels for temporary employment: "I do not check 'my line' [in Gwou'ulu]. In Honiara [the capital

---

2   For a discussion of the overwhelming popularity of Westerns or "cowboy movies" see G. Hobbis (forthcoming).

3   I did not find a digital copy of *The Lau of Malaita* – an ethnographic film produced by Granada Television under their Disappearing Worlds Series, with filmmaker Leslie Woodhead and anthropologist Pierre Maranda – on Gwou'ulu microSDs. While several Lau I talked to expressed interest in a copy of the file, they had been unable to procure one and only very few had ever had the opportunity to see the film. I was also unable to find the file online during multiple trips to internet cafés. The only copy I found was a non-digital VHS tape owned by the National Museum in Honiara. I also did not find any other documentaries on villagers' microSD cards. Most indicated that they had simply never been offered any by villagers returning from town with multi-media files. A young man in his 30s explained that he had watched some during stays in Honiara, but his English had not been good enough to adequately follow the description of events.

city], I use it every day, nearly on a full-time basis. Coverage is a problem [in Gwou'ulu]" (Interview, 18 October 2014). Mark, and others, did however, "bring the Internet" to the village, or at least some of the many multi-media files that can be found there. The same land and sea routes that connect the movement of goods and people between the village and Honiara also facilitate the movement of digital data, offline, in the form of microSD cards which are now also carried through this system. In this case, the village is connected to the World Wide Web by an eight hour truck ride to Auki, followed by a six to eight hour ferry ride to Honiara (assuming a direct connection is available), where microSD cards are fitted into SD card adapters and inserted into a desktop computer at the various urban Internet Cafés and filled with the newest music videos, Hollywood films and at times also memes and pictures more generally, e.g., those portraying famous soccer players.[4]

In the following, I explore this movement of digital multi-media data, along-side the movement of temporary labourers. In my analysis I focus in particular on how the mobility of labour and data, and their interdependency, are entangled in moral debates and how they are possibly transforming social relationships in Gwou'ulu, in dialogue with urban environments and movements. I begin with a brief historical introduction to the role of temporary migration and moral uncertainties. I move from there to a more detailed discussion of the interconnected-ness between remittance networks and multi-media files. In the final section of this article I examine how these rapidly proliferating multi-media files, in partic-ular foreign movies, are integrated into everyday village life, social relationships and their complex moralities.

I build on David Morley's (2009) call for a materialist, non-media centric approach to Media Studies that takes into account movements of digital files, online and offline. Rather than dividing media into "new" and "old," Morley suggests that we "need to investigate the continuities, overlaps, and modes of symbiosis between old and new technologies of symbolic and material communications and the extent to which material geographies retain significance, even under changing techno-logical conditions" (ibid: 115). The anthropology of technology that informed my research in Solomon Islands offers a complimentary approach (cf. Coupaye 2013; Lemonnier 1992). It situates an individual's understanding of a given technological system in its broader social, cultural, historical, economic, political, religious as well as environmental and material contexts. By accounting for, in Morley's words, "material geographies" (Morley 2009: 115) it is possible to develop a better under-standing of the choices users (are able to) make in view of the constraints that they face – in the Solomon Islands case severely limited access to the Internet in rural

---

4   There are also Internet Cafés in Auki. However, Internet access is never the sole reason for going to town, and Honiara is more comprehensively useful (e.g., better health services, cheaper goods, more likely to have relatives there that one could stay with etc.).

areas combined with a flourishing remittance economy and temporary circular labour migration between rural and urban areas.

Methodologically, this article is based on twelve months of multi-sited ethnographic field research (see Marcus 1995). I spent a total of eight months in rural Gwou'ulu and four months in urban Honiara, regularly travelling between the two sites with temporary migrants and the digital technologies and media that they carried, thus both "[following] the people" and "the thing" (ibid: 106). By moving between the urban and the rural, spending time with families from Gwou'ulu in both sites, my goal was to develop a better understanding of urban-rural differences, similarities, and connections in the ways individuals use digital technologies. In addition to participant observation, the core of my data is based on an interview protocol adopted from Heather Horst and Daniel Miller's (2006) research on mobile phones in Jamaica. I implemented this protocol near the end of my fieldwork in Gwou'ulu, after having developed a more concise understanding of the everyday prevalence (and absences) of mobile phones and digital technologies more broadly. With the help of a Lau-speaking research assistant, I interviewed one hundred adult villagers (between ages 18 to 75, men and women) about their mobile phones, their call histories, phone books, application usage as well as the contents of their microSD cards. Interviews were semi-structured to collect comparable data sets, while allowing for enough flexibility to encourage broader discussions with respondents, often about the perceived moral dimension of mobile phones and mobile multi-media files. During my stays in urban areas I completed complementary interviews with executives of the two telecommunication providers. I also talked to owners and users of Internet Cafés and more broadly surveyed the multi-media infrastructures available to urban residents and rural visitors. For example, there were several stores in Honiara that sold copies of Hollywood movies on DVDs, even offering to transfer them directly to USB sticks and microSD cards for easier consumption of these movies on mobile phones.

A Brief History of Malaitan Labour Migration

Temporary labour migration constitutes a cornerstone of Malaita's integration into, but also growing dependency on, the global capitalist economic system. When European traders arrived with goods such as steel tools and guns in the nineteenth century, Malaita had few of the natural resources that traders desired, such as sandalwood or bêche-de-mer. To access European goods Malaitans instead relied on their labour power, or "Malaitan muscle" as it is often called. According to Clive Moore (2017: 86), between 1870 and 1911 Malaitans made up around 58 per cent of all Solomon Islanders working on plantations in Fiji and Queensland. Within the plantation system of the British Solomon Islands Protectorate (BSIP) established in 1893, Malaitans constituted around 68 per cent of all labourers before the outbreak of the Pacific War (ibid: 86). The Lau were particularly well integrated into the labour trade. They offered not only what Corris describes as "probably the largest single source of labour in the group" (1973: 32), but they also served as so-called passage masters or middlemen between inland or "bush" Malaitans and European ships (cf. Corris 1973).

As Malaita (and Solomon Islands) were further integrated into the British Empire, so grew Malaitans need for cash and thus their dependency on indentured labour as the only – somewhat – reliable way to access cash. Especially once the colonial authorities implemented a Head Tax, nearly every young adult man participated in the migratory labour trade, often to obtain the necessary cash income for extended families including older men.[5]

World War II disrupted the labour trade which had already crumbled, e.g., alongside falling copra prices, with the Great Depression (cf. Akin 2013: 94–101). Even more so, the war further nurtured Malaitan discontent with British rule and the dependency on labour migration that it entailed. *Maasina Rule*, an anti-colonial Malaita-wide movement, emerged. One of its primary goals was to refocus Malaitan labour to economic activities on Malaita. While Maasina Rule achieved some of its goals (cf. Akin 2013), it failed at ending Malaitan dependency on labour migration. Even with independence in 1978, temporary labour migration has continued to serve as primary means for Malaitan participation in the cash economy; though Malaitan mobilities have been increasingly confined to the territory of today's Solomon Islands – the international diaspora is nearly negligible.

Large scale development projects remain conspicuously absent from the province. Simultaneously, dependency on cash to buy processed foods, especially rice, instant noodles and if possible canned tuna (cf. S. Hobbis 2016: 124–128) is on the rise. Combined with population pressures, overfishing of coastal areas, and overutilization of garden land, self-provisioning and small-scale trades at bush markets are no longer sufficient to meet everyday needs. Malaitans, above all young men, increasingly *have to* work in the canneries, large-scale logging and plantations located elsewhere in the country. Malaitans have also found employment in the emerging urban core of Honiara on the island of Guadalcanal, where they have come to dominate in both the unskilled and skilled employment sectors (Moore 2007). A growing number of these Malaitan men have been bringing their families to Honiara, sometimes permanently.[6] However, many others leave their families behind, often for several months each year and at times for even longer periods; or they are joined by (some members of) their (nuclear) families for a limited period of time, also to obtain secondary or tertiary education, or to access

---

5   See Keesing (1978) and Akin (2013) for a more detailed discussion of some of the controversies and continued political legacies of British violent enforcement of the Head Tax.

6   Malaitan migration to and dominance in Honiara have been identified as one of the so-called root causes of a civil conflict (1999–2003) that led to the near collapse of the Solomon Islands state and capitalist economic enterprises (cf. Moore 2007).

better medical facilities (e. g., the only x-ray facilities of the country can be found there). What Murray Chapman (1976) suggested in the 1970s remains true today: in many cases Malaitans, especially those working in unskilled, temporary positions, are first and foremost circular migrants, moving back and forth between their home villages and sites of capitalist production.

In this context of prolonged engagement with and dependency on migratory labour, the (domestic) remittance system has come to define Malaitans engagement with the foreign goods and services as increasingly necessary but continuously distant. The same can be said about Malaitans' encounters with foreign values. In response to Malaitans' dependency on temporary migration, those left behind (as well as, at times, those migrating) came to question the morality of migratory lifestyles and the new behaviour and ideas, including religious beliefs, that returnees bring back. Around the turn of the nineteenth century indentured labourers in Queensland and Fiji were exposed to Christian missionaries. Some converted. Some even became missionaries, challenging, upon their return to Malaita, the ancestral beliefs that formed the foundation of the local sociopolitical order.[7]

Urbanization has posed a similar challenge. Honiara, in particular, has come to be viewed as "the opposite of 'home' (hom)" (Berg 2000: 6–7), a place where it is possible for young migrants to be "free" from the social norms of rural communities. From the opposite perspective, Honiara has come to be viewed a place of moral decay. Migrants are often accused of being sexually promiscuous, of wasting the money they earn on alcohol and women rather than contributing to the needs of their families "at home." On a larger scale, especially skilled and more permanent urbanites are often accused of shifting their allegiances away from their kin-networks towards the needs of their work or school colleagues (cf. Berg 2000; Gooberman-Hill 1999).

In the following I outline how Lau conceptualizations and usages of mobile phones and digital multi-media files fit into, and are shaped by these migratory histories, the complex town-village relationships and the moral debates that surround them.

Mobility and Remittances in the Mobile Phone Age

Reciprocal exchange networks are foundational to many Malaitan (and Melanesian) societies. For example, reciprocity is the foundation for the bridewealth system. The groom, often with significant contributions from his extended family, provides a series of goods such as pigs and shell money (and increasingly cash)

---

7   The consequences, and some of the ongoing tensions, surrounding the spread of Christianity in Malaita has been discussed in detail elsewhere (for Lau cf. S. Hobbis 2016; Maranda 2001).

to the family of the bride whose members redistribute the bridewealth among each other. Bridewealth thus reaffirms commitment to reciprocal belonging, in addition to symbolizing the coming together of two families and the shift of a woman's lifeworld to that of her husband's family (cf. Ivens 1930). On an everyday basis and especially in shared spaces, such as village communities, these networks are maintained on a daily basis, for instance by sharing tobacco or freshly caught fish.

Also migratory remittance payments are more than financial contributions to the needs of one's nuclear and extended family. In Malaita as in other areas of Melanesia, remittances are integrated into networks of belonging that transcend the unidirectional flow of cash. While urban-based villagers are expected to send money and goods back to the village, and are frequently called upon to do so, rural residents often supply "home food," *hom kaikai* in Solomon Islands Pijin. The sharing of food, in particular food grown in ancestral soil, is recognized as an important means by which relationships between migrants and villagers are strengthened and a sense of a shared identity rooted in place is reaffirmed (cf. S. Hobbis 2017; Petrou and Connell 2016). Similarly, though disconnected from place, by sending back cash, and at times goods such as rice or mobile phones, migrants restate their commitments to their village-based families and the lands on which they live.

However, a desire for *hom kaikai* is met by a growing dependency on cash to meet everyday needs. The bidirectional remittance system is getting increasingly skewed. More and more pressure is placed on migrants to send cash home, to send more cash home and to send cash more frequently. Mobile phones have complicated this already complex relationship. Mobile phones allow for communicating remittance requests to migratory labourers quickly and, if necessary, repeatedly. Before the arrival of mobile telephony, remittance requests were often only sent through private messengers who travelled between village and town. This long and comparatively expensive trip would never only be taken for the sake of conveying a message. Also not everyone travelling between village and town was deemed a trustworthy enough messenger. Within existing reciprocal exchange networks anyone involved would be entitled to a "cut" from the requested and received remittances. An unreliable messenger may tell others about the possible remittance payment, thus triggering a flood of requests from others. This was also the reason why the two-way transceiver radio that one of Gwou'ulu villagers' owned was rarely used to communicate remittance requests. Many did not trust the operator, and were uncertain as to the operator on the receiving end. In other words, before mobile phones, remittance requests could not be communicated easily, or at least not *that* easily, being predominantly limited to the infrequent travels of trusted individuals.

Many of the temporary (and more permanent) migrants I talked to complained that since the arrival of mobile phones, remittance requests had gotten "out of control." To regain control, Lau migrants have started developing mobile phone-based avoidance mechanisms. Avoiding giving is nothing new. One of the first Lau phrases I was taught was *sui na*, meaning "finished" or "I am out," a common response to requests for tobacco or other common everyday exchange items. *Sui na* is a polite way of saying no, as long as the tobacco is inside a bag and not visible to the person asking. Migrants may use *sui na*, or similar excuses to avoid mobile phone-transmitted remittance requests, but just like a person is likely to ask for tobacco again on the same day, or the next, so would another phone call often follow not long after.

Similar to the mobile phone-based avoidance strategies that Steffen Dalsgaard (2013) observed in Manus Province, Papua New Guinea, my respondents often reacted by managing their SIM cards and thus the phone numbers that they could be reached at. One man reported to me that he was so frustrated with the calls he received from the village that one day he opened his device up and threw out the SIM card, to get a new one and not share it with his village-based relatives for some time. Another, more seasoned urbanite showed me how he maintained seven different SIM cards, each one for a different social network. This urbanite would only use his "family SIM" when he wanted to call them; otherwise, he attempted to keep, e. g., his "work SIM" secret, and thus disconnected from remittance requests.

The most common mobile phone-based avoidance strategy was to refuse to pay for mobile phone credit for their village relatives, so that they were unable to call in the first place. In addition to a shortage of cash for credit in villages, there was, in 2014, no location in Gwou'ulu or the immediate neighbourhood where villagers could buy mobile phone credit. The only in-village option was to give the money to members of Jehovah's Witnesses who visited Gwou'ulu once a week and who could, in another village they visited, purchase credit and thus top up Gwou'ulu villagers' mobile phones. In this context the ideally most reliable source for mobile phone credit is the very migrants who prefer not to receive continued phone calls with remittance requests from their relatives; and accordingly, the most effective avoidance strategy for migrants is not to recharge their relatives' mobile phones or do so only so rarely that villagers, in their "metered mindset," save the available credit to call only in times of emergencies.

However, these avoidance strategies harbour risks for migrants. Most migrants intend to return to the village, for example because they left their wife and children behind, to visit parents at Christmas, or to retire in the village after an urban-based career. To be able to return, it is crucial for migrants to maintain positive relationships with their rural kin (cf. Dalsgaard 2013). In Gwou'ulu, as in most other parts of Solomon Islands, land is communally (clan) owned, and any visit or settlement requires clan approval. Participation in reciprocal exchanges is key to living in rural areas, and to returning there. Networks of belonging need to be maintained. And, as networks of belonging, their continuation is often far more than a "need;" it is desired and at the heart of migrants' sense of self and self-worth.

While the telephonic capacities of mobile phones vex this problem, the multimedia functions provide an answer. Instead of "gifting" credit, migrants bring back, or send back with someone else, multi-media files that villagers enjoy consuming on their mobile phones as a "free" way e. g., to spend time, to relax or to "distract" children. As villagers desire multi-media files, but cannot obtain them without help from urban residents, they are a valued gift that does not come with the immediate "dangers" of mobile phone credit. Urban residents go online, commonly at an Internet Café. There they download movies, music files and at times images and convert them to a file type that can be played on most standard mobile phones. One DVD shop further offered a USB-based movie downloading service. The clerk would turn the desktop monitor to face the shopper who would point to images of movie posters. After paying the SBD 20 fee per download of one movie the shopper was then told when to return to collect the USB drive (depending on the size of the file and Internet speed). This kind of download service is occasionally also advertised on Facebook Groups such as "Buy and Sell in Solomon Islands."

These files are eventually moved to microSD cards, and from there typically transferred via Bluetooth to other mobile phones (and their microSD cards). These files are easily brought into the village. Once obtained, they are free to copy and redistribute, and they can be transmitted by anyone travelling to Gwou'ulu. There is also ongoing demand. Villagers' microSD cards are limited in their storage capacities. To save new movies, old ones are deleted; or a movie or music file may be deleted to take family pictures. MicroSD cards also get lost. As a result, multi-media files are, but also need to be frequently replaced. This fuels a multi-media-based remittance economy that is deemed beneficial by anyone involved, at least at first sight. With multi-media files being folded into mobility patterns the village has experienced an explosion in the consumption of music and movies. The offline social life of these files in Gwou'ulu has become a new source of friction and moral controversy.

The Moral Ambiguities of Offline Digital Media

The offline circulation of digital files has led to an unprecedented access to foreign visual culture. While access to movies, for example, has existed in North Malaita since at least the 1970s it had never been reliable, and it has been controlled by a handful of predominantly male, adult villagers. Now many if not most of Gwou'ulu residents have access to movies (and other multi-media) in the palm of their hand; and many different types of movies are being watched by many different groups of people. With mobile phones movies can be watched privately and by audiences that may not be deemed appropriate. In the following section I briefly outline the historicity of consuming multi-media files with a focus on foreign movies. Then I go on to introduce some of the moral controversies that surround the rapid proliferation of (urban) visual media by focusing in on how foreign movies are used to raise boys to become temporary labourers (and beyond).

From the *Muvi Haos* (Movie House) to Private Viewing

There is a small grove of coconut trees along the side of the school's soccer pitch in Gwou'ulu. It was planted in late 1980s and early 1990s by school boys, who were caught going to the neighbouring village of Mana'abu to watch movies. Mana'abu had a *muvi haos*, a purpose built structure for screening movies with the help of a projector system. The structure was enclosed and a fee for admission was charged. Viewing was primarily restricted to men. While, as Christine Jourdan observed in Honiara, a woman would not be harmed if she attempted to attend a screening, "she would be frowned upon by the men and would most likely be driven away" (1997: 147, note 14). Watching movies was a male prerogative, and the movies chosen were deemed those most interesting and morally acceptable to a male-only audience: commonly Westerns or action movies such as Rambo.[8] Boys were allowed to attend, but their attendance was more controversial. The then-principal of Gwou'ulu Primary School thought watching movies was a distraction from school work and punished whomever he caught with the job of planting a coconut tree.

Gwou'ulu got its own *muvi haos* around 1997. It was owned and operated by an enterprising man who would later become one of the village's more powerful chiefs. Technology had advanced since the Mana'abu *muvi haos* was set up. The new one in Gwou'ulu had a VCR player connected to a television screen. This was also an entrepreneurial scheme that required the control of space. The audience sat on a sand floor, some on a few benches, while they watched the screen in a leaf house with tarpaulin walls. The soon-to-be chief collected a small group of senior men in considerations of censorship, much like had been the case of the Mana'abu *muvi haos*. Their selection similarly favoured action movies and Westerns, with restrictions placed on most sexually explicit material including all movies that were predominantly about love or romance; and their selection was similarly meant to target male-only audiences, this time including boys.

By 2014 the *muvi haos* in Gwou'ulu only existed as a memory amongst adults, having been fully replaced by mobile phones. Ultimately, projectors, VHS and DVD player systems proved too challenging and costly to maintain in the maritime and tropical conditions of the lagoon. In 2014 there was one type of *muvi haos* left near to Gwou'ulu. With a guest house for foreign tourists, Uru'uru Village has a satellite connection, and the guest house operators occasionally facilitate, for a small entry fee, social viewing of live television broadcasts such as the 2014 FIFA World Cup. The Uru'uru *muvi haos* does not show any movies, such as Rambo, that villagers can watch on their mobile phones for free. In comparison to the mobile phone, a *muvi haos* is not versatile enough and too costly to maintain. Besides, because there are plenty of mobile phones redundancy is high; it is easy to watch a movie on a friend's phone, or to obtain a new one through remittance networks.

---

8   Rambo has been recognized as popular movie across Melanesian societies (cf. Wood 2006).

The widespread presence of mobile phones as multi-media players has radically changed the audience experience in Gwou'ulu. What once used to be male-elite-controlled and (semi-)public is now an individualized, privatized experience that includes both men and women – during my fieldwork about half of all mobile phones in Gwou'ulu were owned by women. At the same time, the small screen and individual ownership of mobile phones, microSDs, and digital media does not only favour private viewing, but it also allows for viewing materials that may (or may not) be controversial. In Benjamin's words, a divorced man with two children, "because we now have mobile phones and they have memory cards, you can put all [kinds of] movies inside without someone finding them [...]" (Interview, 7 November 2014). Impossible to control by the male-dominated village elite the private viewing of a wide range of content has become a village-wide controversy.

This individualized control over content is what makes mobile phone movie watching so contentious. Movies are felt to extend the reach of the immorality that is associated with the urban, modern lifeworlds of temporary (and more permanent) migrants who, after all, also choose the movies that they download in town and bring to the village. In turn, villagers worry that movies extend the reach of the "freedom" of town. They worry that the movies bring sexual promiscuity and possibly also a move away from commitment to the village community vis-à-vis individual interests and needs.

This uncertainty in the offline circulation of digital multi-media and its rootedness in migratory movements are particularly reflected in debates about what kinds of movies children should or should not be watching. Especially controversial is this debate for boys who are raised not only to become villagers but also for joining the migratory labour trade. In the following, I briefly introduce this controversy to further highlight the importance of studying the integration of foreign audio-visual media in everyday life and mediated by the domestic remittance economy. This discussion is by no means meant to be exhaustive, in particular not in its treatment of the complex uncertainties that surround broader societal transformations, e.g., continued tensions and negotiations between Christianity and remnants of the ancestral religion.

Raising Boys through Foreign Movies[9]

Shortly before our interview Lucas, a 28 year old father of two boys, had watched *Prince of Persia: The Sand of Time* (2010). The movie features the struggles of a warrior and a princess to defend their kingdom with a magical dagger that can

---

9   I focus on foreign movies as they were most frequently used to nurture desired personality traits in boys, unlike, for example, music videos. Music and music videos open up additional intriguing questions about the role of digital media that go beyond the scope of this article.

control time. Lucas thought *Prince of Persia* was a great movie, and a perfect learning exercise for his sons.

I like all kinds of war movies, war movies with different clans [...] The custom stories that those movies tell, that they show in their acting are somewhat similar to my custom stories. Exemplary are the wars in *Prince of Persia*. They make me think back to all my custom stories [...] I like it because of how the man acted; he is a man who struggles. He struggles and fights for the victory of his people [...] It is a nice story and a helpful one. My mind tells me that it helps prepare for the future of my children. This is my own thinking. This is the reason why I choose this kind of story, why I show it to my children, for the future of my children (Interview, 7 November 2014).

Jason thought *Blood Diamond* (2006), a movie about the violence of the diamond trade during Sierra Leone's civil war, is excellent viewing material for his son and nephews. Jason showed his copy of *Blood Diamond* to a continuously growing number of young boys, and willingly shared his digital copy of the movie with anyone who wanted it. According to Jason, *Blood Diamond* instills the importance of fighting for one's family, and to be prepared to do so at any time, in young, male audience members.

Whatever my brother does outside the village, if he comes here we have to face who he is facing. I must help my brother, if I am strong, [I must do so] together with our other brothers to decrease the demand made by the others [my brother is facing]. Therefore, I must learn how to fight; my children [sons] have to learn how to fight (Interview, 1 November 2014).

Like Lucas and Jason, a majority of Gwou'ulu villagers are confident that children directly learn from what they see in movies, that they will mimic the moralities that are displayed. Hence, caregivers are concerned with identifying movies that they deem to reflect "good" moralities. This is true for all children. However, it is especially true for boys as the historically more significant target audience of foreign visual media, and as preparation for boys eventual encounters with "modernity" during labour migration. The personality that Gwou'ulu men, as experienced temporary labourers, deem to be most appropriate for labour migrants is that of men with aggressive temperament, similar to the war leaders of the past (cf. Ivens 1930). Priest-like personalities, "quiet, dignified, even-tempered, and knowledgeable" (Ross 1973: 55), are those of educated men and deemed the most desirable, but only ideally so. Many of my respondents insisted that few of their sons would be able to obtain adequate education and/or a position as skilled labourers. As adults their sons were more likely to spend time in temporary positions, and they needed to be prepared for this eventuality.

Unskilled labourers spend much time "hanging around" in urban environments. Often they join a *gen* (gang), a support network of similar-aged man who would spend time together without, at least not necessarily, becoming criminals.

According to my respondents, members of a *gen* are increasingly from across Solomon Islands provinces,[10] and they are "recruited" for the personality traits that are most frequently associated with their provinces of origin. Gwou'ulu men are confident that as Malaitan members of any *gen* their sons will be expected to assume a warrior-like position, to be fierce and to serve as protectors for other members. Indeed, Malaitans are often hired as security guards because of their reputation as "warriors." As Tarcisius Kabutaulaka (2001) notes, this stereotype is widespread and accepted (though not necessarily true) by Malaitans, other Solomon Islanders and even the international news media.[11] Gregory, a Gwou'ulu man in his late 30s, who had spent many years as temporary labourer in urban areas, explained that "[you have to be] like a *ramo* [a warrior]. If there is a fight, if someone wants to beat your friend, you can help, you can fight. This is a Malaitan man" (Interview, 4 November 2014). Men like Gregory, Lucas or Jason thus show their sons violent movies to prepare them to live up to this Malaitan ideal of warrior-like masculinity on the move.

In addition to violent movies, Gwou'ulu men also deem it appropriate to show their sons movies with explicit sexualized content, most popularly *Titanic* (1996). While sexual activity outside of marriage is frowned upon in many Malaitan societies – even a "criminal" offense that can lead to violent repercussions and demands for compensation – being sexually promiscuous during stays in urban areas is recognized as another core component of Malaitan masculinity, at least by men. Many of my male respondents consider sexual activity and aggressive temperaments complimentary personality traits for migratory labourers. These traits will have to be tamed with marriage and growing maturity (and a more permanent return "home"). However, they are also thought to be crucial to get a start in locations like Honiara, to cement one's position in a *gen* as primary social network away from reliable kin, and thus to "make it" away from home to success-fully participate in the remittance economy.

This being said, many women and some of the male village elders frown upon exposing boys to movies with violent and sexually explicit content. While many acknowledge the appropriateness of these personality traits for temporary labourers, they worry that these movies and their moralities increasingly influ-

---

10   Often members of a *gen* are from one language group or province. However, my respondents emphasized that this is changing rapidly, e. g., a *gen* might form because of joint religious affiliation or shared experiences as day labourers, rather than kin networks.

11   Kabutaulaka's discussion directly relates to the civil conflict between 1999 and 2003, which centered around two militias, the Malaita Eagle Force and the Isatabu Free-dom Movement, representing the provinces of Malaita and Guadalcanal respectively. Notably, in this context, both groups (not only Malaitans) embraced the warrior "ideals" represented in movies such as *Rambo* which had been popular in Solomon Islands before the conflict (cf. Jourdan 1997; Woodhead and Maranda 1987).

ence life in Gwou'ulu, blurring the lines between village and town further. Indeed, it was not uncommon for young men to knock on my door at night. They would ask for a movie with romantic contents, explaining that they use these movies to seduce women, sometimes their wives but many times not. These nightly requests for romantic movies are exemplary for how sexual promiscuity appears to be seeping into the village alongside digital multi-media. Boys have also been caught punching holes through house walls after watching martial arts movies, thus bringing what some described as "migratory" aggressiveness to rural environments.

In response, mothers and village elders who are predominantly based in Gwou'ulu – in comparison to many of the male caretakers – fight with men about the movies that they show to boys; and they attempt to undermine men's influence by exposing boys to competing movie-based narratives. Women in particular collect cartoons such as *Finding Nemo* (2003) or *The Prince of Egypt* (1998) on their microSD cards for the purpose of instilling a non-violent and family-oriented morality in boys (and girls). *Finding Nemo* portrays a natural environment comparable with the Lau Lagoon, emphasizing a positive, collaborative relationship with one's home. *The Prince of Egypt*, on the other hand, furthers Christian values and ideals among their audiences – at the time of my research a vast majority of Gwou'ulu residents were active members of the Anglican Church. Women also go through their male relatives' microSD cards and delete particularly controversial movies or music videos that are "too" sexually explicit to counteract their redistribution to boys.

Despite their efforts, none of these groups, women, men, elders (and others) are able to fully control what movies boys (as well as girls)[12] are able to watch. This is the case due to the technological tendencies of mobile phones – the privacy and mobility that they encourage – and the particular socio-cultural and economic context that fuels the rapid proliferation of digital media – the dependency on temporary labour migration and the significance of reciprocal remittance networks described earlier. For example, files that women delete are often quickly obtained again, possibly directly from another villager or if necessary via request from urban residents. The offline circulation of digital media, as a way to maintain social relationships between villagers and labour migrants, has then created new, controversial links between urban and village environments. It has become a growing source of uncertainty and conflict among village residents. This is especially true as they look into the future and imagine what this future may hold for their children, the personalities they should develop and the roles that foreign movies play therein.

These concerns about the possible moral consequences of consuming foreign visual media echo Brian Larkin's (2008) observations in Kano, a Hausa city in Nigeria, and those of Marie Gillespie's (1995) among Punjabi families in Southall, London. My findings in Gwou'ulu re-reveal how foreign visual media have the potential to "[catalyse] [...] processes of cultural change" (ibid: 76) when audiences

---

12   For a discussion of the moral uncertainties surrounding the raising of girls cf. G. Hobbis (2017a: 223–251).

mimic some of the (controversial) practices that they observe on their screens such as "Western" dating practices; and they re-emphasize the significance of accounting for the particular sociotechnical systems and "modern" anxieties in which media practices and the controversies that surround them are fashioned (cf. Larkin 2008). The brief ethnographic snapshot presented here is merely, if at all, the tip of the iceberg, best understood as a call for further research on how foreign visual media are connected to historical and contemporary conceptualizations and transformations of masculinity, femininity, youth cultures, and Lau personhood more broadly.

Conclusion

There is a growing literature on the proliferation of digital technologies, particularly mobile phones, in Melanesia. This literature has offered important insights into the ways individuals use digital technologies, how these usages are situated in their respective socio-cultural contexts, and the moral uncertainties that these technologies foster. However, existing research has predominantly focused on urban contexts, and thus on contexts where access to cash and paid mobile phone usages is more widespread. As a result, research has highlighted the telephonic capacities of mobile phones and the controversies that surround them. For example, in urban Papua New Guinea (Andersen 2013), Vanuatu (Servy 2012) and Solomon Islands (G. Hobbis 2017b) mobile phones have been found to be used to find new sexual partners through cold calling, further nurturing narratives that connect urbanity, mobile phones, and sexual promiscuity.

Far less attention has been paid to the integration of mobile phones in villages, and even less attention has been paid to their non-telephonic usages and to how moral concerns about mobile phones in town may (or may not) seep into rural environments.[13] This article attempts to begin filling this gap in ethnographic knowledge on digitization processes in Melanesia. It highlights how even if villagers cannot easily use mobile phones for telephony, texting or Internet access, "free" multi-media usages are similarly imbued with potential for moral controversies, especially so as digital multi-media is increasingly popular. The moral controversy that I briefly outlined here – the question if boys should be shown violent and sexually-explicit movies – is but one example for the uncertainties that surround the presence of digital media in Gwou'ulu as well as the broader links between digital media and "modern" anxieties in Gwou'ulu, the Lau Lagoon, Malaita and Solomon Islands. Others controversies that require further research and analysis include the relationship between religion and digital media – does digital media

---

13   Village-based research has more strongly focused on if and how mobile phones are used to improve access to social services and, more broadly, how they are integrated into existing communication technologies (cf. Watson 2010; Watson and Duffield 2016).

decrease Church attendance? How does it affect the authority of the priest and other church leaders? How and to what extent does it fuel tensions between Christianity and ancestral belief systems? – the morality of sexually-explicit visual materials more broadly – should men (and women) be allowed to watch it? What are the consequences? – as well as a more concise understanding of differences between the types of foreign visual media that are being consumed – What, if any, are notable differences in localized adaptations of movies produced in Hollywood, China, Nigeria or elsewhere (cf. Larkin 1997)? To what extent are music videos conceived of differently than feature films, accounting also for the increasing local production of music videos? Each of these questions, and many more, require elaborations and research in comparable settings to tease out the extent to which these moral controversies may be transforming everyday (rural) life over the long term and how they link to broader sociocultural, political, economic and religious changes and struggles in the Lau Lagoon and elsewhere in Solomon Islands.

Building on Morley's (2009) call for a move beyond a media-centric analysis towards one that looks at media alongside the movement of people, I argue that these controversies cannot be understood without accounting for how digital media files find their ways into the village and what this movement of files represents. I have shown how moral uncertainties are directly intertwined with the reciprocal exchange networks that form the foundation for Malaitan labour migration; and how a growing need for cash and thus growing demands on labourers have encouraged migrants to develop different kinds of remittance strategies. These strategies include gifting of digital media files instead of complying with more costly demands or instead of avoiding remittance requests altogether. While the gift of digital media allows migratory labourers to maintain networks of belonging they are, however, also an important source of friction, at least in Gwou'ulu. The rapid proliferation of foreign digital media represents a growing linkage between urban and rural areas that, so it seems from a village perspective, brings some of the moral uncertainties of urban lifestyles to their rural homes.

References

Andersen, Barbara (2013): "Tricks, Lies, and Mobile Phones: 'Phone Friend' Stories in Papua New Guinea." In: Culture, Theory and Critique 54/3, pp. 318–334.

Akin, David (2013): Colonialism, Maasina Rule, and the Origins of Malaitan Kastom, Honolulu: University of Hawai'i Press.

Berg, Cato (2000): "Managing Difference: Kinship, Exchange and Urban Boundaries in Honiara, Solomon Islands." MA diss., University of Bergen.

Chapman, Murray (1976): "Tribal Mobility as Circulation: A Solomon Islands Example of Micro/Macro Linkages." In: Leszek A. Kosinski/John W. Webb (eds.), Population at Microscale, Christchurch: New Zealand Geographical Society and the Commission on Population Geography, International Geographical Union.

Coates, Jamie (2017): "Key Figure of Mobility: The Flâneur." In: Social Anthropology/Anthropologie Sociale 25/1, pp. 28–41.

Corris, Peter (1973): Passage, Port and Plantation: A History of Solomon Islands Labour Migration, 1870–1914, Carlton: Melbourne University Press.

Coupaye, Ludovic (2013): Growing Artefacts, Displaying Relationships: Yams, Art and Technology amongst the Nyamikum Abelam of Papua New Guinea, New York: Berghahn.

Dalsgaard, Steffen (2013): "The Politics of Remittance and the Role of Returning Migrants: Localizing Capitalism in Manus Province, Papua New Guinea." In: Fiona Mccormack/Kate Barclay (eds.), Engaging with Capitalism: Cases from Oceania, Bingley: Emerald, pp. 277–302.

Donner, Jonathan (2015): After Access: Inclusion, Development, and a More Mobile Internet, Cambridge: MIT Press.

Gillespie, Marie (1995): Television, Ethnicity, and Cultural Change, New York: Routledge.

Gooberman-Hill, Rachel J. S. (1999): "The Constraints of 'Feeling Free': Becoming Middle Class in Honiara (Solomon Islands)." Ph.D. diss., University of Edinburgh.

Hobbis, Geoffrey (2017a): "A Technographic Anthropology of Mobile Phone Adoption in the Lau Lagoon, Malaita, Solomon Islands." PhD diss., École des hautes études en sciences sociales and Concordia University.

Hobbis, Geoffrey (2017b): "The Shifting Moralities of Mobile Phones in Lau Communicative Ecologies (Solomon Islands)." In: Oceania 87/2, pp. 173–187.

Hobbis, Geoffrey (forthcoming): "Cowboys and Aliens: Body Techniques and Audience Reception in Malaita, Solomon Islands." In: Visual Anthropology.

Hobbis, Stephanie (2016): "An Ethnographic Study of the State in Rural Solomon Islands (Lau, North Malaita): A Quest for Autonomy in Global Dependencies." PhD diss., École des hautes études en sciences sociales and Concordia University.

Hobbis, Stephanie (2017): "Peacebuilding, Foodways and the Everyday: A Fragile Confidence in Post-Intervention Solomon Islands." In: Social Anthropology/Anthropologie Sociale 25/4, pp. 470–484.

Horst, Heather/Miller, Daniel (2006): The Cell Phone: An Anthropology of Communication, New York: Berg.

Ivens, Walter G. (1930): The Island Builders of the Pacific, London: Seeley, Service & Company Limited.

Jourdan, Christine (1997 [1995]): "Stepping-Stones to National Consciousness: The Solomon Islands Case." In: Robert J. Foster (ed.), Nation Making: Emergent Identities in Postcolonial Melanesia, Ann Arbor: The University of Michigan Press, pp. 127–150.

Kabutaulaka, Tarcisius Tara (2001): "Beyond Ethnicity: The Political Economy of the Guadalcanal Crisis in Solomon Islands." In State, Society and Governance in Melanesia, Project Working Paper 1/1 (https://openresearch-repository.anu.edu.au/bitstream/1885/41949/1/tarcisiusworkingpaper.htm).

Keesing, Roger M. (1978): "Politico-Religious Movements and Anticolonialism on Malaita: Maasina Rule in Historical Perspective Part I." In: Oceania 48/4, pp. 243–261.

Larkin, Brian (1997): "Indian Films and Nigerian Lovers: Media and the Creation of Parallel Modernities." In: Africa: Journal of the International African Institute 67/3, pp. 406–440.

Larkin, Brian (2008): Signal and Noise: Media, Infrastructure, and Urban Culture in Nigeria, Durham: Duke University Press.

Lemonnier, Pierre (1992): Elements for an Anthropology of Technology, Ann Arbor: University of Michigan Press.

Macintyre, Martha (2008): "Police and Thieves, Gunmen and Drunks: Problems with Men and Problems with Society in Papua New Guinea." In: The Australian Journal of Anthropology 19/2, pp. 179–193.

Maranda, Pierre (2001): "Mapping Historical Transformation through the Canonical Formula: The Pagan vs. Christian Ontological Status of Women in Malaita, Solomon Islands." In: Pierre Maranda (ed.), The Double Twist: From Ethnography to Morphodynamics, Toronto: University of Toronto Press, pp. 97–121.

Marcus, George E. (1995): "Ethnography in/of the World System: The Emergence of Multi-Sited Ethnography." In: Annual Review of Anthropology 24, pp. 95–117.

Moore, Clive (2007): "The Misappropriation of Malaitan Labour: Historical Origins of the Recent Solomon Islands Crisis." In: The Journal of Pacific History 42/2, pp. 211–232.

Moore, Clive (2017): Making Mala: Malaita in Solomon Islands, 1870s-1930s, Canberra: ANU Press.

Morley, David (2009): "For a Materialist, Non-media-centric Media Studies." In: Television & New Media 10/1, pp. 114–116.

Petrou, Kirstie/Connell, John (2016): "Food, Morality and Identity: Mobility, Remittances and the Translocal Community in Paama, Vanuatu." In: Australian Geographer 48/2, pp. 219–234.

Ross, Harold M. (1973): Baegu: Social and Ecological Organization in Malaita, Solomon Islands, Urbana: University of Illinois Press.

Servy, Alice (2013): "'As-tu un petit copain? Non je n'ai pas de téléphone.' Moralité, progrès technique et sexualité en milieu urbain au Vanuatu." In: La Revue Hermès 65/1, pp. 137–143.

Watson, Amanda H. A. (2010): "'We Would Have Saved Her Life': Mobile Telephony in an Island Village in Papua New Guinea." In: eJournalist 10/2, pp. 106–127.

Watson, Amanda H. A./Duffield, Lee R. (2016): "From Garamut to Mobile Phone: Communication Change in Rural Papua New Guinea." In: Mobile Media & Communication 4/2, pp. 270–287.

Wood, Michael (2006): "Kamula Accounts of Rambo and the State of Papua New Guinea." In: Oceania 76/1, pp. 61–82.

Woodhead, Leslie/Maranda, Pierre (1987): The Lau of Malaita. Manchester, UK: ITV Granada.

In the Footsteps of Smartphone-Users

Traces of a Deferred Community
in *Ingress* and *Pokémon Go*

Anne Ganzert, Theresa Gielnik, Philip Hauser, Julia Ihls,
Isabell Otto

Abstract

In this article, the authors carry out conceptual and theoretical reflec-
tions on smartphone communities by closely investigating two apps:
Ingress (Niantic 2012) and Pokémon Go (Niantic 2016). While the
games' narratives fabricate reasons for the players to move, it is the
Smartphone – understood as an open object between technological
and cultural processes – that visualizes and tracks players' movements
and that situates and reshapes the devices, the users and their sur-
roundings. A central aspect is that the 'augmented' cities that become
visible in the apps are based on the traces of others: other processes and
technologies, as well as other players. These traces of practices and
movements structure the users' experience and shape spaces. Traces
are necessarily subsequent and we therefore develop the concept of a
deferred (smartphone) community and analyse its visibility within
the apps. By close reading the two case studies, we examine poten-
tial "smartphone communities" in their temporal dimensions, as well
as their demands and promises of participation. In order to gain a
perspective that is neither adverse to new media nor celebratory of
assumed participatory community phenomena, the article aims
to interrogate the examples regarding their potential for individua-
tion/dividuation and community building/dissolution. In doing so,
the games' conditions and the impositions placed on the players are
central and include notions of consent and dissent. Drawing upon
approaches from community philosophy and media theory, we con-
centrate on the visible aspects smartphone-interfaces. The traces left
by the various processes that were at work become momentarily actu-
alized on the display, where they manifest not as a fixed community,
but as a sense of communality.

DOI 10.14361/dcs-2017-0204
DCS | Digital Culture and Society | Vol. 3, Issue 2 | © transcript 2017

Introduction

Pokémon Go and *Ingress* are two Augmented Reality Games (ARGs) produced by the North-American software developer Niantic, Inc.[1] Both games appeal to their players to go out and move while the app augments mapped representations of their surroundings.[2] The ARGs challenge the blurring borders between the physical and the virtual world,[3] between game narrative and reality, based on locative media technologies with a Global Positioning System (GPS) (cf. Buschauer/Willis 2013). Shortly after it was launched, *Ingress* was praised in marking a turning point in the changing social acceptance of gaming and virtual realities (Stingeder 2013: 7). In the case of *Pokémon Go,* Niantic was able to fall back on Nintendo's trademark and a pre-existing fan base from various previous iterations of the game's world.[4]

In the public debate and scientific research about both games, the question of community has been one of the core topics: since its release for Android in 2012, *Ingress* has often been discussed in relation to its innovative character and ability to evoke new forms of 'communitarization' (Stingeder calls it "Vergemeinschaftung" in German [2014: 4]). It has been said to harbour the ability "to build transformative and collaborative communities both regionally and globally" (Chess 2014: 1108). According to Karl H. Stingeder (2013: 4), *Ingress* supports 'social condensation' and the 'social communitarization' through the possibility of In-Game-Communication, e.g. game-chat and log windows, and external networking in

---

1   In her 2017 article about "Pokémon GO as an HRG", Adriana de Souza e Silva defines four main aspects of an HRG (hybrid reality game): "mobility, sociability, spatiality, and surveillance." (ibid: 21). While her approach to both games is compelling, the visible alteration of space through interfacing and visualizations is what this article focuses on and the reason for describing the games as ARGs first.

2   An Augmented Reality Game builds upon the implication that one's individual environment becomes the playground, or more specifically, the field of play. These games are taking place in what we might call 'reality', but with the difference that this reality is in some way augmented. It can in fact be argued, "that our realities have always been augmented in a fundamental way by our collective and individual imaginaries, and more recently (as exemplified by Pokémon GO), by the instrumental and mediatic extension of our narrative worlds through (mobile) media games." (Hjorth/Richardson 2017: 7)

3   The border itself between the real and the virtual space – if it ever existed – is certainly highly questionable. In this regard, we prefer to operate with the term of the 'hybrid space', as the augmented reality and mobile game researcher Adriana de Souza e Silva (2009) has suggested.

4   Starting in 1996, many generations of Game Boy games, twenty movies, a long running anime series, and a multitude of merchandise have attracted fans and players worldwide. This might be one of the reasons for the popularity of the ARG, which was so popular in the first weeks after its release that it provoked crowds of players to gather in public spaces all over the world (Chen 2017: no pag.).

communities on Facebook, Google+ or websites with forums that have been set up specifically. Majorek and du Vall (2015) describe *Ingress* as "a tool for [sic!] new kind of socialization; it helps people return to typical interactions and frees individuals from functioning only in the virtual world" (2015: 685). They continue to write about the game's capability of "restoring coexistence in the real world and of utilizing new technologies to create true bonds" (ibid: 685 f.) and include other games of this kind.

Pokémon Go certainly qualifies as a similarly 'communitarizing' game, but is more often discussed in a much less optimistic manner, particularly regarding its (social) health impacts. (cf. Clark/Clark 2016: 1, Raj/Karlin/Backstrom 2016). Taking this public visibility of mobile gaming into account, this article asks about new forms of community that arise from the practices and interactions of players. Putting the emphasis on the medial conditions of community means neither investigating (self-regulatory) player communities (cf. Pearce 2009), nor empirically approaching player groups with a shared experience (Ducheneaut et.al. 2005: 407) or values (Egenfeldt-Nielsen/Smith/Pajares Tosca 2016: 182), nor focusing on producer supported online communities (cf. Ruggles/Wadley/Gibbs 2005). Instead, we are interested in the appearances of communality on smartphone displays; a "smartphone communality" that precedes, accompanies, and follows the (crowded) visibility of players. Hence, we seek to explore the medial dimension of "smartphone communities" as well as their demands and promises of participation. In order to gain a perspective on *Ingress* and *Pokémon Go*, that is neither adverse to new media nor celebratory of assumed participatory community phenomena, this article aims at analysing the examples regarding their potential for individuation/dividuation and community building/dissolution. Therefore, our focus lies on theoretic, fundamental research, with the aim that examinations of actual gameplay by researchers in game studies can substantiate the claims made in this article. In doing so, the conditions of the games and the impositions placed on the players demand further elaboration, as do notions of consent and dissent. Prerequisite to any of these considerations are, of course, the smartphone apps, which will be explained briefly, especially with reference to their narrative justification for community building on the one hand and to their impulses for player movement on the other.

Playing the game(s)

"The future is in danger and the world is not what it seems to be" – what sounds like a dystopian surveillance report is in fact the teaser for *Ingress*. In the game world of *Ingress,* the smartphone user, or rather the game player, becomes an agent in a hidden global war, fighting for the survival of humanity, which is endangered by an alien invasion. Therefore, the players have to choose sides between the alien faction, the 'Enlightened' (marked as green) and the 'Resistance' (blue). To achieve victory,[5] each side tries to cover the globe with a net of strings and fields, which they can establish between so called portals that are typically prominent places like historic buildings, artworks in the public space or other exposed sites. These portals are visible within a radar simulation on the smartphone screen that enables the user to only interact with portals in a twenty-meter range.[6] In order to be able to interact with a multitude of portals, 'it is time to move'. The game logic forces the agents to actually move to the respective locations of the *Ingress* portals [Figure 1]. While moving, players also collect the 'Exotic Matter' (XM), a form of in-game currency that is needed to perform any interaction with the portals and that has been scattered during the alien invasion.

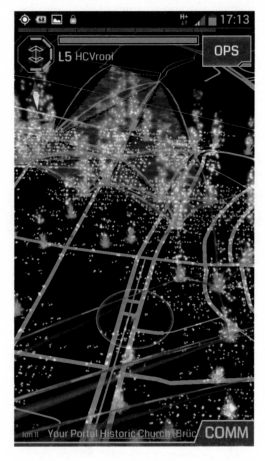

Figure 1: Player/Arrow with scanner radius and linked portals. Screenshot taken from *Ingess*.

The narrative set up of *Pokémon Go* is much less apocalyptic. The players are supposed to take on the role of a Pokémon Trainer and roam their personal local space to find and catch Pokémon – a portmanteau of pocket and monster. In this diegesis, containing Pokéstops, Pokéballs and arenas, the driving idea is in fact to 'catch them all'. To fulfil this goal, players must move through neighbourhoods and cities, different landscapes or countries and look for Pokémon on their map, which appear when a player is close enough to them. Fittingly, the

---

5   Which is always elusive and seems unreachable, even after three years of worldwide gameplay with over 14 million downloads. Players have deployed 5.64 billion resonators and walked a total of 258 million kilometers (Niantic 2016: no pag.).

6   It is an interesting idea to consider whether a map mirrors the territory all the better as it becomes smaller and more fragmentary (cf. Thielmann 2013: 53).

slogan with which the game is advertised in *Google Play*, is: "Go out and catch a Pokémon in the real world." The mention of *Google Play*, or the *App Store*, refers to a seemingly simple fact: potential players have to use a smartphone to play *Pokémon Go* or *Ingress*, at least if they want it to play in the way the game is supposed to be played. Without a proper device, players will neither be able to sense a nearby Pokémon, nor catch it. For that matter, the same goes for creating a net for the players' *Ingress* faction. Furthermore, without movement by the player and the device, the in-app-in-game scanner cannot detect Pokémon or collect XM either. Without movement, players cannot be led to portals or Pokéstops and the apps cannot force them "to visit, revisit [historical sights], and reconsider the value of that space that they may not have noticed before playing the game" (Chess 2014: 1113).

This is precisely why the smartphone, as a device of mobility, is the crucial subject of the following investigation. There is no question that the user can play *Ingress* and *Pokémon Go* with tablets or even desktop computers (provided that they use some hacks to 'virtually' move through the space).[7] However, it is part of this article's thesis and presumption that the smartphone, its medial qualities, mobility and practices intertwine with any practice the two games can create. The way of using the smartphone both fabricates and is fabricated by the games. Furthermore, it is essential for contemporary individuation processes as well as considerations of locality and community dynamics in relation to the apps.

In order to analyse any of these topics, we suggest (re)focusing on the appearances, namely, that which becomes visible, audible or tangible through smartphone interfaces in the respective app. Display symbols, sounds and vibrations enable the interaction between the user and the app via the gaming interface.[8] In our research, we have concentrated on the visible side of this interaction and documented the gameplay through screenshots, which were subjected to a close reading process. The insights gained from this are combined with approaches borrowed from community philosophy and media theory. We have structured the following thoughts based on an implicit subtitle that is assignable to both games:

---

7   It can be argued that players who play *Ingress* or *Pokémon Go* on their personal computer in their warm and dry home have an unfair advantage over those players who have to walk around by themselves to reach the arenas and Pokéstops and who need good endurance and luck (and battery power) to get hold of the truly rare Pokémon. However, that does not change the fact that they still have an advantage over smartphone players in a smartphone game, even if they never use a smartphone themselves. The smartphone remains relevant as a basic condition and prerequisite, even in such practices of undermining or dissent.

8   Other aspects, such as economical background information about the apps or considerations about the games' engine or aesthetics, cannot be considered within the scope of this article.

"I was here". This sentence will be split up and emphasis put on its different constituents to form chapters, and to serve as a guiding expression throughout the following explorations.[9]

I was here

When considering the expression "I was here", one of the first questions might be, who or what exactly was here? Who is uttering this statement? At this point, there are two aspects that merit a closer look. First, the relation between the user, the smartphone and the app. While, intuitively, these three entities seem to be ontologically distinct, if we draw attention to the processes between them, we can find reciprocal interplay that makes a precise distinction nearly impossible. It is therefore insufficient to claim that *I* might be a *me* who plays the game, because since *I* is now playing the game, it is no longer the same *me* as it was before. *Me* as an *Ingress* or *Pokémon Go* player is another *I* than the *me* as a non-player. Hence, the question of "who was here?" is not so much aimed at a human subject, but at a player subject.

However, the player subject is generally a user being, since it is a human smartphone user who is addressed in the *App Store* or in *Google Play* to download *Ingress*; it is the human *Pokémon* fan who is addressed by the specific subject. It is also the human non-smartphone user who might be motivated to buy a smartphone because he or she has been caught up in the hype and wants to play either game. The player subject that may be the *I* that was here, is therefore not 'just' a human user, but the human user with their smartphone. In this aspect, the *I* we describe is for example different to the "I" that utters the "Here, I Used to Be", which Frith/Kalin (2016) have described as the equivalent of the inscription of place in the context of apps such as *Foursquare*, where a "digital network memory" emerges from individual and collective mobilizing practices. The player subjects as we understand them are a specific aspect of the smartphone users, who "experience and practice the relationship between memory and place." (ibid: 44) A common denominator of the two concepts is that in each case both the human user and the smartphone are constituted as black boxes in relation to each other: the human user must, for example, have the potential to move and to operate via the smartphone display, while the smartphone has to be able to connect to the internet via mobile sources as well as be equipped with an appropriate operating system that is capable of running the app. The latter point, in particular, leads us to a third constitutive aspect of the player subject: the player subject is always the human user *with* their smartphone *with*

---

9   "I was here" also marks a first distinction from other community building or participative smartphone applications, where, for example, *Grindr*'s comparable statement would be "Who else is here and gay?" (cf. Liegl/Stempfhuber 2016).

the *Pokémon Go* or *Ingress* app. A statement that is as simple, as it is essential (cf. Latour 1999).

An example is given here to elaborate on this connection: during the gameplay of either app, the user is simultaneously located on a map in the game via the GPS capability of their smartphone and in the street or room they are currently located in. If the body of the player moves in the physical world, an abstraction of this movement (e.g. no height information) is mirrored on the screen. Moreover, the interactions in the game world that become visible on the smartphone display, for example, the hacking of an *Ingress* portal or spotting a Pokémon, affect the players' behaviour in the 'real world': they pause in unusual places, take detours or walk in circles.

Another example of the undeniable interrelation between human user, app and device is when the smartphone runs out of battery and thereby interrupts the gameplay. There are plenty of possible examples for this phenomenon, which we want to describe as a constant shifting between dedication and dependence – a form of relatedness that Antoine Hennion described as *attachement* (2011: 93). As a consequence, we want to refrain from regarding the human user, smartphone and app as three different parties, but rather as one interwoven entity, which permanently individuates (cf. Simondon 1958) through practices in the process of playing.

Accordingly, it is this triad of human user/smartphone/app that we nominate to constitute the player subject. Other aspects are included within this nomination, such as an Internet connection. However, since the 'smartness' of the smartphone contains mobile Internet access, as well as a touchscreen and location services (GPS), these aspects are subsumed under the smartphone. The same applies to the movement that is demanded by the apps, which requires the dual mobility of the human subject and of the mobile device. Similarly, mobility is inherent to both – at least within the discourse of the game. The proposed triad is hence adequate for considering the player subject.[10] It takes important aspects into consideration and is detailed enough to ensure that the different black boxes can be handled without losing important aspects. Finally, it clarifies who might be the source of "I was here".

---

10   The aforementioned player, who plays the game at home on a personal computer, makes the proclaimed trinity seemingly obsolete, or at least questionable. To run the apps on, e.g., a windows system, an emulator is required, a second program or application that simulates the intended device. The player subject then becomes a conglomerate of human being/personal computer/app/emulator. We can adapt our formula and preserve the trinity since the smartphone can be considered as a kind of computer and both app and emulator can be subsumed as programs. Accordingly, the player subject now consists of human being/computer/program, which is nothing less than the widely known classification of hardware, software and wetware, but with the crucial distinction that the player, who was previously always determined in the demarcation of hard- and software, now emerges in the union.

I *was* here

The second interesting aspect in *Ingress* and *Pokémon Go* is the map as part of the game design, and – based on this – the trace or mark. Maps form the core for the interface design of both apps. *Ingress* is built upon the data and map material created and provided by *Google Maps*, which itself plays a crucial part in the (inter) action of users, smartphones and apps.[11] The following section elaborates on how appearance and address merge with aspects of temporality and community-building in the *was* of "I was here".

Considering the display visibilities as the object of our investigation, we need to follow the traces of the *Ingress* agents on the screen. *Ingress* players see themselves represented by a small arrow within the map on the screen. Concentric circles emanate from this arrow, similar to the aesthetics of a radar sending radio waves that locate enemies. The Pokémon trainer's position is also visualized by an avatar on the respective map and, like in *Ingress*, concentric circles scan the surrounding area. However, even though these maps depict streets and buildings and locate in-game points of interest, no other player subject answers the scanner's signal, at least not instantly. This is because the player always acts alone on the screen. Or, put differently: the avatar that visualizes the player's position on the map is the only one that appears on the apps' maps.[12] There are no visualized traces in the actual game play, that the player has to follow, or, put differently, tracing is not practice of playing *Ingress*.[13] Even if there are thousands of other co-players around, they are never visualized as additional 'arrows' on the screen. Instead, they remain invisible, a fact that – in our consideration – highly influences the question of a potential game 'community'.

In this context, we would like to differentiate between two kinds of potential community: on the one hand, a form of 'instantaneous' community that forms physically when players meet, e. g., to plan game actions [Figure 2].[14] On the other hand, a 'deferred' community that is strongly characterized by an inherent asynchronous temporality and posteriority. This concept understands the deferred community as a

11   Niantic was started as an internal start up at Google and became an independent entity in October 2015.

12   The avatar can be both the arrow and the human figure. Exceptions for *Pokémon Go* are in the arenas and in the very few dialogue or cut scenes. In *Ingress*, on the other hand, no human-looking avatar appears whatsoever.

13   In an early version of Pokémon Go, small paw prints indicated the distance to nearby Pokémon, but it was the number of paws that determined how close they players where, not a trace on the map itself.

14   In the summer of 2017, Niantic added 'Raid Battles' to the game, promising a "cooperative social gameplay experience" (Niantic Press Release, June 19, 2017), a development that also warrants further research. Yet this development does not change the fact, that the 'deferred community' as it is developed here is a condition for this newer option as well.

necessary condition for the formation (and collapse) of other communities, reaching from small co-present player groups to large online communities.

Figure 2: *Ingress* players coordinating their efforts. Picture taken by the research group.

For example: When an *Ingress* agent interacts with a portal, they have the option of attacking it, if it is an enemy portal; refresh it, if it is a friendly one; or conquer it, if the portal is neutral. If they choose any of these actions, they brand the portal with their agent name. Then, however, as the game logic commands, the agent has to move on, because the main goal of the game is to establish links between the portals and to connect them to create fields. In other words: a player leaves their mark or trace on a portal and only becomes visible to another player *afterwards*, as an absence that was previously present. Subsequent players can then respond to this trace in different ways: acknowledge it, support it, erase it, or overwrite it. Because this can only happen as a temporarily succeeding action, however, any potential community of *Ingress* players it is eternally split up and fragmented through time. This is a deferral that, according to Nancy (2007), is necessary, because the process of interplay and therefore of individuation would otherwise stop.

In summary, appearance is highly tied to disappearance in both apps, such that we can only read the traces of an absent presence of community (cf. Krämer 1998). Nonetheless, there is in fact an ongoing process of tracing, acknowledging, erasing, and overwriting. However, the very object of investigation – the visibility on the smartphone screen – is a rather fragmented actualization in this constant interplay. The trace is therefore strongly connected to updates of the GPS coordinates, which are visualized on the *Ingress* screen as coloured marks (portals) or an arrow (the user-smartphone-app-subject) and on the *Pokémon Go* screen as coloured pols (Pokéstops) and an avatar that represents the player (the user-smart-phone-app-subject). We understand traces as inscriptions or markings within the game, rather than literal traces that are actively or unconsciously left by the players through their game play.

In *Pokémon Go*, for example, such a trace is left when a player captures an arena. To do so, a Pokémon from the player's stock has to be left in that arena, which also results in further rewards in the form of Pokécoins and Stardust. This reward is maximized with every Pokémon the player places. To mark an arena therefore requires giving up on a previously acquired possession. This mark, just like the hacked *Ingress* portal, is temporary, as other players will subsequently claim the arena for themselves. When they succeed, they find the previously placed Pokémon. They can also see an image of the player's avatar that was previously present, including their trainer name and current level. Leaving a Pokémon in an arena is therefore also a message to a succeeding addressee. It is a delayed "I was here" and also means: "This arena was mine for a certain period". If the succeeding player is in the same team as the previous player, the capacity of the arena can be expanded by adding a further Pokémon. This means that every captured arena will inevitably either be reclaimed or shared. If the currently occupying team does not frequently return and maintain their claim to an arena, it can constantly change its tenancy.[15] Players can therefore only leave traces of having been there and having taken part. Similar to a tagger, who sprayed their name or the sentence "I was here" on a wall, but does not own the building, the Pokémon trainer does not own the arena. They can only claim it temporarily with the knowledge that their mark will be overwritten in the not-so-distant future.

Yet the traces can be read for as long as they exist and, as it stands with most traces, it is also hard, or even impossible, not to leave a mark. This holds even more true when we extend the understanding of trace to the gestures of using the smartphone interface. It can then be said, that "[t]he gesture that transpires in real time at the mobile interface is a deictic 'doing' that produces a fleeting trace in the form of activating a click or moving a map view." (Verhoeff/Cooley 2014: no pag.) 'Tracing' the movement of throwing a Pokéball by swiping the finger on the touch screen towards the Pokémon is such deictic trace. These traces are conditional for the deferred community as it is understood here and most gesture in the gameplay can be interpreted like that. Furthermore, the traces that highlight the deferral emphasize a different facet. Even if a player chooses not to leave a Pokémon behind after clearing an arena, a mark is left showing *that* someone has in fact cleared the arena, even though it is unclear who. In the case of *Ingress*, the former owner of a portal receives a message stating that his or her portal has been attacked or taken over by 'an unknown player'. Similarly, the information on

---

15   Here, effects of repetition and seriality are of the essence. For example, Winkler (2015: 96) writes: "The everyday notion of traces at least has a quantitative side. And a privileged reference either to the mass or to the *repetition*."

when this (re)marking took place is not legible, only the fact that it has happened in the recent past is implicit. The *was* in "I was here" hence clearly refers to a past, a before, and relates to a present or future, depending on the standpoint. Nevertheless, the player who left the mark *was* present and *now* they are absent: this is what, by definition, turns the mark into a trace (Krämer 2007: 14).

As much as players are incapable of not leaving traces, they are also incapable of not following the inevitably existent tracks of their precursory co-players, e.g. in the case of an arena. Whereas Pokéstops allow a different reflection on temporal deferral, as they may all have been previously visited by other players, this does not become visible on the screens. Instead, a player's individual "I was here" is directed at themselves: when a player visits a Pokéstop, they can tap the respective symbol on the map. An icon then appears with a picture of the site where this specific Pokéstop is located in relation to the player's surroundings, such as a clock tower, a statue, a fountain or a unique building. This picture is framed by a blue circle, which turns purple after the icon is swiped and the obtainable items have been collected. For as long as a Pokéstop's icon on the map stays purple, the player cannot spin it again for the next five minutes. [Figure 3] To the player, a purple symbol therefore means that they themselves have been there recently. The icon, as such, is visible to all players, but the purple "I was here (within the last five minutes)" is individual to each player's screen. The deferred temporality of the *was* is nonetheless similar, whether "I was here" addresses the players themselves or subsequent players.

Figure 3: Avatar, Pokéstops, Arena etc. as visible traces of gameplay on the map. Screenshot taken from *Pokémon Go*.

I was *here*

In order to complete the contemplations of this article's guiding expression, we now have to ask about the place or space to which the *here* might refer in the context of the two apps. At least three features characterize this *here*: the maps, GPS tracking, and the position of the players as they relate to their surroundings.[16] On a first level, the maps in both apps function as typical maps, in that they are guiding devices that lead players to Pokéstops and portals. In a second step, these maps reveal themselves as interfaces that mediate between the player and the game. On a third, and perhaps most important level, the maps become a tracking device that enables players to identify the traces of those who were *here* before them.

Generally speaking, *here* refers to the place from which the utterance occurs and – as an act of deixis – to the *I* who speaks. But what does *here* mean in the context of *Ingress* and *Pokémon Go*? At first glance, the situation again seems simple: arenas, Pokéstops, and portals are sites that are only visible when mediated by the map on the smartphone display. However, they also relate to a 'real' place which existed in the actual terrain before being integrated and augmented by the apps. Hjorth and Richardson describe this relationship as "a transformation of the local environment into a game resource, where place is literally made relevant by the extent to which it is populated by virtual currency, game objects, and rewards." (2017: 10) Due to this relation between the in-game places and the actual territory, and the relationship to the user-smartphone-app-subject who 'utters' this relation by referring to a place both in the game and in the territory, the *here* becomes concrete. To make matters even more complicated, those 'real' places are also coordinates on a virtual map. In the context of the apps, the crucial aspect of the *here* is not that a player is at a specific topographic location, but that the (mobile) device sends and receives the corresponding GPS data. Only then can the game's maps appear in full with all the aspects mentioned above. Furthermore, only then can the app determine if the players have reached a defined range and are therefore able to interact with a specific virtual object on their maps (cf. Hui 2012). It does not make any difference to the apps whether this GPS data is in fact the result of a mobile device having moved with its user or the result of a GPS hack.[17] In

---

16   The movement of players could certainly be measured and marked for example in a real-world diorama as Hägerstrand (1982) suggested. However, neither this methodology, nor comparable approaches from time geography, are applied in this article.

17   Potential circumventions of the gameplay (practices like hacking or modding) have to be considered elsewhere. Most developers, for example, do not offer the players to the option of freely manipulating their GPS data and, instead, demand that they change their data output by physically moving. Accordingly, the so called *softbans* are not a penalty imposed by the program code but rather a sanction imposed by the developer.

any case, the assumed topographic *here* becomes a topological *here* (see below). It is no longer a player with a smartphone at a 'real' location that matters, it is an individual mobile GPS receiver in relation to a common static GPS location. It is a matter of a virtual *here* that can be updated in different ways with a player subject that individuates in accordance with their state of being, past and present, and their location.

The attached and interwoven assembly of user, smartphone and app permanently individuates itself through the practice of playing, as was stated earlier. However, regarding the processes of mapping, tracing and tracking it becomes more and more questionable if this term is not missing the plurality of a deferred community which is (dis)connected through time via the trace on a map. For this reason, we would like to introduce the additional term of *dividuation*, coined by media scholar Michaela Ott (2015). Ott describes in-/voluntary forms of participation and reciprocal entanglement in which we find ourselves in the media ecology of the 21st century. Following Ott's train of thought, the map should be considered less topographically, but rather more topologically. A map can never be thought of as a self-contained entity, but rather a dividuated phenomenon of 'being-in-relation', like the community that is at work on it. This dividuation is, unlike sharing, to be understood as a form of involuntary participation that applies to modifiable as well as fixed maps.[18] Consequently, it is in this constant oscillation between individuation and dividuation where an asynchronously deferred smartphone community temporally manifests. In this regard, every pixel or shining dot on the screen, every short sound or GPS signal and every user who leaves their 'virtual' mark with their smartphone is part of a highly interwoven complex of dividuated player subjects. It is therefore all the more important to take the described appearances seriously and to adequately trace individuation and dividuation practices.

"I was here" can thus only ever be considered as processual and non-static. Every instance of the sentence can change its status at any time and inevitably will do so. The transition of the personal, temporal and spatial determination is constitutional for the technological condition: exemplified by the GPS, on which both *Ingress* and *Pokémon Go* are based upon. Localization through GPS is made possible by a network of satellites that is dispersed across the Earth's orbit. A connection to four satellites is required to obtain a correct topographic position. The data that are continuously sent by those satellites are their individual identifier: the exact time based on their embedded atomic clock and their specific coordinates (cf. Misra/Enge 2006). Put differently, the satellites send an endless

---

18 *Ingress* players used to be quite literally be able to work on the map, as they had the option of adding new portals that other players could then interact with. In September 2015, this was suspended by Niantic, due to the large amount of submission (Niantic Post 2015) and the formerly changing map was stabilized by the cooperation. Consequentially, *Pokémon Go* players never had the opportunity to shape the map of the game other than leaving their traces as it is intended by the game.

stream of "I am here" to Earth. This signalling happens in so called 'real time'. Nevertheless, time has passed once the signal reaches earth (a fraction of a second) and the satellite's position is no longer the same. This means that when the signal is received by the GPS navigation device, the satellite's "I am here" has already changed into an "I was there". This temporal shift indicates that GPS tracking inevitably entails following a trace from the past, even though this past might barely be distinguishable from the present. Playing *Pokémon Go* or *Ingress* means that the player does not merely navigate an avatar across a digital map by moving through actual territory. The players also follow their own digital path, which enables the emergence of a game through technical conditions that accumulate with the smartphones in the players' hands. In this sense, each player subject is in the process of a deferred individuation as it is part of a deferred community of multiple in-/dividuated player subjects.

I was here *at work*

When we read a statement like "I was here" tagged in a public bathroom, the place it refers to is pretty obvious. The tagger might have vanished, but their place of having-been-at-work[19] persists. The same situation can be described for the *Pokémon Go* arenas. The most recent player might be still around, but doesn't need to be. Either way, their work is still present, for much longer than any other trace. To be more accurate: it is not the player who leaves a trace, it is their being-at-work which is inscribed.[20] The readers of this trace enter into a temporarily delayed connection with the worker, such that the deferred community that was described above emerges between traces of absent players and present players who were reading these traces while simultaneously leaving new traces of their work themselves.

Unbeknown to many *Pokémon Go* players, they also follow the footsteps of countless *Ingress* players before them, who worked on establishing sites for portals in their maps. Niantic took advantage of their pre-existing data when they created the interactive map for *Pokémon Go*.[21] The *Ingress* players' work, their mobile

19 We understand 'work' here as strictly differentiated from 'labour'. What we want to describe has nothing to do with the 'free labour' of users in digital cultures, as described, for example, by Tiziana Terranova (2000). We rather want to refer to 'at work' as a process of making something.
20 These work traces do not have to be intentional. Footprints in sand are not necessarily intentional either, but nonetheless they are the marks of a person's feet and can be read as the trace of the person as such.
21 A benefit for those users who play both games is the fact that areas where the amount of XM that is present is particularly high coincide with areas in which Pokémon will appear. However, running both games at the same time can significantly drain both battery power and data allowance.

devices, GPS tracking and cameras, plus the *Ingress* app, which is operated by the developers with their computing systems, find their way into *Pokémon Go*, where all this work is then visible on the screen and readable as a trace. [Figure 4] It is this trace, we argue, which leads to a different kind of community, which derives from those common online or offline communities, where players meet to play together or share their experience to gain advantages or generate new codes of behaviour, may it be in videos or in discussion forums or special game wikis. This different kind of community occurs beforehand and in a belated fashion. In the present, it is almost invisible. However, it leaves traces on the smartphone screen as momentary actualizations, not as a fixed community but as a sense of communality. We consider this communality of a deferred community to be essential to understanding the impact and popularity of ARGs like *Ingress* and *Pokémon Go* and for future considerations of mobile ARGs and related smartphone applications.

Figure 4: Push Notification "Ingress Portal Close by" overlaying the Pokémon Go screen. Screenshot taken from *Pokémon Go*.

References

Buschauer, Regine/Willis, Katharine S. (2013): Locative Media – Medialität und Räumlichkeit, Bielefeld: transcript.

Chess, Shira (2014): "Augmented regionalism: Ingress as geomediated gaming narrative." In: Information, Communication & Society 17/9, pp. 1105–1117.

Chen, Joyce (2016): "Pokemon Go: Crowed Stampedes Through Central Park After Rare Vaporeon Sighting." In: Us Weekly July 16, 2016 (http://www.us

magazine.com/celebrity-news/news/pokemon-go-crowd-stampedes-after-spotting-rare-pokemon-w429525).

Clark, Alexander M./Clark, Matthew T. G. (2016): "Pokémon Go and Research: Qualitative, Mixed Methods Research, and the Supercomplexity of Interventions." In: International Journal of Qualitative Methods 15/1, pp. 1–3.

Davis, Michael (2016): "Ingress in Geography: Portals to Academic Success?" In: Journal of Geography 116/2, pp. 89–97.

De Souza e Silva, Adriana (2009): "Hybrid Reality and Location-Based Gaming: Redefining Mobility and Game Spaces in Urban Environments." In: Simulation and Gaming 40/3, pp. 404–424.

De Souza e Silva, Adriana (2017): "Pokémon Go as an HRG: Mobility, sociability, and surveillance in hybrid spaces." In: Mobile Media & Communication 5/1, pp. 20–23.

Ducheneaut, Nicholas/Yee, Nicholas/Nickell, Eric/Moore, Robert J. (2006): "'Alone together?' exploring the social dynamics of massively multiplayer online games." In: CHI 2006 April 22–27, New York: ACM, pp. 407–416.

Egenfeldt-Nielsen, Simon/Heide Smith, Jonas/Pajares Tosca, Susana (2016): Understanding Video Games, New York: Routledge.

Frith, Jordan/Kalin, Jason (2016): "Here, I used to be: Mobile media and practices of place-based digital memory." In: Space and Culture 19/1, pp. 43–55.

Hennion, Antoine (2011): "Offene Objekte, offene Subjekte?" In: Zeitschrift für Medien und Kulturforschung 2/2, pp. 93–109.

Hinsliff, Gaby (2016): "Why Pokémon Go Really is a National Health Service". In: The Guardian July 22, 2016 (https://www.theguardian.com/commentis free/2016/jul/22/pokemon-go-health-service-silly-mobile-phone-game-parent ing-holy-grail).

Hjorth, Larissa/Richardson, Ingrid (2017): "Pokémon GO: Mobile media play, place-making, and the digital wayfarer." In: Mobile Media & Communication 5/1, pp. 3–14.

Hui, Yuk (2012): "What is a Digital Object?" In: Metaphilosophy: Special Issue on Philosophy of the Web 43/3, pp. 380–395.

Krämer, Sybille (1998): "Das Medium als Spur und als Apparat." In: Sybille Krämer (ed.), Medien, Computer, Realität. Wirklichkeitsvorstellungen und Neue Medien, Frankfurt am Main: Suhrkamp, pp. 73–94.

Krämer, Sybille (2007): "Was also ist eine Spur? Und worin besteht ihre epistemologische Rolle? Eine Bestandsaufnahme." In: Sybille Krämer/Werner Kogge/Gernot Grube (eds.), Spur. Spurenlesen als Orientierungstechnik und Wissenskunst, Frankfurt am Main: Suhrkamp, pp. 11–33.

Latour, Bruno (1999): Pandora's Hope. Essays on the Reality of Science Studies, Cambridge: Harvard University Press.

Liegl, Michael/Stempfhuber, Martin (2016): "Intimacy Mobilized: Hook-Up Practices in the Location-Based Social Network Grindr." In: Österreichische Zeitschrift Für Soziologie 41/1, pp. 51–70.

Majorek, Marta/du Vall, Marta (2015): "Ingress: An Example of a New Dimension in Entertainment." In: Games and Culture 11/7-8, pp. 667–689.

Misra, Pratap/Enge, Per (2006): Global positioning system. Signals measurements and performance, Lincoln, MA: Ganga-Jamuna.

Nancy, Jean Luc (1991): The Inoperative Community, Minneapolis: University of Minnesota Press.

Nancy, Jean Luc (2007 [2001]): Die herausgeforderte Gemeinschaft, Zürich: diaphanes.

Niantic: Three Years of Ingress and the Road for Niantic, January 28, 2016 (https://www.nianticlabs.com/blog/three-years/).

Ott, Michaela (2015): Dividuationen. Theorien der Teilhabe, Berlin: b-books.

Pearce, Celia (2009): "Communities of Play. Emergent Cultures in Multiplayer Games and Virtual Worlds." Cambridge, MA. and London: The MIT Press.

Pias, Claus (2000): Computer Spiel Welten, Munich: Sequenzia.

Raj, Marc Alexander/Karlin, Aaron/Backstrom, Zachary K. (2016): "Pokémon GO: Imaginary Creatures, Tangible Risks". In: Clinical Pediatrics 55/13, pp. 1195–1196.

Ruggles, Christopher/Wadley, Greg/Gibbs, Martin R. (2005): "Online Community Building Techniques Used by Video Game Developers." In: Fumio Kishino/Yoshifumi Kitamura/Hirokazu Kato/Noriko Nagata (eds.), ICEC 2005: 4th International Conference, Sanda, Japan, September 19–21. Proceedings, Berlin/Heidelberg: Springer, pp. 114–25

Simondon, Gilbert (1958): On the Mode of Existence of Technical Objects, Paris: Aubier.

Stingeder, Karl H. (2013): "Googles Augmented-Reality-Game 'Ingress'." In: medienimpulse 4/2013, no pagination.

Terranova, Tiziana (2000): "Free Labor: Producing Culture for the Digital Economy." In: Social Text 18/2, pp. 33–58.

Thielmann, Tristan (2013): "Auf den Punkt gebracht: Das Un- und Mittelbare von Karte und Territorium." In: Inga Gryl/Tobias Nehrdich/Robert Vogler (eds.), geo@web. Medium, Räumlichkeit und geographische Bildung, Wiesbaden: Springer, pp. 35–59.

Verhoeff, Nanna/Cooley, Heidi Rae (2014): "The navigational gesture: Traces and tracings at themobile touchscreen interface." In: Necsus #5: Traces (http://www.necsus-ejms.org/navigational-gesture-traces-tracings-mobile-touchscreen-interface/).

Winkler, Hartmut (2015): "Traces: Does Traffic Retroact on the Media Infrastructure?" In: Marion Näser-Lather/Christoph Neubert (eds.), Traffic. Media as Infrastructure and Culture Practices, Amsterdam: Brill Rodopi, pp. 92–113.

Digital Mediation, Soft Cabs, and Spatial Labour

Donald N. Anderson

Abstract

Critics of digitally mediated labour platforms (often called the "sharing" or "gig economy") have focused on the character and extent of the control exerted by these platforms over both workers and customers, and in particular on the precarizing impact on the workers on whose labor the services depend. Less attention has been paid to the specifically spatial character of the forms of work targeted by mobile digital platforms. The production and maintenance of urban social space has always been dependent, to a large degree, on work that involves the crossing of spatial boundaries – particularly between public and private spaces, but also crossing spaces segregated by class, race, and gender. Delivery workers, cabdrivers, day labourers, home care providers, and similar boundary-crossers all perform spatial work: the work of moving between and connecting spaces physically, experientially, and through representation. Spatial work contributes to the production and reproduction of social space; it is also productive of three specific, though interrelated, products: physical movement from one place to another; the experience of this movement; and the articulation of these places, experiences, and movements with visions of society and of the social. Significantly, it is precisely such spatial work, and its products, which mobile digital platforms seek most urgently to transform. Drawing on several recent studies of "ridesharing" (or soft cab) labour platforms, I interrogate the impact of digital mediation on the actual practices involved in spatial work. I argue that the roll-out of digital labour platforms needs to be understood in terms of a struggle over the production of social space.

"Technology is Inevitable"

In November of 2012, representatives from a half-dozen young startups – Cabulous, Hailo, Get Taxi, Taxi Magic, and others – gathered in a Washington, DC hotel for a talk hosted by the International Association of Transport Regulators (IATR). All the startups in attendance were presenting their apps for "e-hailing" – using smartphones to request taxi service – and responding to the IATR's proposed model regulations for governing the roll-out of this new dispatch technology. The lanky young CEO of one e-hailing startup began his presentation by taking a deep breath, and giving the audience a serious look. "Technology," he intoned, "is inevitable." The audience members nodded knowingly at this sage wisdom; but it is worth pointing out that, while the statement is profoundly true in a certain sense, it is completely nonsensical in the way that it was meant. What the speaker meant was that technological change is inevitable, and more specifically, that the emerging technology of e-hailing was inevitable. This is simply not true. Technological change or progress in any direction is not inevitable, no more than any of the technologies and institutions which the speaker and his audience were taking for granted – smartphones, automobiles, concrete-lined city streets, bodies of regulators, startups, conferences, hotels, etc. Each and every one of these formations is historically contingent. Specific technologies, and technological change, are not inevitable, but are instead dependant on the variable outcomes of complicated webs of human practice.

In a deeper sense, of course, the speaker was quite correct. Technology *is* inevitable, if by "technology" we understand the interaction of humans with their environment through prostheses of one sort or another (Stiegler 2010). The smartphone apps being presented at the conference were only one of the most recent means by which tools were to be inserted into, and used to mediate and transform, the relationships between human and human, and between humans and their surroundings. Yet the ends to which such apps would soon be put, and the transformation they would bring about, exceeded the imaginations of those present.

Another taxi and limousine-hailing startup, Ubercab (which had only recently shortened its name to Uber), had declined an invitation to the conference, but instead took up residence in a nearby suite in the same hotel, offering an open bar to meet with regulators on its own terms. This end-run around the conventions of the conference presaged the end-run Uber and similar companies would make or attempt around taxi regulations in the US and elsewhere. Uber's aggressive approach toward regulators went hand in hand with its more aggressive use of the potential applications of e-hailing software (Slee 2015): the Uber app would be used, not only to enable more efficient car dispatch, but to more effectively and intrusively govern the labour of drivers, and the interactions between drivers and passengers. While the traditional taxi-app startups envisioned their e-hailing apps as momentary interventions in the existing practice of cab-hailing (replacing arm waving or phone calls), Uber and a few other e-hailing startups (e.g., Lyft and SideCar) recognized the transformative power of their apps as persistent digital openings onto the space of the cab ride, of the work of the drivers, and even of the everyday life of its customers. Using Latourian terminology, we could say that the taxi startups imagined the e-hailing app as an *intermediary* serving the same function as older means of communication; whereas Uber recognized the app's transformative potential as a *mediator* (Latour 2005).

That transformative potential was just coming to light in 2012. That year, three companies – SideCar, Lyft, and Tickengo – started e-hailing services in San

Francisco under the legal cover of "ridesharing" (traditionally a non-profit activity, and thus exempt from taxi regulation in the State of California). Uber joined these companies in the "ridesharing" game early the next year. Instead of merely serving as a dispatch service, these companies used the digital mediation of the app to regulate the behavior of drivers and passengers and to pre-empt, at least in principle, the rationale for traditional regulation through the control of information and reputation systems. The outcome of this transformation was a controversial new assemblage which has gone by a variety of names, almost all of which are unsatisfactory:[1] here, I will refer to them as *soft cabs*, insofar as they rely on "soft regulation" by means of software, to supplant the traditional "hard" regulatory controls of the past; and because they make use of a *soft meter* (the term of art for an e-hailing app which also calculates the fare to be charged) in the place of that older mediating device, the taximeter, which had given its name to the "taxicab" a century earlier (Gilbert and Samuels 1982).

These soft cab services form the beginning of the roll-out of digital labour platforms (Fish and Srinivasan 2012) into the realm of mobile work. The term *digital work* has been used to describe the work of social reproduction in a digital context; Fuchs and Sevignani (2013) identify three kinds of digital work (cognitive, communicative, and cooperative).[2]

The earliest digital labour platforms – sites such as Elance, UpWork, and above all, Amazon Mechanical Turk – connected globally dispersed networks of on-demand workers and clients through the internet; though some observers have heralded the freedom and economic opportunity brought by these platforms, critics have focused on the extent of the protocological control exerted by these platforms over both workers and customers, as well as the precarizing impact on the workers on whose labour the services depend (the very low cost of "hits" on Amazon Mechanical Turk, for instance, is made possible by the developing-world location of much of its poorly paid workforce) (Fish and Srinavasan 2012; Fuchs and Sevignani 2013; van Doorn 2017). Such platforms, however, were largely limited by the nature of the work that could be conducted and distributed online.

The ubiquitous connectivity of smartphones has created the potential for a much broader range of services to be brought under the management of such digital platforms. The rise of the soft cab marked the advent of mobile digital labour platforms, tracking and managing a workforce doing non-online work.

---

1   The name "ridesharing" properly refers to a distinct set of shared and/or not-for-profit services; see Anderson 2014. Other recent suggestions, such as "transportation network companies" (coined by California regulators) and "ridesourcing" (Rayle et al. 2016) fail to clarify the soft cab's actual practical differences from other services and/or means of dispatch.

2   In this text I will be using the distinction made by Engels in a footnote to Capital between work as a qualitative creation of use value, and labour as a quantitative creation of value for exchange, i.e. paid work (Marx 1967: 47, 186).

So far, little attention has been paid to the specifically spatial character of the forms of work targeted by such platforms. "Social relations," according to Henri Lefebvre, "have no real existence save in and through space" (Lefebvre 1991: 404); space, for Lefebvre, is thus inherently social space, and the production of space is inherently a focus of political struggle. The production and maintenance of urban social space has always been dependent, to a large degree, on work that involves the crossing of spatial boundaries – particularly between public and private spaces, but also crossing spaces segregated by class, race, and gender. Though this *spatial work* is diffuse, and intricated with other forms of work and interaction, its fraught political character comes to the fore when such work is concentrated in particular paid activities; that is, when it takes the form of *spatial labour*. Delivery workers, cabdrivers, day labourers, home care providers, and similar boundary-crossers all perform spatial labour in moving between and connecting spaces physically, experientially, and through representation. Spatial work contributes to the production and reproduction of social space; as I will describe below, it is also productive of three specific, though interrelated, products: physical movement from one place to another; the experience of this movement; and the articulation of these places, experiences, and movements with visions of society and of the social.

Significantly, it is precisely such spatial work, and its products, which mobile digital platforms seek most urgently to transform, and as these platforms spread and are deployed in new kinds of spatial work, it is crucial to understand just how and why this is happening. The use of mobile digital labour platforms has spread far beyond car services, as "Uber for X" startups have sprouted offering a wide variety of on-demand spatial labour. Apps either already exist, or are in development, for home care workers, domestic workers, day labourers, home repair workers, and sex workers.[3] Below, I will define spatial work and outline the three fundamental products it creates, each of which is a target of particular attention for mobile digital labour platforms. Because the soft-cab platforms have, so far, had the most dramatic and controversial roll-out, and have attracted far more media and academic attention than other spatial labour platforms, I will draw primarily on ethnographic and sociological analyses of taxicab and soft-cab drivers, their occupational context, and the degree of control exerted over them by digital labour platforms. However, the focus on soft cabs should be read as the outline of a research agenda which will interrogate the impact of digital mediation on the actual practices involved in all forms of spatial work. In the conclusion, I will argue that the roll-out of digital labour platforms needs to be understood in terms of a struggle over the production of social space.

---

3   Examples include TaskRabbit, Cleanify, ClearCare, and Rendevu.

Mobility and Spatial Work

Within the broad literature that has emerged in the wake of the "new mobilities paradigm" (Sheller and Urry 2006), the most relevant for present purposes is that addressing the "politics of mobility" (Cresswell 2006, 2010). Defining spatial work necessitates a focus on the mobility of people (or "corporeal mobility" [Urry 1999: 56]) without losing sight of other kinds of mobility (e.g., of objects, images, communications, etc.; cf. Larsen et al. 2006: 47–61). In this context, *mobility* depends on the relative capacity to move, in other words, power; it is necessary that agents have and exercise this ability to connect the dots; to move, for instance, from place of rest to place of work to place of play and back again, for territorializing projects to function; and for large scale, enduring territorializations such as cities it is necessary that as a population they do this as repeated and shared practices of mobility. As a productive practice, mobility is constrained, conducted, and channeled through various means, but nevertheless agentive and subjectifying, and hence potentially unstable (Foucault 1983). To theorize mobility politically, it must be understood in its productive context and so cannot be treated as pre-existent or outside of power. However, to treat mobility solely as produced is to deny it causality; it must be considered as both produced by, and outside of limiting, constraining structures.

Thinking of mobility in terms of this two-way production and responsiveness, we come to the apparent paradox that mobility is *outside* power because mobility *is* power; or, more accurately, employing the Foucauldian understanding of power as diffuse in all social relations, mobility is an aspect of the excess of power – its extension, intrication, backgroundedness, unassimilable complexity – in which any given practice of power is inserted. Any program of fixedness, planning, or legibility is born in the midst of a multitude of ongoing processes and relations, and from this standpoint that which threatens to disable or limit these is mobility, to the extent that mobility is the excess of presence of objects, the excess spatial agency of subjects. Mobility is then, a species of power taken as an object of power, an object upon which power (as constraint, production, compulsion to circulation) is to be exercised.

Since domination must always be practiced within the networks and context of power more generally, projects of "power over" must make use of and draw on (and thus contribute to) the rhizomatic threads of "power to." The excessive power of mobility is in this sense, not merely a threat, but also a vast resource to projects of territorialization and social control. As an excess of power, mobility reacts excessively to its constraints, in part like a river which moves faster when it is channeled; but it is also excessive in that, without producing them per se, it imparts force to the very constraints that operate on it. Mobility thus has a transferable or commutative power which is what makes it an object of productive constraint.

Much of the productive capacity of mobile practices takes the form of *spatial work*, the work of moving between and connecting spaces – connecting, that is, physically, experientially, and through representation. Spatial work contributes to the production and reproduction of social space; it is also productive of three specific, though interrelated, products: physical movement from one place to another; the experience of this movement; and the articulation of these places, experiences, and movements with visions of society and of the social.

This triad is influenced by, and formulated in response to, two other triads outlined by scholars of space. The first is Lefebvre's tripartite discussion of the production of social space:

1. *spatial practice* (all the practices involved in the relations of social production and reproduction, the ways that people move and act in space; the way in which a sense of reality is produced through daily routine);
2. *representations of space* (which, as explicit representations, order space, in alignment with the existing relations of production and their ideological justification; the privileged product of scientists, planners, urbanists, and social engineers); and
3. *representational spaces* (a complex set of often implicit spaces of experience and familiarity, influenced by representations but not reducible to them; the lived space of inhabitants) (Lefebvre 1991: 33, 39).

Each of these three plays a role in the production of space, though Lefebvre argues that *representation of space* is typically dominant, particularly in modern capitalism, insofar as privileged representations crucially order, and give sense to, spatial practices and the more experiential "representational" spaces. This is related to the hierarchy Lefebvre finds in forms of knowledge, with *savoir*, the field of explicit propositions and laws which forms the basis of (for example) scientific knowledge, playing a dominant role over *connaissance*, the less explicit realm of familiarity and experience. Representations of space – as representations – are more closely embedded with *savoir*, while spatial practices and representational spaces are primarily associated with *connaissance*. Lefebvre's triad is useful for emphasizing the fact that the experience of space is not independent of the practices and representation that produce it, as well as for his insistence on the political implications of different forms of representation and of knowledge. Nevertheless, Lefebvre overemphasizes the dominance of *savoir* and the representation of space, painting *connaissance* and representational space as relatively passive. I argue that the concept of spatial work helps to correct this imbalance. Spatial work is not passive, but active, it is interactive and productive. Within Lefebvre's triad, spatial work is primarily a spatial practice, shaped by, and operating in context with, other spatial practices; it draws on the ability for, and takes place within the experience of representational space; and it is regimented by, and can reinforce or undermine, representations of space.

Tim Cresswell (2010: 22) also outlined three aspects of the politics of mobility:

1. *movement,* "the fact of physical movement;" the "motive force" and expenditure of energy involved in getting from one place to another;
2. *representation,* "the representations of movement that give it shared meaning;" and
3. *practice,* "the experienced and embodied practice of movement."

Cresswell's triad, not surprisingly, is clearly based on Lefebvre's, though simplified (while Lefebvre's triad are imagined as interacting dialectically, Cresswell's are simply three different "aspects" of mobility; Lefebvre is concerned more generally with space and its production while Cresswell is considering mobility in particular). Also, while Lefebvre's triad, which insists on the dominant influence of representations of space, is largely meant to explain how enduring power structures are reproduced at the level of social space, Cresswell's is meant to problematize the immediate politics of the production of space at the moment of movement itself (and of outcomes such as why a person or thing moves, how fast, in what rhythm, by what route, with what feeling, and how it stops) (Cresswell 2010).

Drawing from these triads, spatial work can be defined as contributing to the production and reproduction of social space; and as furthermore productive of three specific, though interrelated, products: A. The *physical movement* of people, of things, etc. from place to place; the physical connection this establishes between "point A" and "point B;" B. The *experience of movement,* or of the connection of those places; in the case of the taxicab this relates to the affective experience of the ride, though in general this should refer to any affective impact of spatial work (the exhaustion of the commute or of driving in traffic, the pleasant surprise of receiving a package mailed by a distant friend); and C. The *articulation* of these places, movements, and experiences *with visions of society and the social.* This linkage is created in many ways, before, during and after travel; it is the field explored through concepts such as psychogeography, rhythmanalysis, and cognitive mapping; it is the sense in which the "mattering maps" by which we make sense of society are more than metaphorical (Grossberg 1992). Every journey is a "spatial story" (de Certeau 1984), telling the expected or unexpected connections between place and place, and between the people who live in and pass through them.

The politics of spatial work revolves around the control of these products. Spatial workers have always been the subjects of a range of disciplinary controls targeting their movements, affective interactions, and knowledge. The transportability and multifunctionality of smartphones and other mobile communicative devices – along with the tracking and computational power of the networks they are linked to – have brought an unprecedented opportunity for the rollout of projects to control spatial workers and their products. The transformation of analog space and practice through the ubiquity of digital interfaces is arguably one of the most important developments of our time; and it is not surprising that a profusion of metaphorical terms and theoretical approaches have arisen in response. Thus, digital connectivity is described as "ubiquitous" and "persistent;" "augmented" social space is *transduced* by the logic of software (Kitchin and Dodge 2011); or becomes a *hybrid*, simultaneously analog and digital (de Souza e Silva 2006). As Aurigi and de Cindio put it,

> In the augmented city, 'virtual' and 'physical' spaces are no longer two separate dimensions, but just parts of a continuum, of a whole. The physical and the digital environment have come to define each other and concepts such as public space and 'third place', identity and knowledge, citizenship and public participation are all inevitably affected by the shaping of the reconfigured, augmented urban space. (Aurigi and de Cindio 2008: 1)

Nevertheless, it is important to keep in mind the differences between the digital and analog spaces in which mobility is practiced, as well as what these differences are *not*. One is not more "real" than the other; one is not "physical" and the other ethereal; the augmentation of analog with digital space is made possible by a very physical global apparatus of servers, satellites, mobile devices, etc. (Bratton 2015). These spaces are, however, founded on different kinds of relationships, which can be illustrated through the differing ways in which space is measured by taximeters and by soft meters. Relationships in analog space are founded in adjacency and connectivity; relationships in digital space are founded in calculability. This is not to say that analog spaces can never be calculated or calculatable. Insofar as to be "analog" is to be comparable or in proportion with some standard of comparison, analog space is a space already in a relationship of measurement or representation: the analog is not the immanent. Digital practices can exist in analog space; for instance, counting the sheep that pass through a gate begins with direct indexical relationships which, once established, may be transformed into abstract symbols for calculation (Anderson 2011). The analog taximeter, invented in 1891, measures the distance of the trip by counting the rotations of the vehicle's wheels or axle (Gilbert and Samuels 1982: 34). Modern taximeters may use digital displays and integrate with digital payment systems, GPS, etc., but these remain founded on the initial analog measurement of space.

Digital space, in contrast, begins with symbolic relationships and calculability, and is only afterwards applied to indexical or analogous relationships. The digital space of the soft meter is composed of global positioning coordinates which exist independently of the cab trip, and indeed, of the geographic points to which they are plotted. The soft meter calculates the vehicle's successive positions in terms of these coordinates, then uses them to calculate the distance traveled. A foundationally digital space is created, even as drivers and passengers interpret these coordinates in terms of the analog space of the built environment and of human interaction.

Differing sets of practices are enabled and constrained by the differing logics and material affordances of digital and analog spaces (Galloway 2012). In analog space, mobility is a never-fully contained or calculated excess, which produces spatial relationships (for example, the path worn across a field would not exist without the mobile practices of animals, human walkers, etc.). But in digital space, the relationships between places are already determined – programed, or "emplaced" in De Certeau's terms – and mobility is simply the acting out of moves on the already inscribed "gamespace" of the map (Wark 2007). Anything that does not conform to the existing protocols simply is not registered and/or fails to take effect (Galloway 2004). This means that, whereas mobility in analog space is always to some degree *polytropic* – indeterminate, untrackable, and potentially deceiving – mobility in *protocological* digital space is inherently trackable, known, and circumscribed. The capacity for deception afforded by this polytropic mobility has long been a problem for analog projects of measurement or control; one of the appeals of digital space is that such *polytropoi* are eliminated in advance (cf. Nietzsche 1974: 344).

Of course, the actual digitally-enabled movements of humans and non-humans in cities take place in both analog and digital spaces, simultaneously. As Brian Massumi has argued, it is within the analog that power exists; to have any impact, the digital must operate through, and by means of, the analog (Massumi 2002). Next, I will describe in turn each of the three products of spatial work, and the means by which the mediation of such work through digital media is used to control and transform it in the case of the soft cab.

The studies from which the following descriptions are derived were almost completely conducted in the United States, where the soft cab originated. Donald Anderson conducted participant observation and ethnographic interviews with soft cab, taxi, and limousine drivers in San Francisco and in Tucson, Arizona (Anderson 2014, 2015), and analyzed the writings and video blogs of soft cab drivers in several US cities (Anderson 2016). Barry Brown, Marieke Glöss, and Moira McGregor interviewed taxi drivers, soft cab drivers, and passengers in San Francisco and London (Glöss et al. 2016). Min Kyung Lee, Daniel Kusbit, Evan Metsky, and Laura Dabbish analyzed soft-cab driver discourse in online forums, and interviewed soft cab drivers and passengers in Pittsburgh, Pennsylvania (Lee et al. 2015); Brenton J. Malin and Curry Chandler, also in Pittsburgh, followed a similar methodology (Malin and Chandler 2017). Alex Rosenblat and Luke Stark analyzed discourse on soft-cab driver forums, followed by ethnographic inter-views with drivers (Rosenblat and Stark, 2015, 2016). Benjamin V. Hanrahan, Ning F. Ma, and Chien Wen Yuan analyzed driver discourse on the online forum *uberpeople.com* (Hanrahan et al. 2017).

Moving and connecting places

Spatial workers are boundary crossers; a practice which entangles their image and identity with fears and concerns about the other and the alien, or even with the impure and the profane. This is particularly true for those workers who cross the boundaries between public and private space. Most obviously, domestic workers intrude upon the intimate space of middle and upper-class homes, as do, to a more limited extent, repair personnel and on-call health workers (cf. Gutierrez-Rodriguez 2014; Stacey 2005). The intimate nature of on-call sex work is self-evident. Cab and "ridesharing" drivers share the intimate interior of the car with their passengers for the duration of the ride, a fact which has spurred a long history of micropolitical contestation over the boundaries and meaning of in-cab interaction (Anderson 2004). Even delivery workers, when food is involved, impose upon the domestic sphere due to the affectively-imbued practice of serving food. The boundary crossing of these workers is rendered all the more volatile in that much of this work is performed by workers of a different class and ethnicity than their customers. (Boris and Nadasen 2008; Schaller 2004).

Liminal and precarious status incites further surveillance, and this is rolled out through the digital mediation of spatial work. By means of this digital mediation, spatial workers become constantly trackable, with an analyzable data trail. In the case of soft-cab services such as Uber and Lyft, the insertion of mobile labour platforms into the relationship between drivers and passengers has made possible a new form of "algorithmic management" (Lee et al. 2015), and transformed the car into a "digitally mediated workplace" (Hanrahan et al. 2017). A growing set of surveillance mechanisms are deployed to track, evaluate, and police the movement of drivers, in order to increase company control and assuage the concerns and fears of passengers (Lee et al. 2015; Glöss et al. 2016). The acceptability of drivers in the view of passengers is managed through driver profiles, which use a five-star rating system (discussed in more detail below), and, depending on the platform, additional details such as driver name, photo, car make and model, and even information on what kinds of music interests are shared by both driver and passenger. The larger soft-cab companies have developed means for tracking and evaluating the driving style of drivers based on smartphone sensor data, using algorithms to tag excessive braking, speeding, etc. Though not all of the potential applications of this information have yet been deployed, the intent is clearly to make use of the ubiquitous digital tracking of the smartphone app to render knowable the movements and behavior of drivers, for the purpose of more effective control.

The extent to which cabdrivers manage their own movements in urban space has long inspired projects of surveillance and control, from vehicle licensing and numbering, through police monitoring of cabstands, mandatory waybills and trip reporting, to (of course) the taximeter (Anderson 2012). Soft cab platforms make use of digital tracking and assymetrical access to information to further influence and control the movements of drivers (Rosenblat and Stark 2015). While the author's early research on soft cab drivers documented them recreating many of the spatio-temporal strategies long employed by cabdrivers (such as "deadheading" to busy areas, or "sandbagging" the locations of likely trips) (Anderson 2014), subsequent studies have detailed the increasing effort by soft cab companies to develop greater control over drivers, including in particular their movements in space (Lee et al. 2015; Rosenblat and Stark 2015; Malin and Chandler 2017). Dynamic pricing is used to lure drivers onto (and off of) the platform, and to attract them to specific areas where demand is expected to be high; hourly promotions and income guarantees based on number of trips completed, along with targeted "nudges" by text and email, bring drivers out on the road during specific hours, and keep them on the road, accepting calls (Malin and Chandler 2017; Rosenblatt and Stark 2015).

Soft-cab companies emphasize the role of their platforms in "connecting people" (i. e., drivers and passengers), and many drivers describe this as a primary benefit of the apps (Anderson 2015). The soft cab is established as a space purified of the taxicab's old, pre-digital means of connection, signification, and control, through an appeal to the technological prestige of algorithms (or what Rosenblat and Stark [2015: 8] call the "appeal to the concept of algorithms"). In this discourse the responsibility, and the agency, for the production of social space through connections is assigned to these mobile digital platforms, without which such connections come to be imagined as impossible.

Spatial Work as Affective Interaction

The intimacy of much spatial work is linked to the affective or emotion work involved. Hochschild used the concept of "emotion work" to describe the work done by workers whose jobs include the need to strictly manage one's own emotions, or at least the display thereof, in the work environment and during interactions, especially with customers; as well as the associated work of maintaining a (usually) positive relationship and atmosphere in the workplace. Such work involves guiding interaction towards certain feelings and/or meanings, which are then associated with the workplace or the service performed (Hochschild 1983). All forms of spatial work which entail interaction with clients involve some form of emotion work. Because all interactants are invested in the meaning and outcome of the interaction, the micropolitics are all the more fraught.

Platform apps work to control the affect of these interactions through ratings systems and controls over the performances of workers and to a lesser degree, of customers. The use of ratings systems to recruit customers into policing workers has begun to spread in many retail sectors, but is most marked, and most controversial, in the soft cab (Anderson 2016; Rosenblat and Stark 2016; Malin and Chandler 2017). With such a system, both drivers and passengers rate each other, on a scale of one to five, at the end of each ride. Drivers and passengers, thus, each accrue a personal rating, averaged from all those they have received, which forms part of their profile. The rating serves two purposes; first, both drivers and passengers are able to see each other's ratings as part of their profiles, and may choose not to request or accept rides with those who are low-rated. Second, both drivers and passengers who fall below a set rating run the risk of being removed from the system.

Although the ratings system ostensibly helps drivers identify and avoid potentially troublesome customers, the ratings system actually has little effect on customers, and other controls exerted on drivers limit their opportunities to exclude passengers based on ratings. The primary function of the ratings system is to induce a sense of anxiety in drivers, and to mediate the policing of drivers by passengers. The anxiety experienced by drivers, and the effect of this in making them a compliant workforce, is often emphasized in studies of soft-cab platforms (Anderson 2016; Rosenblat and Stark 2016). Drivers are encouraged to maintain as high a rating as possible (close to a 5.0), and are threatened with deactivation when their rating falls below 4.6 (depending on the app and the city). When their ratings go down, drivers do not receive a clear indication of what passenger rated them poorly, or why. The result is that drivers inculcate a generalized fear of upsetting customers, which governs their behavior during each ride.

Similar ratings systems have been used by other spatial labour platforms, such as those for home care workers and day labourers. Ratings systems seem especially suited for assuaging the fears of clients over sharing intimate or personal space with the potentially dangerous others involved in spatial labour. By disciplining the performance of workers, and labelling these performances with an ostensibly objective numerical value, the polytropic quality of the worker is resolved through digital mediation into a trackable, objectified quantity – a "data double," which is used against the drivers as a tool of control (Haggerty and Ericson 2000). Hanrahan et al. (2017: 1) argue that "the replacement of the relationships between the stakeholders by the platform [...] is a contributing factor to the decrease in contractual responsibilities each stakeholder has to one another," resulting in the enabling of bias and discrimination between passengers and drivers, as an effect of platform mediation.

Spatial Work as Articulation of the Social

Through their boundary crossings and affective interactions, spatial workers help create and disseminate visions of the city and of the social. Spatial labour relates different spaces of the city, tying them together – or separating them – in meaningful ways. As a result of their movement across the spatial boundaries of social stratification, and their affective labour in intimate circumstances with diverse clients, each kind of spatial worker must develop some particular form of occupational knowledge which doubles as a cognitive mapping, or an auto-ethnographic image of the social space of the city. Examples of such practical ethnographic knowledge will be found among occupations in which one deals regularly with individuals from a broad spectrum of society (electricians and plumbers, for instance, spend their days travelling through town seeing how other people live and work, in their homes and offices; even more intimate is the view of domestic workers working for on-demand house-cleaning services); or among any of those who, moving through different communities or social strata, must keep relearning "what people do" and how to interact (Heider 1975). At the same time, in practice spatial workers, for their clients and employers, often obscure this "hidden transcript" of subaltern knowledge and the "hidden injuries of class" behind a performance which reinforces an apologetic image of the social order (Sennet and Cobb 1972); this too is a product of spatial work.

The production of this social image, and whether it will challenge or reinforce social order, has long been at the heart of the ambivalent cultural image of cabdrivers; whether envisioned as city "ambassadors" in Toronto (Berry 2006), spreading rumors and news across Bangkok (Sopranzetti 2013), or telling spatial stories about driving to their passengers in San Francisco (Anderson 2004). While London cabdrivers famously train to learn "the Knowledge," an officially recognized understanding of the spatiotemporal ground for navigating their city, the same name and concept is applied unofficially by cabdrivers in cities around the world.

The digital labour platforms governing soft cab work seek to harness and control this same productive power. Through the app interface, soft-cab drivers are fed carefully measured portions of relevant information – locations of fares, routes to follow – that replace and pre-empt the traditional taxi drivers' need to develop a "knowledge" of the city. In place of the complex and polytropic performance of the cabdriver (Berry 2006), soft-cab drivers are given work doled out into a series of guided tasks – tap to accept hail, follow map navigation to location and destination – and are provided a narrative to follow which positions the soft cab and its driver as friendly, "sharing" alternatives to taxicabs and taxi drivers. As described in Anderson (2016) this narrative becomes an *allegorithm* when drivers use it as an (analog) "allegory" to interpret the algorithms governing their performance through the app's digital mediation. Recalling de Certeau's distinction between the perspectives of urban "walkers" and "voyeurs": it is as if the (analog) walkers came to understand their own actions through the mediation of the (digital) voyeurs' perspective (de Certeau 1984).

Malin and Chandler note, with irony, that many drivers internalize the "celebratory rhetoric of the digital workforce" which soft-cab companies promote (Malin and Chandler 2017: 384). This rhetoric emphasizes the freedom of choice and flexibility offered to drivers by the soft-cab platforms. Several authors have pointed out the contradiction between such claims to freedom, and the influential controls exerted over drivers through the "algorithmic management" of the app (Lee et al. 2015; Rosenblat and Stark 2015; Malin and Chandler 2017). Drivers resolve this contradiction by assuming the responsibility for their own submission to these controls, as a result of their free choice to enter into the job; this means, however, that drivers feel they should cede the right to complain about or contest the controls exerted by the companies; that drivers should "get over yourself" (Anderson 2015: 419) and "just deal with it as a driver" (Malin and Chandler 2017: 386).

Such submission is not only likely to "discourage the political activism that might help challenge the systemic problems facing these workers as a whole" (Malin and Chandler 2017: 397); it surrenders the very ground on which such problems could be contested. To the mediating platform is attributed the power to connect people and places, to manage the affective performances of drivers and passengers, and, in the end, to produce social space. The "right to the city" (Lefebvre 1996) becomes a privilege for properly behaved users of mobile platforms.

Mobile Digital Mediation and the Production of Social Space

Mobile labour platforms have made it possible for workplace control to extend beyond the mere interaction between customers and workers, and beyond the control of the immediate products of labour, to attempt new forms of control over the production of social space itself, as this is achieved through spatial labour. The struggle over the production of social space centers on the three parts of Lefebvre's "conceptual triad:" spatial practices, representational space, and representations of space. I have argued above and elsewhere (Anderson 2015) that Lefebvre's classic account overemphasizes the power and importance of the representation of space vis-a-vis representational spaces and spatial practices; this leads his theory into a somewhat static condition, which has, arguably, resulted in a greater contemporary interest in Lefebvre's more fluid account of rhythmanalysis (Lefebvre 2004) than in his theory of the production of space. The concept of spatial work as the mobile work involved in producing social space is intended to open up the politics of the production of social space to a more fluid analysis of the interaction of practices and affects.

Technology may be inevitable, but particular forms and effects of technology are not. The uses and outcomes of new technologies depend on the practices adopted by developers, producers, and users. The new forms of control exerted over spatial labourers through the digital mediation of mobile labour platforms, which I have detailed above, are projects in the making, not inevitable outcomes; and they have already sparked controversy and resistance. Although many drivers submit to the control of information through the company apps, others seek alternative channels of information, via other media such as online driver chat rooms, websites, and Facebook pages – there are even smartphone apps providing soft-cab drivers with the functionality of old-fashioned walky-talkies. Although many soft cab drivers embrace the affective framing of the allegorithm and the image of the "ridesharing" driver promoted by companies (Malin and Chandler 2017), others develop a critical stance and identity as working drivers; some even organize politically to challenge the companies' control over their work (Anderson 2015, 2016).

The politics of spatial labour in the soft cab illustrate the new sites of struggle over control and the production of social space which will take place as mobile digital labour platforms continue to develop. And although these platforms primarily focus on spatial *labourers*, the ubiquitous character of connected, hybrid space means that all kinds of spatial work can be transformed through similar projects of digital mediation – and beyond this, all of the work of social reproduction (Urry 2007: 41). As mobile digital platforms are used to mediate, track, and analyze more and more of our interactions and social lives, value extraction and means of control become ubiquitous as well; we are all mobile digital workers, now. But just what this will come to mean, and how it will transform the production of social space, depends on our response.

References

Anderson, Donald N. (2004): Playing for Hire: Discourse, Knowledge, and Strategies of Cabdriving in San Francisco, MA Thesis: California State University, Hayward.

Anderson, Donald N. (2011): "Major and Minor Chronotopes in a Specialized Counting System." In: Journal of Linguistic Anthropology 21/1, pp. 121–141.

Anderson, Donald N. (2012): "The Spy in the Cab: The Use and Abuse of Taxicab Cameras in San Francisco." In: Surveillance & Society 10/2, pp. 150–166.

Anderson, Donald N. (2014): "Not Just a Taxi"? For-profit Ridesharing, Driver Strategies, and VMT." In: Transportation 41, pp. 1099–1117.

Anderson, Donald N. (2015): In Cisio Scribere: Labor, Knowledge, and Politics of Cabdriving in Mexico City and San Francisco, Doctoral Dissertation, University of Arizona.

Anderson, Donald N. (2016): "Wheels in the Head: Ridesharing as Monitored Performance." In: Surveillance & Society 14/2, pp. 240–258.

Aurigi, Allesandro/De Cindio, Fiorella (2008): "Introduction: Augmented Urban Spaces." In: Allesandro Aurigi/Fiorella De Cindio (eds.), Augmented Urban Spaces: Articulating the Physical and Electronic City, Burlington, VT: Ashgate, pp. 1–3.

Berry, Kimberly (2006): The Independent Servant: a socio-cultural examination of the post-war Toronto taxi driver, Doctoral Dissertation, University of Ottawa.

Boris, Eileen/Nadasen, Premilla (2008): "Domestic Workers Organize!" In: WorkingUSA: The Journal of Labor and Society 11, pp. 413–437.

Bratton, Benjamin (2015): The Stack: On Software and Sovereignty, Cambridge, MA: MIT Press.

de Certeau, Michel (1984): The Practice of Everyday Life, Berkeley: University of California Press.

Cresswell, Tim. (2006): On the Move: Mobility in the Modern Western World, New York: Routledge.

Cresswell, Tim. (2010): "Towards a Politics of Mobility." In: Environment and Planning D 28, pp. 17–31.

Fish, Adam/Srinavasan, Ramesh (2012): "Digital labor is the new killer app." In: New Media & Society 14/1, pp. 137–152.

Foucault, Michel (1983): "The Subject and Power." In: Hubert Dreyfus/Paul Rabinow (eds.), Michel Foucault: Beyond Structuralism and Hermeneutics, Chicago: University of Chicago Press.

Fuchs, Christian/Sevignani, Sebastian (2013): "What is Digital Labour? What is Digital Work? What's their Difference? And why do these Questions Matter for Understanding Social Media?" In: tripleC 11/2, pp. 237–293.

Galloway, Alexander R. (2004): Protocol: How Control Exists After Decentralization, Cambridge, MA: MIT Press.

Galloway, Alexander R. (2012): The Interface Effect, Malden, MA: Polity Press.

Gilbert, Gorman/Samuels, Robert E. (1982): The Taxicab: An Urban Transportation Survivor, Chapel Hill, NC: University of North Carolina Press.

Glöss, Marieke/McGregor, Moira/Brown, Barry (2016): "Designing for Labour: Uber and the On-Demand Mobile Workforce." In: Proceedings of CHI 2016.

Grossberg, Lawrence (1992): We Gotta Get Out of This Place: Popular Conservatism and Postmodern Culture, New York: Routledge.

Gutierrez-Rodriguez, Encarnacion (2014): "Domestic work–affective labor: On feminization and the coloniality of labor." In: Women's Studies International Forum 46, pp. 45–53.

Haggerty, Kevin D./Richard V. Ericson. (2000): "The Surveillant Assemblage." In: British Journal of Sociology 51/4, pp. 605–22.

Hanrahan, Benjamin V./Ma, Ning F./Yuan, Chien Wen (2017): "The Roots of Bias on Uber." In: Proceedings of 15th European Conference on Computer-Supported Cooperative Work – Exploratory Papers, Reports of the European Society for Socially Embedded Technologies.

Heider, Karl (1975): "What do people do? Dani Auto-ethnography." In: Journal of Anthropological Research 31, pp. 3–17.

Hochschild, Arlie Russell (1983): The Managed Heart: The Commercialization of Human Feeling, Berkeley: University of California Press.

Kitchin, Rob/Dodge, Martin (2011): Code/Space: Software and Everyday Life, Cambridge, MA: MIT Press.

Larsen, Jonas/Urry, John/Axhausen, Kay (2006) Mobilities, Networks, Geographies, Burlington, VT: Ashgate.

Latour, Bruno (2005): Reassembling the Social: An Introduction to Actor-Network-Theory, New York: Oxford University Press.

Lee, Min Kyung/Kusbit, Daniel/Metsky, Evan/Dabbish, Laura (2015): "Working with Machines: The Impact of Algorithmic and Data-Driven Management on Human Workers." In: Proceedings of the 33rd Annual ACM Conference on Human Factors in Computing Systems, pp. 1603–1612.

Lefebvre, Henri (1991): The Production of Space, Cambridge, MA: Blackwell.

Lefebvre, Henri (1996): Writings on Cities, Malden, MA: Blackwell.

Lefebvre, Henri (2004): Rhythmanalysis: Space, Time, and Everyday Life, New York: Continuum.

Malin, Brenton J./Chandler, Curry (2017): "Free to Work Anxiously: Splintering Precarity Among Drivers for Uber and Lyft" In: Culture & Critique 10/2, pp. 382–400.

Marx, Karl (1967): Capital, Vol 1.: A Critical Analysis of Capitalist Production, New York: International Publishers.

Massumi, Brian (2002): Parables for the Virtual: Movement, Affect, Sensation, Durham, NC: Duke University Press.

Nietzsche, Friedrich (1974): The Gay Science, New York: Vintage Books.

Rosenblat, Alex/Stark, Luke (2015): Uber's Drivers: Information Asymmetries and Control in Dynamic Work. Brussels: Data & Society Research Institute.

Rosenblat, Alex/Stark, Luke (2016): "Algorithmic Labor and Information Asymmetries: A Case Study of Uber's Drivers." In: International Journal of Communication 10, pp. 3758–3784.

Schaller, Bruce (2004): The Changing Face of Taxi and Limousine Drivers, New York: Schaller Consulting.

Sennett, Richard/Cobb, Jonathan (1972): The Hidden Injuries of Class, New York: Alfred A. Knopf.

Sheller, Mimi/Urry, John (2006): "The New Mobilities Paradigm." In: Environment and Planning A 38, pp. 207–226.

Slee, Tom (2015): What's Yours is Mine: Against the Sharing Economy, New York: OR Books.

Sopranzetti, Claudio (2013): The Owners of the Map: Motorcycle Taxi Drivers, Mobility, and Politics in Bangkok, Doctoral Dissertation, Harvard University.

de Souza e Silva, Adriana (2006): "From Cyber to Hybrid: Mobile Technologies as Interfaces of Hybrid Spaces." In: Space and Culture 9/3, pp. 261–278.

Stacey, Clare L. (2005): "Finding dignity in dirty work: the constraints and rewards of low-wage home care labour." In: Sociology of Health & Illness 27/6, pp. 831–854.

Stiegler, Bernard (2010): For a New Critique of Political Economy, Malden, MA: Polity Press.

Urry, John (1999): Sociology Beyond Societies: Mobilities for the Twenty-First Century, New York: Routledge.

Urry, John (2007): Mobilities, Cambridge, UK: Polity Press.

van Doorn, Niels (2017): "Platform labor: on the gendered and racialized exploitation of low-incomeservice work in the 'on-demand' economy." In: Information, Communication & Society 20/6, pp. 898–914.

Wark, McKenzie (2007): Gamer Theory, Cambridge, MA: Harvard University Press.

So 'Hot' Right Now

Reflections on Virality and Sociality from Transnational Digital China

Jamie Coates

Abstract

A reflection of both the intensity of sharing practices and the appeal of shared content, the term 'viral' is often seen as coterminous with the digital media age. In particular, social media and mobile technologies afford users the ability to create and share content that spreads in 'infectious' ways. These technologies have caused moral panics in recent years, particularly within heavily regulated and censored media environments such as the People's Republic of China (PRC). This paper uses the spread of a 'viral' sex video among young Chinese-speaking people who live transnational lives between Japan, China, and Taiwan, to reflect upon the question of 'viral' media as it is conceptualised more broadly. Their position both inside and outside Sinophone mediascapes affords a useful case study to think beyond purely institutional discussions of Chinese media, and focus on the ways media practices, affects, and affordances shape patterns of content distribution. It examines the language and practices of 'virality' among Chinese-speaking people in Tokyo and shows how the appeal of content like the sex video 'digital stuff' on WeChat are typically a digital amplification of pre-existing social practice. Described in terms of 'sociothermic affects' (Chau 2008) such as 'fever' and 'heat' (re/huo), the infectious nature of media is imagined in different but commensurate forms of virality that precedes the digital age. In the digital age however, virality is also made scalable (Miller et al. 2016) in new ways.

Introduction

In July 2015, I was sitting in an old coffee shop in Shinjuku, Tokyo, when a 'viral' phenomenon broke out among my Chinese informants living in the city. I had been researching how media practices of young Chinese people in Japan effect their local social lives and political attitudes. I was passing the time with one of my closer friends and informants, who was a language student from Northeast China. Lin had completed her undergraduate degree in Beijing before moving

DOI 10.14361/dcs-2017-0206

DCS | Digital Culture and Society | Vol. 3, Issue 2 | © transcript 2017

to Japan for further studies, and had hopes of doing something creative such as photography or fashion. We had been lounging with one eye on our phones and another on the overfilled ashtray on the table, occasionally commenting on something and holding up our smartphones to show each other what we were looking at. This mode of hanging out, co-present in both digital and corporeal terms, was the most common way we would spend time together, our interpersonal commentary serving as a meta-commentary on various social media. As she often did, Lin cursed and chuckled as she held her phone up to my face. 'Look, look' she taunted, as I started to work out what I was seeing. It was a video of a young man and woman having sex while standing in a changing room, the woman topless and pressed up against the mirror as the man held his smartphone up to film them. The few words spoken were mostly muffled by Chinese-language service announcements and banter from outside the changing room. Lin laughed and said 'people are such perverts' and, after I mistakenly asked if the film was taken in Japan and whether the people were her friends, she said 'no, no, this is just something that has blown-up and become a craze *(bao re)* in China.'

This is how I first came to know about a video of a young Chinese couple having sex in the Sanlitun, Beijing outlet of the Japanese clothing store 'Uniqlo'. The impact of this one piece of footage was such that it was reported in several major English-speaking news outlets (cf. Phillips 2015; News.com.au 2015; Sola 2015). Translated to the Anglophone world, the terms 'viral' and 'meme' were often repeated as a common way of describing how popular and widespread the video had become. Moreover, the video became a focal point for discussions of censorship in China, and the punitive measures taken to curb sexually explicit content on the 'Chinese' internet. These acts of translation, and the idea of a censorship created digital-divide between China and the world, struck me as fruitful ground to reflect upon the mobile practices and emic terminology that inform Sinophone digital practice, particularly as a form of alterity that might complicate our understanding of 'virals' and 'memes'. Events such as the sex video often pepper the news outside of China, but are typically reduced to debates around the Chinese government's efforts to censor the 'Chinese' internet. While these issues are of concern, I am equally concerned by how little Chinese digital practice informs the theorization of media, and the degree to which popular media terms from the Anglo-European context are unreflexively applied to alternative digital media ecologies.

Why was this 'craze' *(re)* called a 'viral' in English-language media? What does 'viral' mean? In popular Anglophone usage, the term 'viral' is associated with the rise of digital media, even more so since the advent of social media (Burgess 2008). The concept of 'viral media' has been attributed to several people. Some trace the origins of 'viral media' to the 'viral marketing' campaigns of the 1990s (Nahon et al. 2011; Jurvetson and Draper 1997) whereas others have shown how its early academic inception can be found in the 1994 book *Media Virus* where Douglas Rushkoff argues 'media events are not *like* viruses. They *are* viruses,'

(Rushkoff 1994: 9). The tendency to equate the spread of media content with biological processes however, has a long history extending beyond the term 'viral' (Shifman 2014). For example, it is often quoted that current popular understandings of 'viral' media are strongly influenced by another term: 'meme' (Dawkins 1976). Borrowing from the Greek term for imitation *mimema*, Richard Dawkins coined the term 'meme' to argue that 'Cultural transmission is analogous to genetic transmission' (1976, 189), defining 'memes' as units of culture that replicate across milieu. Eager to suggest that 'memes' seek reproduction in ways akin to genetic survival, Dawkins and many 'meme' enthusiasts have suggested that phenomena as wide as ideas, linguistic patterns, and faith in God can be attributed to the virus-like propagation of 'memes'. From the late 1980s into the early 2000s, a field intended to study the spread of memes, *mimetics*, grew in popular discourse. Public advocates for mimetics, such as Susan Blackmore (Blackmore and Dawkins 2000), have tried to explain almost everything as 'memes'. Somewhat deservingly, clumsy efforts to sidestep the empirical findings of fields such as anthropology, sociology, and linguistics attracted many critics of 'memes' (Aunger 2001; Downey 2008; Sperber 1996) and over the same time and in a similar fashion, the concept of 'viral' media attracted its own critics (Arauz 2008; Chapman 2010; Yakob 2008).

The major objections with both the concepts of 'meme' and 'viral' largely revolve around a perceived misattribution of agency, as well as various inconsistencies in the conceptualization of *what* is transmitted and *how* it is re-produced. For example, in suggesting their own concept of 'spreadability' as a solution to 'viral' metaphors, Jenkins, Ford and Green argue that the term 'viral' overlooks the active role people play in producing participatory cultures, where media content is spread as a part of social practice (Jenkins, Ford, and Green 2013). Similarly, the terms 'viral' and 'meme' have been criticized for their appeals to 'scientistic' authority (Aunger 2001). Greg Downey summarizes these criticisms in his sarcastically phrased 'We hate memes, pass it on' (Downey 2008) where he shows how the attribution of personality-like qualities such as 'selfish' to cultural phenomena overlooks the role of people, institutions, and pedagogy.

Despite the many analytic shortcomings of 'virals' and 'memes', the rapid spread and seductive qualities of media content are common topics in popular discourse, and these terms are part of how we understand digital media in everyday Anglo-European life. For example, popular commentators such as Bill Wasik have suggested that America is now a 'viral culture' (Wasik 2009), and google trends searches for both 'memes' and 'virals' show consistent growth in the use of these terms in English-language net culture since 2004 (Google 2017). With the widespread debate and everyday use of the term 'viral' within Anglophone worlds it would seem disingenuous to dismiss popular understandings of 'virals' and 'memes', as these phenomena play reality altering roles in many social contexts. Rather, in the spirit of the 'ontological turn', perhaps we should take the gap between emic and etic understandings of viral media as a methodological and epistemological opportunity (Holbraad and Pedersen 2017). As John Postill has shown in positing the term 'viral reality', the rapid spread of media content and the ways they reshape political and social processes in Europe is 'real' (Postill 2014). What is more, as Postill clearly outlines, concerns about the viral qualities of social media and digital practice have caused many to debate the very 'real' consequences these practices might have for democracy, particularly in relation to the activism in Egypt in recent years (cf. Almiraat, 2011). The question remains however, whether there are alternative 'viral realities'. Investigating what it means to be 'viral' within highly mobile Chinese digital cultures serves as a methodological injunction to rethink our approach to media events and the processes that allow them to spread.

Within this paper I reflect upon the terms we use to conceptualize 'viral' content as a window onto the relationship between digital content, sociality, and practice. Thinking from the Chinese context I trace an alternative genealogy of 'virality' to show that, in as much as digital practice has accelerated the spread of media content, the rapid and seductive spread of meaning has a long history that precedes digital life. Building on this genealogy, I concur with Miller et al.'s recent social media research cohort that it is the scalable sociality of contemporary media that distinguishes it from previous media forms (Miller et al. 2016). I extend the concept of scalable sociality to include scalable content as a means to understand virality, and in turn argue that digital practice is perhaps best understood as a form of scalable virality. Understanding the virality of content as it spreads through Chinese networks, particularly networks that operate on transnational scales, helps us explore the relationship between digital life and mobility. It demonstrates the role of digital affordances in making content 'mobile', while also attending to the the differing ways this semiotic mobility is described and imbued with meaning.

The alterity of digital China

It is difficult to avoid speaking about the 'Chinese' internet and its related terms and practices, without veering towards the language of 'techno-orientalism' (De Seta 2016a; Morley 1995). And yet, it is important to understand the ways infrastructure development, the politics of censorship (Wallis 2015), and their occasionally carnivalesque practices (Herold and Marolt 2013), have led to an alternative ecology of media practices (De Seta 2016a; Lum 2014). These practices are not relegated to the PRC but spread out, rhizomatically (Bateson 1958; Deleuze and Guattari 1987), among Chinese-speaking peoples worldwide. Rather than treating the alterity of Sinophone digital practices as a bounded site of difference, I interpret it as a methodological opportunity to reflect upon the potentially taken-for-granted ontological suppositions of terms such as 'viral' and their associated practices (Holbraad and Pedersen 2017). In order to situate the terms mentioned above, and the practices I will go on to explain, it is important to understand some of the general history and layout of China's digital landscape.

Although the 'Chinese' internet developed over a similar time period as the internet in the rest of the world, the legal and infrastructural processes that have shaped it ensure that it has a history that distinguishes it from broader narratives about digital globalization (Herold and Marolt 2013; Herold and De Seta 2015; Qiu and Chan 2013; Yang 2011). Today, the advent of mobile technologies and Sinophone media developers' efforts to capture this market has created an inseparable link between digital life and everyday mobilities. However, much like in other parts of the world, this widespread access and popularity was less so the case twenty years ago. Private use of digital networks at home was not made legally available to citizens of the People's Republic of China (PRC) until 1997, and a significant rural-urban divide exacerbated unequal access to digital technologies in the early 2000s. For example, only 1.8% of the population had access to the internet in the PRC in 2000 (CINIC 2017). Government policies surrounding censorship created an image of China's online world as bounded and regulated, epitomized in the term 'the Great Firewall of China', which was purportedly coined by Sinologists Geremie Barme and Sang Ye for a *wired* magazine report (De Seta 2016b). The 'Firewall' is a cluster of government campaigns, technologies and practices, such as the 'Golden Shield Project' initiated in 1998; the failed 2009 software filter 'Green Dam Youth Escort' *(Lüba Huaqi Huhang)*; and, the 2014 campaign 'Clean Web: Sweeping Away Pornography and Striking Illegality' *(Saohuang Dafei Jingwang)*. It is patchy, porous, and relatively ineffective against the motivated and tech-savvy, but 'the Great Firewall' serves as an imagined barrier between China and the rest of the world, informing digital practices in various ways. For example, Facebook and Twitter were banned in China in 2009 following reports that rioters in Xinjiang were using the services to communicate. And Google and its associated services, such as Youtube, withdrew from China in 2010 after disputes over censorship. The common practice of using VPNs to side-step official bans have been called 'crossing over the wall' *(fanqiang)*, and they have enabled motivated fans of international pop culture, such as fans of the Japanese celebrity Aoi Sola (Coates 2014, 2017), to participate in Twitter and Facebook discussions. At the same time, censorship measures have ensured that, in practice, non-Chinese social media platforms that appear seemingly ubiquitous worldwide, are far less popular than their Chinese counterparts.

At the end of 2016, 53.2% of the PRC population officially had internet access amounting to over 731 million users, 27.4% of these users lived in China's rural areas (CINIC 2017). However, these figures are difficult to verify and are likely conservative. The use of internet cafés and phone sharing in rural areas, for example, suggests that shared access may be more prevalent than official figures. The popularization of mobile technologies has dramatically changed the landscape of digital practices in China over the past 10 years. In 2007 a little over 10% of the Chinese population had internet access and were largely dependent on desktop computers. 24 % of net users utilized mobile technologies in 2007, while today 95.1 % predominantly use smartphones (CINIC 2017). Due to these changes, mobile internet access is not only reshaping urban lives, but plays increasingly important roles in rural people's lives (McDonald 2016), and the lives of rural-urban migrant workers (Wang 2016).

In many senses, Chinese digital life constitutes the largest network of alternative platforms, practices and meanings in the world. There are information services akin to Google such as Baidu; originally browser based social networks such as QQ, the ICQ-like messaging service founded in 1999 which has grown to become a multi-media platform; microblogs that have been equated to Twitter, like Sina Weibo; and, most recently a variety of smartphone based apps such as WeChat, which was started in 2011, and Tantan, established in 2014. While these services are often touted as alternatives or even 'copies' of Facebook, Twitter, and Tinder, they are distinct assemblages of socialities, meanings, and practices. Historically, China's most popular microblogging platform, Sina Weibo has been one of the major focuses of scholarly attention. Launched in 2009, Sina Weibo is a publicly visible platform with functions originally similar to Twitter, but it has since evolved to incorporate a range of other content and uses that hold similarities with Instagram, Facebook and Youtube. Due to its public visibility and longer history, it has been easier to study in an ethically justifiable way (Svensson 2017), and has attracted a range of methodologies with a focus on politics and online discourse in China (Schneider 2015; Svensson 2015; Wu et al. 2011; Wu et al. 2013; Yuan, Feng, and Danowski 2013). Complimenting this microblog research, recent ethnographic work has come to the increasing consensus that platform choice differs between locales, performances, and socialities (Miller et al. 2016), and that microblogs may not best reflect everyday practice. For example, Tom McDonald has shown in his study of social media use among rural villagers that Sina Weibo was not very popular and that his informant's choice of QQ as their favoured platform related to the degree of visibility and the socialities this visibility affords (2016). As one of China's oldest social media platforms, QQ provided his informants the most services and possibilities to manage their presentation of self (Goffman 1959), using functions as varied as music and video streaming to private and group-based messaging. In contrast, recent work on rural-urban migration (Wang 2016), and other Chinese urban contexts (De Seta and Proksell 2015; De Seta 2016a; Holmes et al. 2015; Sun 2016) have found WeChat to be the fastest growing and most popular form of social media among young urbanites.

In line with most findings over the past 5 years of urban digital practice research in China, I found WeChat had become the most common way Sinophone socialities were produced in Tokyo. A relative latecomer to the social media game, WeChat (*Weixin* lit. Micro-message) has grown to become almost synonymous with Chinese smartphone-based social media. In early 2017, 80 % of Chinese mobile internet users surveyed reported using WeChat (CINIC 2017), with 938 million users worldwide in the first quarter of 2017 (Hariharan 2017). It is the second largest messaging app in the world, after Facebook Messenger. WeChat was started as an app by Tencent in 2011, the same company as QQ and one of the oldest social media developers in China. Originally a side project in 2011, its purely app-based functionalities have since become one of Tencent's most successful products, and in many ways heralds an increasingly inseparable marriage between digital practices and mobility. The app itself requires verification through a telephone number, and was originally only intended for smartphone use, although online and PC-based versions have since been made that you can log into by verifying them on your phone. Each quarter WeChat gains new functionalities, making it difficult to summarize in many ways. As of early 2017, WeChat consisted of a cascading wall (called moments in English) where you can share general content with your personal contacts; group walls formed out of your contacts and their own contacts; official accounts that act as news services and interest groups; financial services that allow the gifting of money, and immediate payment for services and commodities in China; and, a range of other apps and games that operate in conjunction with WeChat. In terms of messaging content, WeChat encourages the mixing of text, audio-messaging, videos and images, and has developed a complex ecosystem of Gif-like animations and emojis that are designed to only work within WeChat.

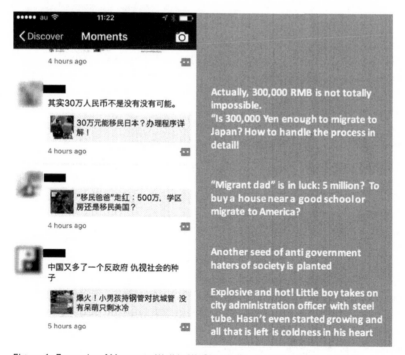

Figure 1: Example of Moments Wall in WeChat (left), and translation (right).

The WeChat users I met in Tokyo spanned mainland Chinese and Taiwanese users, with occasional speakers of standardised mandarin *(Putonghua/Guoyu)* who had no ethnic Chinese heritage, such as myself. In this sense, although dominated by mainland Chinese users, WeChat was more an assemblage of Sinophone sociality than it was a form of 'Chinese' social media. It was not simply made up of citizens from the PRC, but also people who were linguistically and culturally competent in Chinese-languages. Its Chineseness depended on shared and approximate semiotic logics rather than strictly defined ethnic identifications. For example, the ability to joke and understand the many layered references encompassed in other people's humorous content shaped group-membership more than ethnic or national identity. Similarly, the written script shared between many Sinophone and other North East Asian languages ensured that WeChat afforded forms of conviviality and connection between people who might otherwise not associate with each other. Yet, this pattern of sociality grew out of largely embodied encounters with each other in Tokyo. The WeChat users I followed were a series of overlapping networks grown out of face-to-face interactions within various spaces of consumption and play within Tokyo. Exchanging WeChat contact details was incredibly common, and often served the function of a handshake within crowded clubs and restaurants. 'Do you use/play with *(wan)* WeChat?' followed by a quick exchange of details using either a proximity based search or the scan of a QR code, became a phrase and practice that invited strangers to become acquaintances. The term *wan* (use/play) embodies the way communication, utility, and play, are often collapsed into each other in Sinophone sociality. It also demonstrates how the linguistic idiosyncrasies of one language might elucidate the experiences of other sociocultural worlds. As a native English-speaker it is easy to understand how social media might be understood as a field of play, and yet it also evokes different associations than saying 'Are you on Facebook, or can I find/follow you on Twitter', as we might in English. Using the same method as my interlocutors I asked for permission to become contacts with, and eventually follow, several networks on WeChat. One group was specifically formed for the purpose of my research and several others relating to various specific interest groups spanned both Tokyo, Taiwan, and mainland China. There was a group for the employees and followers of a local Chinese-language news service; a group of billiards enthusiasts; one group was for a bar and one was for a group of artists and their friends. There were also two groups for specific businesses, two for fans of dining in Tokyo, and two were general chat rooms for separate networks of friends. Overall the groups covered roughly 300 people. Despite the varied nature of these groups, the sex video spread throughout their varied discussions. Over the 48 hours following when I first saw the sex video with Lin, I witnessed the short video repeated several times in differing forms within each of the groups. A range of creative responses built on the original video were passed from group to group. And they combined group-member created responses, with other popular user-generated images and jokes from the wider ecology of Sinophone digital content.

A Chinese Viral, Meme or 'Craze'?

As part of a practice-oriented approach to digital media, it is worth interrogating the terms used to describe these practices. Within this section I interrogate Chinese 'virals' from a keyword perspective (Williams 1985), seeing whether alternative terms for the contagious qualities of media might add to the 'concept-metaphors' (Moore 2004) we use to understand these practices. The words 'meme' and 'viral' have been translated into Chinese but serve different conceptual and metaphoric purposes than their English counterparts. Meme has been translated as either *miyin* or *moyin*, which connotes the 'charming' *(mi)* or imitative *(mo)* elements *(yin)* of popular cultural assemblages. However, in daily practice this translation of 'meme' is not widely used among Chinese speakers, save for when reporting on international discourses on 'memes' which already feature the term. Similarly, although there is a translated term for 'contagious media' *(chuanran meiti)* and 'viral broadcast' *(bingdushi/xing chuanbo)*, discussions of 'virals' are either business-oriented, such as in viral marketing, or they are used by Chinese government censors to describe the malicious qualities of certain media content. The Uniqlo sex video is one example of the use of 'viral' in official government rhetoric.

Although the official details of the case are difficult to verify, the predominant narrative surrounding the sex video is as follows. After deciding to break up, the couple made the video as a risqué memento sometime before the film was circulated. However, around the 13th of July, the young woman lost her phone, and the person who found it distributed the film through her WeChat account. The sex video was subsequently posted on the more publicly visible Sina Weibo on July 14th, and spread quickly in the following 24 hours (YahooHK 2015). After spreading quickly, many 'netizens' *(wangmin)* suspected the film was an advertising prank on the part of 'Uniqlo' itself. This suspicion attracted the attention of the Cyberspace Administration of China (CAC) officials because the distribution of sexually explicit material for profit is a serious offence in the PRC, and an advertising campaign using these tactics would constitute a violation of Chinese law. However, these accusations were later dismissed by the CAC after a public statement from Uniqlo-China's manager (Thepaper.cn 2015). As the sex video spread, a search for the couple turned into the popularly called practice of 'human flesh search engine' *(renrousousuo)* (Shuimu 2015), a term used to describe situations where large numbers of users engage in a carnivalesque search for individuals' identities (Herold and Marolt 2013). This led to a string of false identifications of the couple involved, before two business students from Beijing Union University were identified and admitted to being the couple in the film. 5 people were arrested in relation to the Uniqlo sex video, including the couple in the film and three others charged with circulating the film.

Two days after the initial circulation of the Uniqlo Sex video, the CAC issued a statement declaring: "The online *'bingdushi'* (virus-style) dissemination of the 'vulgar *(buya)* changing-room video' breaks the '7 foundational clauses' *(qitiao dixian)* of the CAC, and seriously violates the core of socialist principles" (CAC 2015). As this statement suggests, in the eyes of Chinese officials the term 'viral' speaks as much to their uncontrollable and violating qualities, as they do to their spreadability. As Elizabeth Povinelli argues, the 'Virus' acts as a powerful figure in current regimes of governance (Povinelli 2016). Describing contemporary governance as *geontopower*, which depends on regulating the distinction between Life and Nonlife, Povinelli argues the 'Virus' antagonizes power structures because 'It confuses and levels the difference between Life and Nonlife while carefully taking advantage of the minutest aspects of their differentiation' (2016: 19). In a similar way, the CAC statement is suggestive of the capacity for images and meanings to spread and seemingly take on a life of their own, challenging the Life-Nonlife distinctions of meaning and media, and disrupting any government-level pretence of a responsible Chinese citizenry. In this sense, describing virals as virals is in many ways 'seeing like the state' in the Chinese context (Scott 1999).

From the perspective of the groups of Chinese youths in Tokyo I conducted my fieldwork with, the sex video was not a 'viral video' or a 'meme', but rather 'fiery' *(huo)*, explosive *(bao)* and 'hot' *(re)*. It was defined by its qualities, rather than as an object. The terms they used reflected a wider trend within Chinese discourse to describe the popularity of a joke, term, or video, through metaphors of heat. Much like in earlier English-language descriptions of celebrity and popularity that precede the internet, a character or media event in contemporary Chinese vernacular can be described as 'hot' *(re)*, as 'on fire' or 'fiery' *(huo)*, as well as other qualities associated with heat, such as the colour red *(hong)*. These references to heat invoke equally contagious but less biomedical images of virality in the Chinese context. Moreover, they show connections to an older history of social crazes in China, with some ethnomedical connotations akin to, but also different from, the English term 'viral'. Heat can spread in virus-like ways for example, and an excess of heat and energy, such as the condition of *shanghuo* (literally 'rising fire'), is often prescribed as a cause of poor health within Chinese ethnomedical systems (Rongrong and Hiroshi 2008). Taking on heat can be caused by the overconsumption of heat-inducing foods within Chinese ethnomedical classifications, such as dog meat, but has also been associated with certain patterns of thought and workplace stress in recent years.

Although not directly equated with illness, the contagious qualities of social crazes in reform era China have also been described using the term 'hot/heat' *(re)*, which has in turn been translated using terms such as 'fever' and 'craze'. As David Palmer describes *re* in *Qigong Fever*:

A 'fever' is a form of collective effervescence in China's post-totalitarian phase which occurs when official policies and informal signals sent from above correspond with, open the space for, and amplify popular desire, which appropriates these spaces in unexpected ways, simultaneously complying with, appropriating, disrupting and mirroring the projects of state hegemony (Palmer 2007: 81).

Since the early 1980s there have been countless 'fevers' and 'crazes' including, a 'Chairman Mao *re*' (Barme 2016), a 'Culture *re*' (Wang 1996), a 'Stock Trading *re*' (Hertz 1998), and a 'Leaving Country *re*' (Louie 2004). In more recent years, the tendency for *re* has accelerated and proliferated in micro-blogging networks, with reports of ethno-patriotic crazes like the Ming Dynasty *re* (Shui 2007) and an anti-Japanese *re* (Kanke 2012).

The concept-metaphor *re* and other heat-related terms thus stand for an emic conceptualisation of the virality of everyday social life. Adam Yuet Chau has explored these themes in his discussion of the 'red-hot sociality' *(honghuo)* of festivals and events in China as part of his call to focus on the sensory production of sociality (Chau 2008). Drawing on a longer history of scholarship on 'heat' *(re)* and the positive valuation of 'heat and noise' *(renao)* in religious activities and markets in China and Taiwan (Weller 1994; Yu 2004), Chau suggests 'sociothermic affect' (499) as a 'native conception' (498) of sociality and effervescence (Durkheim 1965) in China and Taiwan. Sociothermic affects are 'more diffused than "feelings" and more complex than simple excitement' (499). They are a mode of social excitement reminiscent of Durkheim's 'collective effervescence' (1965), although they attend more to the dynamics of intimacy and estrangement between actors, rather than the effervescence of society as a whole. Prosocial affects are associated with heat, whereas antisocial affects are associated with cold. According to Chau the distinctly social nature of these affects ensures that they also evade a simple interpretivist framework, because they not only involve acts of communication but also 'the body, the senses and being-in-the-world' (500). In his other work Chau has used Actor-Network Theory (Latour 2005) to show the central role the amassing of 'non-human actants', such as pigs and consumable intoxicants, plays in the production of festive sociality and its sociothermic qualities (Chau 2013).

These terms and metaphors imply a native concept of 'spreadability' (Jenkins, Ford, and Green 2013) that both posits media content as 'catching' in an affective sense, if not 'contagious' in biological ways. The contagious image of sociothermic affects indicate that the enthusiastic re-production of sociality can take on properties beyond the control of lone interpretants without succumbing to an understanding of media and meaning as somehow having a personality of their own. Chinese understandings of sociality as spreadable, seductive, and affective, suggest that social life has always been contagious. And indeed, emic understandings of sociality, encapsulated in terms like *guanxi* (connections) and *renqing* (human sentiment), underpin a large part of the anthropological and sociological understanding of China (Kipnis 2002; Gold, Guthrie, and Wank 2002; Sun 1990; Yang 1994). From the language used to describe sociality, to the preponderance of pre-internet era 'crazes' it is clear that the enthusiastic social spread of meaning is by no means relegated to social media. If, as Postill suggests, we live in 'viral reality' today (Postill 2014), then from a Sinophone perspective we might say that we have always been viral.

Scalable Virality

As the official Chinese response to the sex video suggests, there is a difference between positing media content *as a virus*, and recognizing the tendency for media content to spread and gain popularity. To call media content a virus, or its associated metaphor of 'memes', is to take a political stance on the sociality of media, one where ideas and meaning are either a threat to control (virus) or a force to be contended with in a survivalist interpretation of social life (Dawkins and Blackmore etc.). However, recognizing the *virality* of media content does not necessitate calling media content 'viral'. As Postill (2014) and Dan Sperber (Sperber 1996) argue, we can be interested in the 'epidemiographic' and/or 'epidemiological' qualities of media practice without agreeing with the use of 'memes' and 'virals' among mimetics enthusiasts. Sperber has shown how 'memes' and 'virals' misattribute a 'survival of the fittest' logic to the spread of media content where the content itself is imbued with intentions and desires. In making this point, Sperber suggest an epidemiological approach where the vectors and attractors that afford the spread of a symbol, image or term, are closely analysed. Postill shows how Sperber's insights might be applied to recent debates about media and activism, arguing that we can move away from the approaches of Dawkins and Blackmore while maintaining an interest in why and how meanings spread.

As the case of Chinese concept-metaphors for sociality and digital practice show, media content and its 'spreadability' (Jenkins, Ford, and Green 2013) can be understood from the affective and sociality producing qualities of media without reference to viruses per se. In this spirit, I suggest a hard etic distinction between the terms viral and virality. Virality is a term that has already become popular among some scholars (Shifman 2014) and in many ways captures some of the meaning of the Chinese term *re*. For example, Jeff Hemsley and Robert Mason define virality as:

A word-of-mouth-like cascade diffusion process wherein a message is actively forwarded from one person to other, within and between multiple weakly linked personal networks, resulting in a rapid increase in the number of people who are exposed to the message. (2013: 138)

Helmsley and Mason's definition provides us with a useful way of describing the social distribution of media content. However, Chinese emic terms of similar processes remind us of the need to incorporate an understanding of the affective qualities necessary for a 'cascade diffusion process' to take place. Without asking everyone to learn standardised mandarin *(Putonghua/Guoyu)* I would like to suggest that we build off Chinese understandings of *re* to conceptualize the virality of media content in terms of both its affective appeal, and its social distribution. I would define virality as:

A form of sociality whereby the affective appeal of an assemblage of meaning and practices leads to its rapid diffusion and re-production between multiple weak-ties, resulting in an increase in the number of people participating in that assemblage of meaning and practices

There is still however one shortcoming in applying this definition of virality to the case of the sex video among my interlocutors in Tokyo. How can we differentiate digital practice, the mobility of digital content, and the role of mobile life, from other social practices inscribed with 'virality'? If Chinese social life has always been viral, what is different about digital practices today, particularly in migration contexts, or contexts of rapid urban mobility?

As the video spread to each group among my informants in Tokyo, complex dynamics of intertextuality, cut up the signifiers of the event into smaller forms of content, and recombined them with other pre-existing terms, images, and animations popular within each group. The originally 6.5-megabyte video was converted into short GIFs and stills, and catalysed the swapping of other lewd and transgressive images and animations within friendship groups. One of the groups affiliated with a business quickly admonished the person who posted the video, but otherwise, most groups engaged in a torrent of jokes, banter and animation. The sex video itself and the images taken from it soon stopped circulating, but the terms Uniqlo *(youyiku)* and 'changing room' *(shiyijian)* remained as playful substitutions for the term sex. It became the euphemistic 'Netflix and chill' (Langmia and Tyree 2016) for many young Chinese in Tokyo for the second half of 2015, and was deployed in a variety of ways. At times it was misogynistic, such as a GIF with the term 'Women are like clothing, I like to wear them in Uniqlo', and responses from women stating that 'You couldn't even book a Uniqlo changing room, and you want to shag me *(yuepao)*? You're dreaming *(zuomeng)*'. Another GIF was a complex assemblage that was specific to Chinese social media in Japan. Its image was taken from the popular GIF which substitutes a submitters face into a cartoon character with a goofy bob haircut called 'mushroom head' *(mogutou)*. And the caption combined Japanese and Chinese language, using the Chinese slang *zhuangbi* that can be literally translated as 'adorning female genitalia' but typically means 'to show off or be a faker', and the Chinese characters for Uniqlo *(youyiku)*, while constructing the sentence out of Japanese terms and syntax:

'somebody is *zhuangbi*-ing about their *Uniqlo* skills! Unbelievable!'
dareka 'youyiku' (ch) ni tsuite, 'zhuangbi' (ch) shite imasu! Mō yabai yo!

As Uniqlo is a common Japanese brand found at almost every train station in the city, and most of the group members were in Tokyo, the sex video also translated and intensified several ways of interacting with the city, and with each other. Many of my friends and interlocutors started taking photos of local Uniqlo outlets with captions in Chinese such as 'dare I go in?', 'want to be my Uniqlo-friend?', and engaged in a series of selfies where they joked about stealing each other's boyfriends and girlfriends and 'taking them to Uniqlo'. Six weeks after the sex video blew up *(bao re)* and became 'hot' *(huo)*, a group of my informants had gone out to a bar to celebrate one of their birthdays. As they each pealed-off to go home, a final pair, who everyone knew liked each other but had not started dating, lingered as we all left. The next morning everyone in the group speculated on WeChat as to whether the pair had 'been to Uniqlo to change clothes', but there was no response from the couple. Later that evening however, one of them confirmed that they were now dating by saying that they had, indeed, been to Uniqlo.

The spread of this one video among a series of overlapping networks outside of China, is suggestive of its virality. Moreover, its proliferation through creative user responses to the original video, indicates the appealing sociothermic affects it generated. It was not simply that the video was exciting or transgressive, but also that it provided the means to proliferate a range of playful engagements, from in-app banter and image swapping to selfies within the city. Practices similar to those of my informants in Tokyo, such as taking selfies out the front of Uniqlo, became popular in mainland China too, but they also differed in terms of the localized language play and image taking. What these various dynamics imply is the multiple scales at which the virality operates.

A large cohort of social media ethnographers recently coined the term 'scalable sociality' to better define social media (Miller et al. 2016). Taken from a perspective where all media have social qualities, and interact with each other as 'polymedia' (Madianou 2012), Miller et al. argue that the current social media ecology of apps, platforms and devices, are distinguishable in their capacity to scale between public and private, as well as intimacy and estrangement.

From the maintenance of intimate relationships to the possibilities of forming relationships with strangers, social media can be seen as a form of 'scalable sociality' enabling people to better control their social lives. This may be through adapting existing social norms to different contexts or allowing for the creation of entirely new forms of social relations and sociality by exploiting this register of degrees of intimacy and distance (Miller et al. 2016: 109)

Miller et al. focus largely on the social scale and form of media interactions, and although it is not the focus of their research, they wager that in the near future all media are likely to become scalable to the degree that the term 'social media' becomes irrelevant. However, there is another scale that receives less attention within their work, but may help us understand the virality of phenomena such as the sex video. The Chinese media ecology suggests that content has also become increasingly scalable, as is evidenced within debates of the 'micro-era' of Chinese media.

The ubiquity of apps like WeChat and its services, including former social media platforms that now work in conjunction with WeChat, has heralded what De Seta, borrowing from broader commentary in China (Tao 2014), has called the *weishidai* (Micro-Era):

While software development in Euro-American contexts is couched in buzzwords empha-sizing the acts of sharing, networking, and personalization (social, smart, personal), the *wei* prefix of the Chinese micro-era summarizes a series of cultural patterns emerging from the local developments of digital media: decentralization, fragmentation, dispersion, and immediacy. (De Seta 2016a: 132)

De Seta analyses the complex semiotics of vernacular creativity to show how miniaturization has led to the increased blurring of distinctions between sociality, devices, digital practices, and everyday life. The prefix of *wei* (micro) adorns a range of popular apps and services today, including micro-messaging such as WeChat *(weixin)*, micro-blogging *(weibo)*, micro-business *(weishan)*, and micro-novels *(weixiaoshuo)*. Beyond this prefix, we also see other miniaturizing terms such as in the short video app *miaopai* (1 second video). These references to miniaturization demonstrate the appeal of scalable content, which are both part of scalable sociality and the virality of certain media content and crazes. From a more technologically-oriented perspective, we could argue that the translation of everyday phenomena into a series of 0s and 1s, or in other words digitization, is itself a means of making life scalable. Here we see that everyday Chinese discourses resonate with recent anthropological discussions of the ontology of the digital, whose 'distinctiveness resides in an inherent capacity to be distorted and transformed, to be continuously other than they are' (Knox and Walford 2016). Scalable content affords a degree of 'detachability' and 'reproducibility' (Spitulnik 2002) which helps explain the virality of certain media events and content (Postill 2014).

Often when we think of the scale of digital media and 'virals' we think of the trajectory from micro to macro, from small to big, or private to public. In many ways, the treatment of viral media and memes has followed this emphasis, partic-ularly among diehard advocates for the application of biomedical understandings of viruses to the realm of media. However, in the micro-era, the seductive quality of media content and its scalability, is dependent on its ability to fit into, and occa-sionally create, niches (Postill 2014). It produces new interpersonal convialities, and shifts scales from micro to macro and micro again. In this sense, scalable sociality and scalable content are co-constitutive. The success of platforms such as WeChat is predicated on its attention to aligning its application's affordances with the social practices of Chinese-speaking peoples (Hariharan 2017). From gifting money through 'red packet' *(hongbao)* games (Holmes et al. 2015; Wang 2016) to payment services that work from smartphone to smartphone in night markets, to a convivial messaging system that allows the easy combination of sound, image, text and animation into streams of constant banter. WeChat is increasingly scaling pre-existing content and practices, riding tandem to already prevailing vernacu-lars. In their scaling however, they can also increase and translate the intensities of many of these phenomena, such as in the spread of transgressive and comical material.

How might the case of this 'hot' and explosive sex video in China's 'Micro-Era' help us better understand digital practice? The rapid spread, affective language, and recombinant practices that surrounded the sex video case during my field-work in 2015, suggest that there is much to be learned from thinking beyond Facebook and Twitter. On the one hand, the alterity of Sinophone media ecologies, allows us to trace platforms and modes of digital practice divergent from the majority of scholarship on digital and mobile media. At the same time, the subtle differences between the commensurate terms used to describe these practices, helps us look beyond our own concept-metaphors. Instead of embracing the metaphoric language of viruses or treating units of meaning as virus-like objects, we can speak of the virality of media in terms of sociothermal affect. From such a perspective, it is clear that the virality of meaning has long been an important part of human sociality. And yet, with the advent of scalable media, we can also note an intensification of virality, which in turn have social effects. To recognize the scalable virality of digital practice in China today, then, is to see new media practices in terms of intensities rather than epochs or forms.

References

Almiraat, Hisham (2011): Egypt: Videos are worth a million words. In: Global Voices, 28 January, 2001 (https://globalvoices.org/2011/01/28/egypt-videos-are-worth-a-million-words/).

Arauz, Mike (2008): "Pass-along Is Made of People! Peeeeeeeoplllllle!" Mike Arauz (blog), Dec. 1, 2008 (http://www.mikearauz.com/2008/12/pass-along-is-made-of-people.html).

Aunger, Robert (ed.) (2001): Darwinizing Culture: The Status of Memetics as a Science. 1st edition, Oxford and New York: Oxford University Press.

Barme, Geremie (2016): Shades of Mao: The Posthumous Cult of the Great Leader: The Posthumous Cult of the Great Leader, London: Routledge.

Bateson, Gregory (1958): Naven: A Survey of the Problems Suggested by a Composite Picture of the Culture of a New Guinea Tribe Drawn from Three Points of View, Cambridge: Cambridge University Press.

Blackmore, Susan/Dawkins, Richard (2000): The Meme Machine,. Oxford: Oxford University Press.

Burgess, Jean (2008): "'All Your Chocolate Rain Are Belong to Us?' Viral Video, YouTube, and the Dynamics of Participatory Culture," In: Geert Lovink/ Sabine Niederer (eds.), Video Vortex Reader: Responses to YouTube, Amsterdam: Institute of Network Cultures, pp. 101–109.

CAC (2015): "Guojia wanxinban jiu 'shiyijian buyashipin' yuetan sinlang tengxun fuzere." Cyberspace Administration of China and information guidance office (http://www.cac.gov.cn/2015-07/15/c_1115936596.htm).

Chapman, C.C. (2010): "The Going Viral Myth." C.C. Chapman (blog), Nov. 19, 2010 (http://www.cc-chapman.com/2010/11/19/the-going-viral-myth/).

Chau, Adam Yuet (2008): "The Sensorial Production of the Social." In: Ethnos: Journal of Anthropology 73, pp. 485–504.

Chau, Adam Yuet (2013): "Actants Amassing." In: Nicholas Long/Henrietta L. Moore (eds.), Sociality: New Directions, New York: Berghahn Books, pp. 133–156.

CINIC (2017): "39th China Statistical Report on Internet Development." China Internet Network Information Centre, (http://www.cnnic.cn/hlwfzyj/hlwxzbg/hlwtjbg/201701/t20170122_66437.htm).

Coates, Jamie (2014): "Rogue Diva Flows: Aoi Sola's Reception in the Chinese Media and Mobile Celebrity." In: Journal of Japanese and Korean Cinema 6/1, pp. 89–103.

Coates, Jamie (2017): "Blue Sky Thinking: The Effects of Aoi Sola in a Sino-Japanese Context." In: Celebrity Studies 8/2, pp. 337–343.

Dawkins, Richard (1976): The Selfish Gene, Oxford University Press: Oxford.

Deleuze, Gilles/Guattari, Felix (1987): A Thousand Plateaus: Capitalism and Schizophrenia. Translated by Brian Massumi, Minneapolis and London: University of Minnesota Press.

De Seta, Gabriele/Proksell, Michelle (2015): "The Aesthetics of Zipai: From Wechat Selfies to Self-Representation in Contemporary Chinese Art and Photography." In: Networking Knowledge 8/6, pp. 1–17

De Seta, Gabriele (2016a): Dajiangyou: Media Practice of Vernacular Creativity in Postdigital China. Ph.D dissertation, The Hong Kong Polytechnic University.

De Seta, Gabriele (2016b): "Great Firewall of China." In: Jeremy A. Murray/Kathleen M. Nadeau (eds.), Pop Culture in Asia and Oceania, ABC-CLIO.

Downey, Greg (2008): "We Hate Memes, Pass It On ...." In: Neuroanthropology, June 12, 2008 (https://neuroanthropology.net/2008/06/12/we-hate-memes-pass-it-on/).

Durkheim, Emile (1965): The Elementary Forms of Religious Life. Translated by Joseph Swain, New York: Free Press.

Goffman, Erving (1959): "The presentation of self in everyday life." In: Craig Calhoun/Joseph Gerteis/James Moody/Stephen Pfaff/Indermohan Virk (eds.) (2012): Contemporary Sociological Theory, Third Edition, Oxford: Wiley and Blackwell.

Gold, Thomas/Guthrie, Doug/Wank, David (2002): Social Connections in China: Institutions, Culture and the Changing Nature of Guanxi, Cambridge: Cambridge University Press.

Google (2017): "Google Trends", Accessed June 10, /trends/explore/viral.

Hariharan, Anu (2017): "On Growing: 7 Lessons from the Story of WeChat." In: Y Combinator. April 12, 2017 (https://blog.ycombinator.com/lessons-from-we chat/).

Hemsley, Jeff/Mason, Robert M. (2013): "The Nature of Knowledge in the Social Media Age: Implications for Knowledge Management Models," In: Journal of Organizational Computing and Electronic Commerce 23/1-2, pp. 138–176.

Herold, David Kurt/Marolt, Peter (2013): Online Society in China: Creating, Celebrating, and Instrumentalising the Online Carnival, London et al.: Routledge.

Herold, D.K./de Seta, G. (2015): "Through the looking glass: Twenty years of Chinese internet research." In: The Information Society 31/1, pp. 68–82.

Hertz, Ellen (1998): The Trading Crowd: An Ethnography of the Shanghai Stock Market, Cambridge: Cambridge University Press.

Holbraad, Martin/Pedersen, Morten Axel (2017): The Ontological Turn: An Anthropological Exposition, Cambridge: Cambridge University Press.

Holmes, Kyle/Balnaves, Mark/Wang, Yini (2015): "Red Bags and WeChat (Wēixìn): Online collectivism during massive Chinese cultural events." In: Global Media Journal Australia 9/1, pp. 1–12.

Jenkins, Henry/Ford, Sam/Green, Joshua (2013): Spreadable Media: Creating Value and Meaning in a Networked Culture, New York: NYU Press.

Jurvetson, S./Draper, T. (1997): "Viral Marketing Phenomenon Explained", (http://www.dfj.com/news/article_26.shtml).

Kanke (2012): "Kangri lüyoure (the Anti-Japanese tourism craze)." In: Kanke 202, November 2, 2012 (http://news.163.com/photoview/3R710001/28501.html#p=8EFIUSSK3R710001).

Kipnis, Andrew (2002): "The Practice of Guanxi Production and Practices of Ganqing Avoidance." In: Thomas Gold/Doug Guthrie/David Wank (eds.): Social Connections in China, Cambridge: Cambridge University Press, pp. 21–36.

Knox, Hannah/Walford, Antonia (2016): "Is There an Ontology to the Digital?" In: Theorizing the Contemporary, Cultural Anthropology website, March 24, 2016 (https://culanth.org/fieldsights/818-is-there-an-ontology-to-the-digital).

Langmia, Kehbuma/Tyree, Tia C.M. (2016): Social Media: Culture and Identity, Cambridge: Lexington Books.

Latour, Bruno (2005): Reassembling the Social: An Introduction to Actor-Network-Theory, Oxford: Oxford University Press.

Louie, Andrea (2004): Chineseness Across Borders: Renegotiating Chinese Identities in China and the United States, Durham, North Carolina: Duke University Press.

Lum, Casey/Kong, Man (2014): "Media Ecology." In: Robert S. Fortner/P. Fackler (eds.): The Handbook of Media and Mass Communication Theory, Oxford: Wiley and Blackwell, pp. 137–53.

Madianou, Mirca (2012): Migration and New Media: Transnational Families and Polymedia, Abingdon, Oxon; New York: Routledge.

McDonald, Tom (2016): Social Media in Rural China: Social Networks and Moral Frameworks, London: UCL Press.

Miller, Daniel/Costa, Elisabetta/Haynes, Nell/McDonald, Tom/Nicolescu, Razvan/Sinanan, Jolynna/Spyer, Juliano/Venkatraman, Shriram/Wang, Xinyuan (2016): How the World Changed Social Media, London: UCL Press.

Moore, Henrietta L. (2004): "Global Anxieties Concept-Metaphors and Pre-Theoretical Commitments in Anthropology." In: Anthropological Theory 4/1, pp. 71–88.

Morley, David (1995): Spaces of Identity: Global Media, Electronic Landscapes and Cultural Boundaries (International Library of Sociology), London: Routledge.

Nahon, Karine/Hemsley, Jeff/Walker, Shawn/Hussain, Muzammil (2011): "Blogs: spinning a web of virality." In: Proceedings of the 2011 iConference, ACM, pp. 348–355.

News.com.au. (2015): "China Loses Its Mind over Uniqlo Sex Tape." July 16, 2015 (http://www.news.com.au/travel/world-travel/asia/china-loses-its-mind-over-uniqlo-sex-tape/news-story/c4e0f13c1709053d553d11f20b0aaabb).

Palmer, David (2007): Qigong Fever: Body, Science and Utopia in China, New York: Columbia University Press.

Phillips, Tom. (2015): "Uniqlo Sex Video: Film Shot in Beijing Store Goes Viral and Angers Government." In: The Guardian, sec. World news, July 16, 2015 (https://www.theguardian.com/world/2015/jul/16/uniqlo-sex-video-film-shot-in-beijing-store-goes-viral-and-angers-government).

Postill, John. (2014): "Democracy in an Age of Viral Reality: A Media Epidemiography of Spain's Indignados Movement." In: Ethnography 15/1, pp. 51–69.

Povinelli, Elizabeth A. (2016): Geontologies: A Requiem to Late Liberalism, Durham, North Carolina: Duke University Press.

Qiu, J.L./Chan, J.M. (2013): China Internet Studies: A Review of the Field. In: H. Nissenbaum/M.E. Price. Academy and the Internet, New York: Peter Lang, pp. 275–307.

Rongrong, He/Kurihara, Hiroshi (2008): "Shanghuo Syndrome in Traditional Chinese Medicine." In: World Science and Technology 10/5, pp. 37–41.

Rushkoff, Douglas. (1994): Media Virus!: Hidden Agendas in Popular Culture, New York: Random House.

Schneider, Florian (2015): "Searching for 'Digital Asia' in Its Networks: Where the Spatial Turn Meets the Digital Turn." In: Asiascape: Digital Asia 2/1-2, pp. 57–92.

Scott, James C. (1999): Seeing like a State: How Certain Schemes to Improve the Human Condition Have Failed, New Haven: Yale University Press.

Shui, Yinhe. (2007): "Mingchaore, zhibuguoshi yizhong wenhua ganmao (Ming Dynasty fever is simply a kind of cultural sickness)" (http://news.xinhuanet.com/forum/2007-02/03/content_5688224.htm).

Sperber, Dan (1996): Explaining Culture: A Naturalistic Approach, London: Wiley.

Spitulnik, Debra (2002): "Media Machines and Mobile Worlds: rethinking reception through Zambian radio." In: Faye D. Ginsburg/Lila Abu-Lughod/Brian

Larkin (eds.), Media Worlds: Anthropology on New Terrain, Berkeley: University of California Press.

Shifman, Limor (2014): Memes in Digital Culture, Cambridge, Massachusetts: MIT Press.

Shuimu. (2015): "Zuó wǎn dàjiā dōu zài sōu de sānlǐtún yōuyīkù shìgè shénme guǐ_xīnwén_téngxùn wǎng (Last night we were all trying to figure out WTF happened at Sanlitun Uniqlo)", July 15, 2015 (http://news.qq.com/a/20150715/008887.htm).

Sola, Katie (2015): "Bizarre Uniqlo Sex Video Called Menace To China's 'Socialist Core Values.'" In: Huffington Post, sec. The WorldPost, July 16, 2015 (http://www.huffingtonpost.com/entry/uniqlo-sex-video_us_55a7d917e4b0896514d082ec).

Sun, Longji (1990): Zhonguo Wenhua de Shenceng Jiegou. (The deep structures of Chinese culture), Beijing: TangShan lunyi.

Sun, Xinru (2016): "Self-Narration and Double Articulation: A Study of a WeChat Group of Pumi Villagers." In: Communication and the Public 1/4, pp. 500–503.

Svensson, Marina (2014) "Voice, power and connectivity in China's microblogosphere: Digital divides on SinaWeibo." In: China Information 28/2, pp. 168–188.

Svensson, Marina (2015): "Connectivity, Engagement and Witnessing on Weibo: Understanding New Forms of Civic Engagement and Connective Action in China." In: Jacques deLisle/Avery Goldstein/Guobin Yang (eds.): The Internet, Social Media, and a Changing China, Pennsylvania: University of Pennsylvania Press, pp. 49–70.

Svensson, Marina (2017): "The Networked China Researcher: Challenges and Possibilities in the Social Media Age." In: Asiascape: Digital Asia 4/1–2, pp. 76–102.

Tao, Dongfeng (2014): "Lijie Weishidai de weiwenhua (Understanding the microculture of the micro-era)." In: Jinrong Bolan 2/21, pp. 4–8.

Thepaper.cn (2015): "Yōuyīkù huí yìng bù yǎ shìpín shìjiàn fǒurèn chǎozuò, běijīng jǐngfāng yǐ jièrù diàochá_zhíjí xiànchǎng_péngpài xīnwén – (UNIQLO denies any connection to the indecent video incident, Beijing police further their investigation_The Paper)", July 15, 2015 (http://www.thepaper.cn/newsDetail_forward_1352602).

Wallis, Cara (2015): "Gender and China's Online Censorship Protest Culture." In: Feminist Media Studies 15/2, pp. 223–238.

Wang, Jing (1996): High Culture Fever: Politics, Aesthetics, and Ideology in Deng's China, Berkeley: University of California Press.

Wang, Xinyuan (2016): Social Media in Industrial China, London: UCL Press.

Wasik, Bill (2009): And Then There's This: How Stories Live and Die in Viral Culture, London: Penguin.

Weller, Robert (1994): Resistance, Chaos and Control in China: Taiping Rebels, Taiwanese Ghosts and Tiananmen, Seattle: University of Washington Press.

Williams, Raymond (1985): Keywords: A Vocabulary of Culture and Society, Oxford: Oxford University Press.

Wu, Ming/Guo, Jun/Zhang, Chuang/Xie, Jianjun (2011): "Social Media Communication Model Research Bases on Sina-Weibo." In: Yinglin Wang/Tianrui Li (eds.): Knowledge Engineering and Management Proceedings of the Sixth International Conference on Intelligent Systems and Knowledge Engineering, Shanghai, China, Berlin, Heidelberg: Springer, pp. 445–454.

Wu, Yanfang/Atkin, David/Lau, T.Y./Lin, Carolyn/Mou, Yi (2013): "Agenda Setting and Micro-Blog Use: An Analysis of the Relationship between Sina Weibo and Newspaper Agendas in China." In: The Journal of Social Media in Society 2/2, (http://thejsms.org/index.php/TSMRI/article/view/47).

YahooHK (2015): "Dàlù zuì huǒ huàtí! Yōuyīkù shì yī jiān nánnǚ ` jīzhàn'yǐngpiàn (the hottest topic in mainland China: battle of the 'sexes' video in UNIQLO change room) – Yahoo", June 15, 2015 (http://hk.news.yahoo.com/%E5%A4%A7%E9%99%B8%E6%9C%80%E7%81%AB%E8%A9%B1%E9%A1%8C-%E5%84%AA%E8%A1%A3%E5%BA%AB%E8%A9%A6%E8%A1%A3%E9%96%93%E7%94%B7%E5%A5%B3-%E6%BF%80%E6%88%B0-%E5%BD%B1%E7%89%87-055544926.html).

Yakob, Faris (2008): "Spreadable Media." Talent Imitates, Genius Steals (blog), November 25, 2008 (http://farisyakob.typepad.com/blog/2008/11/spreadable-media.html).

Yang, Mayfair (1994): Gifts, Favors and Banquets: The Art of Social Relationships in China, New York: Cornell University Press.

Yang, Guobin (2011): "Technology and its contents: Issues in the Study of the Chinese Internet". In: Journal of Asian Studies, 70/4, pp. 1043–1050.

Yu, Shuenn-Der (2004): "Hot and Noisy: Taiwan's Night Market Culture." In: David K. Jordan/Andrew D. Morris/Marc L. Moskowitz (eds.): The Minor Arts of Daily Life: Popular Culture in Taiwan, Honolulu: University of Hawaii Press, pp. 129–149.

Yuan, Elaine J./Feng, Miao/Danowski, James A. (2013): "'Privacy' in Semantic Networks on Chinese Social Media: The Case of Sina Weibo." In: Journal of Communication 63/6, pp. 1011–1031.

Twitter in Place
Examining Seoul's Gwanghwamun Plaza through Social Media Activism

Samuel Gerald Collins

Abstract

In Korea, social networking sites are overwhelmingly utilized through smart phones; people tweet or update Facebook with their mobile devices. Like any social networking site, this means that people are making (and remaking) connections with each other, but it also means that people are connecting in complex ways to place. Even if geo-location is disabled, these social media still have this embodied dimension; they're not just tweets, but tweets in a particular space and time. In Seoul, embodied practices of social media infuse spaces with diverse and networked meaning that interact (however weakly) with existing spatial systems. In this essay, I explore the diverse meaning of public space in Seoul through an analysis of Twitter traffic surrounding enormous protests in 2016 at Gwanghwamun Plaza calling for the resignation of President Park Geun-hye. People who protested against the President in Gwanghwamun Plaza were not only calling for her resignation, but they are also making strong claims to space that re-define the heterogeneous site as a space of protest. At the same time, they are not the only groups making claims on the plaza: conservative groups, merchants, commuters, tourists and various bots tweet other meanings through their interactions with the protest site, and these, too, add to the networked representation of Gwanghwamun Plaza. Ultimately, the paper suggests a theory of social media in urban settings which emphasizes complex interactions of space, representation, networked action, absence and presence.

Figure 1: The beginning of a protest against Park Geun-hye. Image from Wikimedia.

DOI 10.14361/dcs-2017-0207

DCS | Digital Culture and Society | Vol. 3, Issue 2 | © transcript 2017

Introduction

In South Korea, the impeachment and removal of former President Park Geun-hye in early 2017 represents the triumph of years of activism, beginning with protests in the wake of the Sewol ship disaster in April of 2014 – an accident off of the southwest coast of South Korea that killed hundreds of students from a high school in a suburb of Seoul, and that led to charges of government complicity and corruption. Like other instances of activism, the campaign to remove Park Geun-hye – while national – was also very much a local event, centred in Seoul. Shortly after the 2014 accident, the bereaved families and their supporters started staging sit-ins in Gwanghwamun Plaza in the centre of old Seoul and, as the weeks went on, the city erected tents to house the protestors. As weeks turned to months, Sewol protestors joined others in a chorus against the Park Geun-hye government, protests that would frequently culminate in dramatic, candlelight vigils along Sejong Avenue *(Sejong-daeno)*.

Figure 2: Sewol ship disaster protest encampment. Photo by author.

But the occupation and frequent protests were also huge media events, framed by countless streams of commentary, photos and reporting through multiple plat-forms of social media, in a way that has become normative in activism: protests are planned on social media, reported on through social media, and reflected on through social media. That is, a physical protest is enacted against the scaffolding of social media platforms, in a way that became famous in Arab Spring protests in 2011 and in the Occupy Movement, although South Korean activists had largely anticipated this in the 2008 protests against then-President Lee Myung-bak and US beef imports (Lee, Kim and Wainwright 2010). While many have been less than sanguine about the impact of social media on organizing and activism, it is no longer possible to bring aggregations of people and groups together in a space of protest without these media platforms (Campbell 2017). With the protests against Park Geun-hye, we see the next stage of development of social media-informed activism. Here, activists were able to organize through South Korea's ubiquitous internet and its near-universal adoption of smartphones along multiple localities nationally and even internationally. While the struggle to remove Park from office echoes earlier struggles both in Korea and elsewhere, they also antici-pate an activist future where "physical" and "virtual" emerge as a seamless, activist interface that unites people, idea and social action across multiple sites.

Figure 3: A candlelight protest against government policies regarding the victims of the Sewol ship disaster. Photo by author.

In the age of social media, the social media campaigns and the physical occupa-tions of urban spaces cannot be separated: they are both part of the "networking" logic of contemporary activism (Juris 2008). But while the interpenetration of social media and urban space in contemporary activism seems like a truism, the ways one maps one to the other is less clear. Clearly, social media *represents* urban space. More than this, it may help in the *occupation* of urban spaces. But what are those representations? How do social media users position themselves in urban spaces? And what is the relationship of one to the other? It is, perhaps, obvious that activists "occupied" Zucotti Park during Occupy Wall Street (OWS), and schol-arship has explored the meanings of space during OWS and other movements (Hammond 2013). But what does "occupy" mean in a world of social media that renders location more ambiguous? Can one "occupy" a space of protest through social media? In this paper, I begin to explore these questions: how does social media help to make sense of urban spaces? How does it help to position people vis-à-vis a politicized city? What is the relationship between people and their media in the context of urban place? And how does the experience of activism re-inscribe the urban scape with meaning and action?

From 2014 to 2017, there have been hundreds of variously organized protests against the Park Geun-hye government. However, allegations of corruption surrounding Park's confidante, Choi Sun-shil, snowballed through 2016 and, by October, protests were reaching historic proportions. Several protests were estimated at over 1 million people (although these numbers are contested by various actors, including organizers, Seoul government officials, the police and the media). The data for this exploratory analysis is drawn from a single, large-scale event: a huge protest and call for the ouster of then-President Park Geun-hye on December 10, 2016.

This paper joins other research that looks to the "cyber-urban," to the confluence of digital mobilities and space that is re-defining both the practice and the ontologies of the urban (Forlano 2015). Our digital devices seem to confirm Lefebvre's insistence on the multidirectionality of social constructions of the city – and even to facilitate that construction through the formation of seamless urban practice, representation and discourse across multiple modalities. We move, reflect, relate, communicate and act through haptic devices that both grant us more autonomy while tethering us to structures of power and capital (Hjorth 2014). While all of these shifts have precipitated changes in the ways we both theorize and represent the urban, the following examines a moment in that transformation: the meanings and uses of space that emerge through Twitter usage during a large-scale protest in downtown Seoul. Twitter users relate to each other (through following, re-tweeting, hashtagging), to discourse (through the content of tweets and hyperlinks), to media (through photos, GIFs and video clips) and, finally, to urban space itself, which incorporates all of these through the mediated practices of smartphone users. These spaces are "emergent" in that they are not given *a priori*. Instead, the interaction of people, space, movement, smartphone, social media and event render certain sites more prominent or more intelligible than others.

Gwanghwamun Plaza

"Gwanghwamun" is a reconstruction of a Chosŏn-era gate that marked the entrance into the Gyeongbok Palace.[1] Over decades of colonization, war and explosive modernization, the gate has continued to mark not just the centre of the old city, but the symbolic centre of the nation. Directly in front of Gwanghwamun, Gyeongbok Palace and the President's home (Cheong Wa Dae, sometimes called the "Blue House" after its tiled roof), Gwanghwamun Plaza is a highly visible

---

1   Romanizations of Korean are consistent with the McCune-Reischauer system, except in the case of names and place-names that follow either the Revised Romanization system developed by the Korean government ("Gwanghwamun") or conventional orthographies established through custom ("Park Chung Hee").

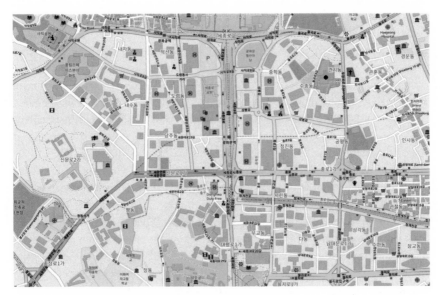

Figure 4: Sejong-daeno, from OpenStreetMap.org.

public space to stage protests, frequently accompanied by large-scale stage performances. Sejong-daeno (Sejong Avenue) runs from Gyeongbok Palace (at the top
centre of the map), down past Seoul Station (beyond the bottom of the map).
During many of the demonstrations, the entirety of the avenue thronged with
protestors, with estimates on the most attended protests at nearly 2 million people.

In many ways, the enormous success of the occupation and the protests
have been enabled by Gwanghwamun Plaza itself. Over the past fifteen tears,
downtown Seoul has been transformed in many ways – new parks, the restoration
of the Cheonggyecheon stream through the centre of Seoul, and the opening of
major thoroughfares all over the city to pedestrian and bicycle traffic (Ryu 2004).
Since its reconstruction in 2008, Gwanghwamun Plaza has provided highly effective visibility for social movements. It is the literal centre of the old, walled city,
and it is also symbolically (and even geomantically) the centre of the nation, with
the reconstructed Chosŏn palace at the north end of Sejong Avenue and, behind
it, the President's house (Yoon 2008). Finally, it is a synecdoche for South Korea's
place in the contemporary, global order, with newspapers, Korean conglomerates,
global corporations and embassies lining both sides of Sejong Avenue as it moves
south from Gwanghwamun. Indeed, the history of the Republic is itself visible
(and embodied) along Sejong-daeno, with the (reconstructed) palace, the occasional example of Japanese colonial architecture (e.g., the Dong-a Ilbo Building)
and the conspicuously atavistic U.S. embassy, itself an artefact of the beginnings
of Korea's developmental state and a reminder of the ambiguities of postcolonial
Korea.

On the other hand, the plaza has also figured into city and national efforts at "branding" and commodification through the creation of spectacle; indeed, there is rarely a day when there are not multiple events and festival-like attractions (Kim 2009). Trade shows, free concerts and tourist events transpire next to protest and direct action. In the span of a few feet, one can sample free food products from a regional food show and then walk past buses of conscripted riot police (kidongdae). In other words, in this relatively small space, each of these events must contend with the other amidst in an atmosphere riven with politics, global capital and, these days, international tourists visiting sites used for popular K-drama.

Nothing has been more contentious than the Sewol protestors themselves, who remained in their tent occupation for almost 3 years. This tent encampment became a rallying point not only for Sewol families, but for a host of others with grievances against the Park Geun-hye government. When the protests calling for Park Geun-hye's removal increased in size, frequency and urgency in the wake of revelations of the corruption of Park's associate, Choi Sun-sil, the Plaza was a natural centre for activism. In August of 2016, large-scale demonstrations were held calling for the President's removal, reaching a crescendo in December, when protest numbers swelled to over one million and large-scale demonstrations were held simultaneously in South Korea's other cities.

Gwanghwamun, December 10

The December 10 protest was the 7th, large-scale mobilization of citizens seeking the ouster of the President. It was the largest yet – and like the others, it was also a media spectacle, with politicians and pop stars joining citizen groups and many, ordinary people and students on a cold, Winter evening in Seoul.

People began to gather earlier in the day. By 4:30 pm there were orchestrated protests. At around 5:30, Park Geun-hye supporters (the counter-protestors) began to congregate around the Gyeongbok Palace Subway Station (next to Gwanghwamun). Known as the "Park Sa Mo" (Park Geun-hye Loving People Meet-up), they clashed with protestors, waved Korean flags, and hurled abuse. At 6 pm the protest formally commenced on the main stage directly in front of Gwanghwamun, led by families of the Sewol ship disaster victims. At 7 everyone extinguished their candles and closed their eyes in remembrance of victims of Park Geun-hye's policies. There was also a concert from the singer Lee Eun-mi and fireworks.

Shortly after the rally had ended, I ran a Twitter search through NodeXL, an open-source spreadsheet and network visualization software that allows queries on multiple social media APIs (Application Programming Interface) (Hansen et al. 2011). Here is a sociograph visualization of tweets downloaded from Twitter's API containing the keyword "Gwanghwamun". In this search, the vertices represent Twitter users whose tweet contains the keyword, and the lines connecting the vertices (edges) represent Twitter users who have replied to a tweet, or who are mentioned in a tweet. Most of the mentions are, in fact, retweets.

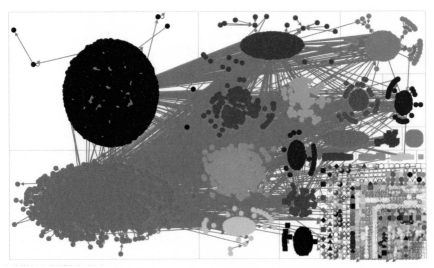

Figure 5: Sociograph visualization of a Twitter search network created around the keyword, "Gwanghwamun".

In Figure 5 above, Twitter users are grouped into color-coded clusters on the basis of their similarity to each other in terms of their connectedness and their attributes, ordered according to the Clauset-Newman-Moore algorithm (Hansen et al. 2011).[2] These groups are also assigned alphanumeric identifiers (used below), moving by size from G1 (top left) to G2 (bottom left) and then to the top row of the middle column (G3). After this, the rows move across to G4, G5 and so on. The largest clusters typically reflect a single tweet (e.g., from a news hub like JTBC) and hundreds of re-tweets, while the lower, right corner of the graph show countless "singletons" – Twitter users who have neither replied to another, nor re-tweeted, been re-tweeted nor mentioned.

Here are the quantitative characteristics of the dataset:
Vertices: 10853
Unique edges: 16043
Edges with duplicates: 2633
Total edges: 18,676

Self loops 1215
Connected components: 1173
Average geodesic distance: 4.070718
Graph density: 0.000137591
Modularity: 0.657418

2   NodeXL's algorithm assigns arbitrary colours and shapes to clusters in order to assist in the visual differentiation of one from the other.

The graph was laid out according to the Harel-Koren Multiscale layout algorithm, particularly useful for large graphs (Harel and Koren 2002). The low density (0.000137591 out of a maximum density of 1.0) of the graph is typical of large scale social media: most Twitter traffic consists of re-tweets of a few, central tweets, with little traffic between different clusters' followers and re-tweeters (Smith et al. 2014). Indeed, despite some connectivity between clusters, the high modularity suggests considerable coherency within the groups (Himelboim et al. 2017).

The groups can be differentiated from each other in several ways and according to a number of different metrics, including different measures of centrality (degree centrality, betweenness centrality and Eigenvector centrality). These measures of centrality are often used as indicators of network importance. For example, vertices at the centre of the two clusters on the left of the socio-graph indicate the highest degree centrality; they have the largest number of edges connected to them. Not surprisingly, many of the nodes with high centrality are media hubs (e. g., Newstapa).

We can also characterize the contents of tweets. NodeXL has added a "sentiment analysis" algorithm in its spreadsheet that identifies keywords through models of "salience" that compute frequencies and relationships between word pairs (Hollander et al. 2016). Although there are more robust models for sentiment analysis derived from natural language processing, the results from NodeXL are useful as a way to suggest common themes from a large dataset. Here are the most frequent word pairs identified for several groups. Note that translations of word pairs from Korean to English may exceed two words.

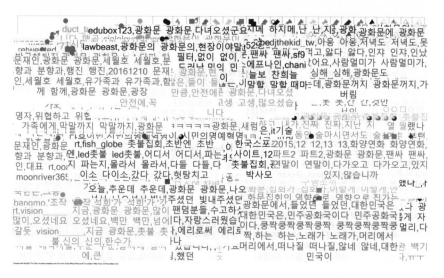

Figure 6: Word-pairs in the "Gwanghwamun" dataset identified through NodeXl sentiment analysis.

After filtering out re-tweets and the groups not concerned with protests at Gwangh-wamun, these are the most prominent word pairs in the tweets, ordered by Group number (e. g., G2):

(G2) Gwanghwamun-Plaza; Gwanghwamun-Candlelight Protest; periscope-Lee Shi-gak; Lee Shi-gak, Gwanghwamun; Can-Not; 12-10; 7th-Candlelight Protest; Daum-News; Gwangh-wamun-700,000; YouTube – Sir.

(G5) Next Café – At the Present; Next – News; the 7th – Candlelight Protest; Candlelight Protest – Cold; Cold – Weather; Weather – 600,000 People; 600,000 people – In Gwangh-wamun Plaza; In Gwanghwamun Plaza – Gathering; Gwanghwamun – Candlelight Protest.

(G6) Today – Gwanghwamun; Last Time – More than Seoul Station; More Than Seoul Station – At Least 20 Times More; From Dongsung – To Gwanghwamun; At Least 20 Times More – Met; Met – From Dongsung; Until Gwanghwamun – Of The Parade; Of the Parade – the End; Absurd – Park Geun-hye; Park Geun-hye – Jongno 3Ga Road.

(G8) Citizen – One Person; One Person – One Person; From Hannam Transport – From Past Days; From Past Days – Operated; Number 129 – Seoul; Seoul – Guro District; Guro District – Gocheok-dong; Gocheok-dong – Departing; Jongno District – From Gwangh-wamun; From Gwanghwamun – To the End.

(G9) Gwanghwamun – In the Plaza; Jeon In-gwon – Patriot (song); Patriot – Of Lee Eun-mi; Of Lee Eun-mi – Patriot; Patriot – 2012; 2012 – Presidential Election; Presidential Election – I; I – First; First – Gwanghwamun Campaigning; Gwanghwamun Campaign – Last.

Most of the tweets concern the protests, its events (e. g., the concert), the large numbers of attendees. These suggest the contours of the public debate around the protests, particularly the contrast between G2, G5 and G9 with the counter-protestor cluster in G6, where the impeachment of the president is being contested.

We can also examine sociograph itself for the particular structures of the self-organized network. In their influential report, "Mapping Twitter Topic Networks," Marc Smith et al. explore the typology of the "Twitterverse" using character-istic shapes for a variety of common, discursive forms, including the "Polarized Crowd," where a contentious issue has separated people into two clusters with little communication between them, the "Community Cluster," where different, but related groups, develop around common topics, the "Broadcast Network," where "many people repeat what prominent news and media organizations tweet," and, finally, the "Brand Network," where otherwise disconnected consumers tweet about popular products (Smith et al. 2014: 3).

In the Gwanghwamun example, we can see a combination of these different graph types. In Figure 1 (above), the large component (G1) in the upper left is typical of "Broadcast Network", with a central tweet being re-tweeted by hundreds of followers. As Smith *et al.* explain, "Twitter commentary around breaking news stories and the output of well-known media outputs and pundits has a distinct hub and spoke structure in which *many people repeat what prominent news and media organizations tweet*" (3).

Many of the central clusters concerned with the protests suggest less of a "broadcast" style than a "Community Cluster Network." Smith *et al.* continue: "Some popular topics may develop multiple smaller groups, each with its own audience, influencers and sources of information. These Community Clusters conversations look like bazaars with multiple centres of activity" (3). Finally, there is even (in the sociograph in Figure 5) evidence of a "polarized crowd" network between broadcast networks, community clusters, particularly in G2 and G5.

Applying this typology dramatically illustrates the salience of social network analysis for our understanding of public discourse in terms of clustering and directionality. With Smith *et al*'s model, we can understand the extent to which the quality of "public" discourse consists in the ways that the public is constituted. Indeed, it is even possible to use their typology as a predictive tool: if we see, for example, two, broad clusters of tweets with few connections between then, then we might surmise that the topic under discussion has been extremely divisive.

But what about location itself? These typologies may be extremely useful in characterizing Twitter's discursive space, but these tweets still refer to actual spaces – at the very least, each contains the keyword, "Gwanghwamun". Since nearly 90 percent of smartphone users in South Korea access the Internet primarily from their mobile devices, apps like Twitter are likely to be used by people on the move (Jung 2015). We therefore need to understand the spatial relationships users form and express through the Twitter platform.

Occupy Gwanghwamun

It seems obvious here that the struggle for justice for Sewol victims, the fight against corruption and, ultimately, the demand for former President Park Geun-hye's resignation take place not just in discourse and in media, but in space. In other words, it matters that the focus for the protests is Gwanghwamun. On the other hand, although protest and civil unrest have always been about space, social media adds another wrinkle (Campbell 2017). "Liberated" from any, single location, social media might seem to obviate the importance of the local. But it seems that the opposite has happened, and that the local has never been more important.

The literature on recent social movements has also been a rich source of insights on social activism, social media and space, including work on the Occupy Movement and the "Arab Spring" (Sharp and Panetta 2016). In these movements, social media have been used to assemble people in space and to communicate something of the meaning of that space (Juris 2012; Tremayne 2014). Here, the social media are themselves an important step in wresting public spaces away from corporate and government hegemony by creating alternative narratives generated through horizontal organizing on Facebook and Twitter. People not only articulate their claims to a "right to the city"; they also recursively define what those rights should be (Harvey 2013). In other words, activism flows from virtual forums to physical space and back again through shared media content. As AlSayyad and Guvenc (2015) write of Tahrir Square: "At many rallies, protestors could be seen holding smart phones in one hand and anti-state banners in the other. And from the tents in occupied squares, Internet users disseminated images and messages of protest to the rest of the world." (2028)

Social media have a well-documented role in organizing people in space and in broadcasting that message abroad. In the Arab Spring, the ability of protesters to upload media and to disseminate their message brought assistance, empathy, embarrassment to the entrenched regimes, and, ultimately, stimulated other protests around the Arab world. It allowed organizers to transcend the physical space of protest to the "mediascapes" that connect like-minded supporters around the world (Appadurai 1996). That social media, AlSayyad and Guvenc argue, was one factor in the spread of the idea and the language of protest throughout the Arab world. But, they remind us, the influence of social media was also tied to the meanings of those places. For example, AlSayyad and Guvenc (2015) outline this fluid movement from mobilization in space to digital platforms.

Simply put, neither the regimes nor the traditional mainstream media would have paid attention to the protestors had they not forcefully taken over symbolic spaces in these cities. Yet we also need to look at the new urban dynamics that resulted from complex social and political relations – where, for example, new social media has become a subversive apparatus in the articulation of politics and the reappropriation of urban space. (2030)

That is, social media become more than the dissemination of reports from the "front lines"; content uploaded to different platforms also had the effect of inflecting Tahrir Square with new, oppositional meanings.

On the other hand, the emphasis on space in recent social movements has also been thought of as more problematic. The Occupy Movement involved the occupation of specific places: Zucotti Park (New York), St. Paul's Cathedral (London), Los Angeles's City Hall, St. James Park (Toronto). But some theorists have questioned whether a global movement should have so closely identified itself with hyperlocal occupations.

During this period, the 'space of representations' of Occupy's networks – a global movement seeking radical structural change – became increasingly tied and trapped to the place of protest (i. e. camps), which acted as a barrier to occupiers' perceived and conceived spaces of activism, limiting the movement's capacity to identify and mobilize across more topological connections. (Halvorsen 2017: 5)

In Halvorsen's account, the attention and energy lavished on the occupation came at the expense of horizontal ties between groups in a network of activists. The resulting split between occupiers and other activists, he suggests, resulted in a weakened, divisive movement. Yet, would an Occupy movement have been possible without a spatial practice? How much of one, and how much of the other? Or can they be parsed so easily? This ambivalence is testament to the deep connections between them – that is, it may not be possible to imagine organizing in "real" space without the "virtuality".

In any case, these scholars raise interesting questions. In activism – and, by extension, in other forms of concerted, human organizing – what is the relationship of the "shape" of social networks to the "shape" of urban space? Other recent political movements have also utilized social media, and have also concentrated on both the symbolic value and the physical occupation of an urban space. The assumption is usually that space is elaborated through social networks – e.g., through "co-presence" people extend their relationships beyond physical spaces (Hjorth 2014; Ozkul 2013). But what does that mean for the city? I have argued elsewhere that social media allow people to establish a latent relationship to space through their social connections, but the relationship to contemporary activism is less clear (Collins 2014).

The transformation of Gwanghwamun Plaza

There is a wide literature on the language of protest in South Korea. For example, the Korean democratic movement has a large body of associated signs, slogans, chants, music and performance associated with it – some of which still has relevance in today's struggles (Abelmann 1996). But this doesn't speak to the more quotidian ways protestors encounter and construct the space of protest through language, text and "geosemiotics" (Rojo 2014). Nor does it address the ways protests transform urban space through their social media practice. There are many ways that vast sociographs of social media connections can be connected to space, but one of the most accessible is through the contents of tweets themselves.

In the following, I filtered the December 10 dataset for prepositions of place – in front of *(ap)* and next to *(yŏp)*. In addition, I also searched for specific places, including "underground" (referring to the subway and connecting tunnels beneath Gwanghwamun) and "tent," referring to the Sewol families tent encampment. Each of these can be represented with its own sociograph as a subset of the twitter users in Figure 5. The following graph shows Figure 5 filtered for the preposition of place "in front of":

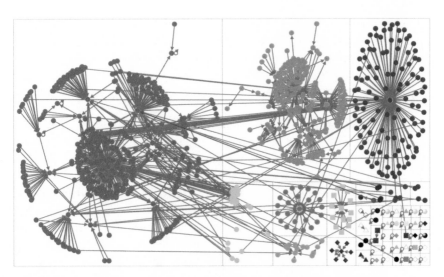

Figure 7: Twitter network visualization showing Twitter users and their tweets with keywords "Gwanghwamun" and "ap".

While most of the tweets from Figure 5 have been filtered out, the graph in Figure 7 demonstrates the widespread usage of "in front of" in tweets containing a reference to Gwanghwamun. Other prepositions and places also suggest widespread usage across clusters. But what are Twitter users in front of? That is, were there patterns in usage across tweets that suggest constructions of space? The dataset visualized in Figure 5 can be filtered for different prepositions, each suggesting different spatial relationships in the content of a connected tweet. The following thematic analysis paraphrases common twitter threads utilizing these prepositions or places to discuss Gwanghwamun Plaza.[3]

Themes: "In front of"

1. Coming within 100 meters in front of the Blue House.
2. A woman in front of the Paris Baguette gives someone candy, and they give it to the person next to them, as they walk towards Gwanghwamun.
3. People are meeting in front of the JTBC truck.

---

3 Some scholars have suggested that reproducing tweets in academic papers is ethical practice, "because tweets are inherently public and readable, when posted to a public account, by anyone with an Internet connection" (Thelwall 2014: 85). But I have tried to consider not just the platform, nor even just the uses that Twitter has authorized for its user data through its API, but the intentions of users themselves. Accordingly, I have not included the tweets themselves (either in the original Korean or in translation) out of deference to users who, while they may have assented to making their work public, have not consented to having their work dissected in an academic paper (Collins and Durington 2014).

4. Counter-protestors meeting in front of the Dong-a Ilbo Building.
5. Wondering if the area in front of the Blue House has become a playground for the left.
6. The Mayor and concerned citizens meeting in front of the "conch tower" sculpture at the Cheonggyecheon.
7. The scene in front of the Gwanghwamun tents is of wind blowing and songs being sung under a cloudy moon.
8. On a cold night, a massive crowd of 600,000 people thronged from Gwanghwamun to the front of the Chosŏn Ilbo building.
9. Complaining that they barely managed to get to the counter-protest in front of the Dong-a Ilbo building because of all the protestors.
10. Got as far as the in front of the Blue House but there's no room in Gwanghwamun so they had to wait far outside the Plaza.
11. Announcement that gobalnews.com, Twitter, YouTube etc., will be mobilizing for a live broadcast in front of City Hall and Gwanghwamun.
12. Meeting citizens in front of the ChongunDong Community Centre at sunset who are there to surround the Blue House.
13. Planning to meet in front of the Anguk Station and then continue to the Blue House.
14. In front of the DongA newspaper Building, but can't hear any sounds because they're listening to their iPhone.
15. Catching a taxi in front of Chogyesa on the way to the counter protest.
16. Setting off a fireworks finale in front of the Cheong-un Hyojadong Community Centre.
17. Critique of democratic party politicians for preening in front of the camera.
18. Calling for counter protestors to group in front of the Gwanghwamun Post Office.
19. Happy that there's a wave of flag-waving counter-protestors from the Gwanghwamun at the intersection in front of City Hall.
20. A scene from Gwanghwamun Plaza – a line of people in front of the Sewol Ship Disaster memorial altar.
22. Standing in front of the stage looking at the crowd of people united in their desire for Park Geun-hye's resignation.
23. Call for counter protestors to confront protestors in front of the Blue House.

Thematic analysis: Next to

1. Walking next to Mun Jae-in.
2. Sitting on the steps of the Hyundai Automotive building next to the Starbucks.
3. Surprised that the person next to you is a Park Geun-hye supporter.
4. Person sitting next to them talking about Lee Eun-mi.
5. Writers group meeting next to the Lee Sun-shin Statue.
6. Volunteers sitting next to the person playing with light wands.

Thematic analysis: "Tent"

1. Right-wing groups are hassling people at the Sewol Families tent. Calls to protect the tents.
2. Calls to protect the tents and the disabled rights activists from the Park Sa Mo group.

3. Reminder that after the rally is over, the Sewol families and supporters will be spending the night in tents in the cold.

4. Criticizing the mayor for tearing down unlicensed residences in Seoul while allowing the Sewol tents to remain.

Thematic analysis: "Underground"

1. People pouring out of the subway,

2. Right-wing groups are abusing the sit-down protestors in the Gwanghwamun Station and taking the banners for "Park Geun-hye Resign Station".

3. Can't get out/in of the subway station because there are so many people waving flags.

4. There's a surge of counter-protestors at the entrance to the subway.

5. Counter-protestors taking Sewol yellow ribbons and ripping down signs in the subway.

6. Reporting that city hall has ordered the subway station to stop selling tickets in order to discourage counter-protestors.

7. As the plaza swells with protestors, the subway reports 'extreme congestion'.

8. The subway reports 790,000 passengers.

9. An older man on the subway was calling everyone a bunch of communists.

10. They walked through a bunch of right-wing lunatics on the way down to the subway.

11. Moving at a turtle's pace after coming out of the subway.

12. Surprised that counter-protestors are tearing down the disabled person's rights tent in the subway station.

13. A drunk guy on the subway exclaiming that he's going to Gwanghwamun.

Discussion: Twitter City

Through Twitter, a version of Gwanghwamun is represented, but it's one that emerges out of the encounter of activists with the Plaza. It is contingent on the logistics of a massive protest, the lines drawn by riot police, and the formation of new structures of protest erected in the square (e.g., the stage, the tents). In these geographic transformations, certain places become important, while others become less consequential – but every site along the Plaza takes on different valences in the time-space of protest. Here are some examples:

a) As symbolic spaces. Many tweets concern the closeness of the protest to the Blue House. Being 100 meters "in front" of the Blue House means challenging the former President directly: 100 meters is the security perimeter. Counter-protestors also use this image in a more alarmist register, one that perhaps references an elite North Korean military unit that was able to come within 100 meters of the Blue House in a 1968 raid that was aimed at assassinating Park Geun-hye's father, Park Chung Hee. Similarly, sitting amidst the Sewol tent encampment, or in front of the stage, and hearing singing from the throngs of protestors is the symbolic heart of the protest. Here, being "in front of" locates one at the centre of protest and activism.

b) As meeting places. The tweets draw an alternative geography of Gwanghwa-mun around the logistics of meeting. These include, for example, the counter protestors in front of the old Dong-A newspaper building (now the Ilmin Museum), the mayor and supporters at the conch shell sculpture *(Sola Tap)* and a group of writers at the Lee Sun-shin statue. The wide Avenue decomposes into a series of rallying points for different groups.

c) As reference point. The size of large-scale protest is always contested, with authorities consistently under-counting protestors in order to minimize and contain the importance of the struggle. Journalists and other people use reference points in the square to evoke the size of the crowd. Photographs and film clips that accompanied tweets emphasized the vast size of the crowd, and the language underscored the unprecedented scale of the protests. Writing that the crowd stretches from Gwanghwamun to the Chosŏn Ilbo building evokes size through easily identified landmarks. Or complaining about the impossibility of entering Gwanghwamun Plaza because of the congestion lends a tactile dimension to numerical reports.

d) As sites of struggle. This iteration of the protests brought a strong, reactionary contingent of pro-Park Geun-hye supporters. Their confrontations with protestors transformed the Gwanghwamun subway station and the 4-way intersection in front of the Gwanghwamun gate into contested spaces, where the signs calling for impeachment *(t'anhaek)* of the former President visibly clashed with Korean flags. In the subway, counter-protestors assailed a tent protest from disability rights activists, and this proved a rallying point for protestors who expressed their disgust and outrage over the attacks and verbal abuse. Finally, the subway itself, as a place (or a non-place) that brings together strangers in close proximity, becomes a space where people perform politics.

e) Other geographies. In a massive demonstration, the crowd itself becomes part of the geography. A crowd or throng *(inp'a, unsu)* becomes something to navigate, to be swept along with, to identify oneself with, to criticize. Absent geographies are also important; the U.S. embassy, the National Museum of Korean Contemporary History and the KT Building are all prominent along Sejong-daeno, yet do not figure in tweets during the protest. Some of these are off-limits, but others lack the symbolic weight to make them significant in the geography of the protest.

But there are many other absences in these tweets:

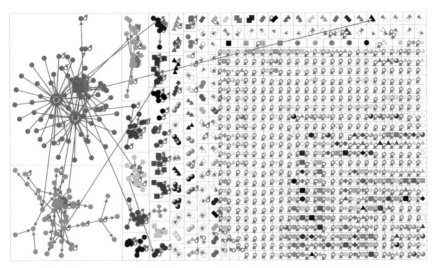

Figure 8: Sociograph of tweets from Figure 1 with re-tweets filtered out.

Comparing the graph above to the sociograph of the entire dataset in Figure 5 at the beginning of the essay, we can see that most of the edges in the original graph are re-tweets. The above graph with the re-tweets removed has 1521 edges: only 8% of the total. What about the remaining 17,155 edges? Some of them, we can surmise, are the work Twitterbots: automated accounts that exist to endlessly propagate messages towards commercial or political ends. For example, an analysis of bot traffic during the Brexit debates in Great Britain showed that bot traffic generated one-third of the tweets about Brexit (Howard and Kollyani 2016). Why would Twitterbots be used here? One reason may be to simply clog the Twitter feed in order to drown out the voices of activists with either reactionary content or with unrelated material tweeted under the same hashtag. This has been a strategy in suppressing dissent since at least 2011, when the Putin government used it to neutralize protests against parliamentary elections (Brunton and Nissenbaum 2015).

There are different tools for the detection of bots, but I have not used them with this dataset.[4] After all, not all re-tweets are the work of automated accounts. People re-tweet for a variety of reasons that can include their subjective alignment with the tweet, their support of the tweet's author, their membership in a community of like-minded Twitter users, and their desire to "piggyback" their own meanings on the original tweet (Weller 2016). Outside of the behaviour of twitterbots, then, we should look to retweeting as a form of social action with

---

4   Bot detection looks to a variety of indicators in order to determine whether a Twitter user represents a real user or institution, or whether it is an automated bot. These include examining tweet behaviour, profile, and social relationships between users followed and following (Mowbray 2014).

its own varied intentionalities. The importance of media content cannot be over-looked: people retweeted evocative photos of the demonstrations, with particular importance placed on the panoptic photos of the protestors extending down Sejong-daeno. Finally, it's entirely possible that people re-tweeted because they were also at the protest: in these cases, the sentiment of the Tweet or the uploaded media resonates with the Twitter user, who may retweet the original or an edited version of the original tweet. But deciding actually who was there and who was not presents formidable challenges.

Problems with Geolocation

There have been various attempts to locate enormous sets of social network data in space. One of the most dramatic has been to utilize geolocational tagging to map social network users onto a city (Neuhaus 2011). But this suffers from an obvious flaw: a very small percentage of social media users have geo-tagged their content – as low as 0.5% – although the power of Big Data is such that geoloca-tional tags are not necessarily needed for data scientists to algorithmically track people in urban space (Mahmud et al. 2014).

But perhaps the difficulty of establishing geolocation may be the point. The data collected through the "Gwanghwamun" search yielded only 39 geolocated tweets: barely 0.21% of the total dataset. In Korea, geolocational data has not been popular precisely because of its problematic relationship to the state and corpora-tions. And, indeed, some scholars have linked the rise of South Korea's impressive information technology infrastructures to the development of State surveillance (Kim 2004). A 2014 scandal involving government plans to collect and monitor private messages on South Korea's universally popular messaging app, KaoKao-Talk, led to a (comparatively) brief period of mass defections to non-Korean plat-forms. It's clear that people in South Korea (and elsewhere) balk at the idea of being tracked through their devices. But is being geolocated a requirement for placemaking and belonging in social media? In this dataset, the "location" data that people include in their Twitter profiles is not especially helpful: "On Earth", "in bed," "In a state of boredom," etc. It is, in fact, a bit subversive – satirizing geolocation by being too broad ("the universe") or too subjective ("in my head").

While people might hesitate to share their location, there may be another dynamic: ambiguous location can mean that one cannot be located, but it can also mean that one can be located anywhere. These "locations" may be less about denying definable geolocation than suggesting a "presence" that can include space, social life and ideas. The ambiguity itself allows for multiple lines of filia-tion and entanglements. After all, as many scholars have argued, the identity of an individual and a place has de-coupled over the development of social media. "Not only have ICTs loosened the relationship between place and community, they allow people to be engaged in communities anchored in multiple places" (Goodspeed 2017: 13). With social media, this "loosening" is not evidence of a *lack* of identification of place; it's an acknowledgement of the desire to be in many places, and in relationships with many people and ideas. In the end, it does not reject the salience of geographic place. For example, as Halegoua et al. (2016) suggest in their work on "jumping" in Foursquare, people who "check-in" in places they have never visited that are impossibly far from their homes in Jakarta may not only give users pleasure, but may form the basis for future face-to-face meetings in Indonesia.

The Rise of the Slacktivist

In his 2010 article, "Small change," Malcolm Gladwell panned the "slacktivism" he saw proliferating through social media – the "likes," "shares" and varied emoticons of a public unlikely to show up for a protest nor donate. The "slacktivist" is ineffective precisely because they have a tenuous, low- or no-risk connection to the cause. On the other hand, in a study of the viral spread of the HRC (Human Right Coalition) Marriage Equality logo in 2013, Vie (2014) asserts that "these kinds of digital activism over time can lead to more substantive off-line action."

I would suggest that the December 10 protests re-create the city along real and virtual dimensions simultaneously, and the ambiguities of location, presence and absence are part of the process of creating an activist potentiality through Seoul (and, by extension, the nation). Through the engagement with sites along Sejong Avenue, and with media created through and about the protests, citizens literally create a space not only for protest, but for the discourse of protest. That is, they achieve a "co-presence" of protest distributed across the symbolic territory of the nation, one that includes both material place and digital presence.

A complex event like a protest exists on many levels. In Okabe's and Ito's original formulation, co-presence is constructed in the shadow of physical presence. That is, people sandwich their face-to-face meetings between co-presences sustained through messaging apps: where will they meet? Who's going to be late? And who had to leave early but still wants to be part of the conversation? As Ito writes,

In the case of text messaging, we found that many messages are exchanged for the purposes of maintaining lightweight contact and co-presence, and don't perform an explicit communication function. Between friends and intimates who one is in regular touch with, text messages do not need to be interesting or newsworthy to be worth sending. (Ito 2005)

Based on Ito's argument, we would expect that smart phone use in Gwanghwamun would fill some of the same functions – that it would, in other words, serve to connect (and re-connect) like-minded activists in order to virtually re-confirm co-presence.

But, in some ways, the ambiguity of location would seem to contradict the point of ICT-mediated co-presence. If you're on the way to Gwanghwamun, you might broadcast your presence. "I'm on the steps next to the Hyundai Building." "Co-presence" in this way precedes, anticipates or simulates physical encounters, and bridges spatial gaps between people who may be active – or merely sympathetic – but not physically present in Gwanghwamun. But what about re-tweets? Agreement, solidarity, and perhaps co-presence? It's unclear what status these tweets suggest. First-person presence? A kind of slacktivism by co-presence?

What smartphones seem to do is to define a social media space that encompasses sentiment, spatial practice and social action. The ambiguity is a by-product of Twitter – spatial, non-spatial, temporal, non-temporal. For example, one person tweeted that, after nine hours, they had gotten as far as the police barricades along Gwanghwamun before knocking off to get something to eat. Having eaten, they felt re-energized and included a photo of the empty bowls from their food in the tweet. Here, the user communicates their presence and their struggle through description "standing in front of the police bus barricades" as well as through a photo. Another user writes that they've found a place to sit outside of the of the Gwanghwamun subway stop in front of the Hyundai Automobile Building, and includes a photo of protestors. Again, the affirmation of presence. But both tweets were also re-tweeted several times by users who were not otherwise present in the December 10 database. What does it mean then? Solidarity with the speaker? Co-presence? Imagined co-presence?

Conclusions

The sociograph has become the iconic representation of networked media; media that connect users, institutions and concepts in complex ways that become visible (and, perhaps, also occulted) in the vertices and edges of the graph. These diagrams (e.g., Figure 5 above) spatialize social and semantic relationships using a variety of algorithms, but this paper has argued that these social networks are simultaneously spatial networks, connecting people to an emergent space of protest even as they network users to each other. Geographies emerge from collective action, even as these protests are shaped by the urban venues in which they are sited. In tweeting place during the Seoul protests, Gwanghwamun Plaza develops into significant touchstones that are not only about the logistics of protest ("Where should we meet?") but about the meanings of these spaces (Gwanghwamun subway stop becoming the "Park Geun-hye Resign Subway Station"). But just as the sociograph includes users who have not produced any content directly (in the form of re-tweeting and following), so, too, do social networks about protesting in Gwanghwamun Plaza feature users without demonstrable relationships to the Plaza itself. Do these matter?

I have argued elsewhere that re-tweets and following (as well as "likes" and other expressions of vague support) are ultimately constitutive of meaning in networked environments. That is, the re-tweets constitute the meaning of a tweet by associating it with (and thereby rendering it visible to) certain classes of user accounts and not with others (Collins and Durington 2014). As many progressive academics have discovered, the tweet that is re-tweeted by like-minded colleagues means something very different than one that is re-tweeted by, say, reactionary conservatives. Likewise, the meaning of space is formed not just through its representation in any one tweet, but through both the repetition of content and through the connections of those repetitions to other users across multiple politics. The challenge of social network analysis in the era of networked activism is precisely this: how to analyse all of these different dimensions of meaning, space and social life through both presence and absence without privileging one over the other? The bias in most social network analysis is to the social relations themselves – as the sociograph as a technological artefact might suggest. Similarly, analyses of social protest focus on spatiotemporal presence to the exclusion of more ephemeral relationships. But through including a spatial dimension in social network analysis that is not premised on geolocation, we can engage networked behaviour that is at once social and spatial through both presence and absence. In Gwanghwamun Plaza, the ultimate meanings will always include (among other things) the physicality of the city, the social connections that people make through it, and large orbits of meaning and connection that include the nation as not only an "imagined community" but also a sphere of imagined connection and spatiality.

Acknowledgments

This research has been partly supported by a Fulbright Grant. My thanks to them and Hanyang University, ERICA campus, where I spent the 2014–2015 year.

References

Abelmann, Nancy (1996): Echoes of the Past, Epics of Dissent, Berkeley: University of California Press.
AlSayyad, Nezar/Guvenc, Muna (2015): "Virtual Uprisings." In: Urban Studies 52/11, pp. 2018–2034.
Appadurai, Arjun (1996): Modernity at Large, Minneapolis: University of Minnesota Press.
Brunton, Finn/Nissenbaum, Helen (2015): Obfuscation, Cambridge: MIT Press.
Campbell, Perri (2017): "Occupy, Black Lives Matter and Suspended Mediation." In: YOUNG 26/2, pp. 1–16.

Collins, Samuel Gerald (2014): "Latent City." In: Anthropology News 55/5 (anthropology-news.org).

Collins, Samuel Gerald/Durington, Matthew (2014): Networked Anthropology, NY: Routledge Press.

Duggan, Maeve/Brenner, Joanna (2012): "The Demographics of Social Media Users – 2012." In: Pew Research Center, February 14 (http://www.pewinternet.org/2013/02/14/the-demographics-of-social-media-users-2012/).

Forlano, Laura (2015): "Towards an Integrated Theory of the Cyber-Urban." In: Digital Culture and Society 1/1, pp. 73–91.

Goodspeed, Robert (2017): "Community and Urban Place in a Digital World." In: City and Community 16/1, pp. 9–15.

Habuchi, Ichiyo (2005): "Accelerating Reflexivity." In: Mizuko Ito/Daisuke Okabe/Misa Matsuda (eds.), Personal, Portable, Pedestrian, Cambridge, MA: The MIT Press, pp. 165–182.

Halegoua, Germaine R./Leavitt, Alex/Gray, Mary L. (2016): "Jumping for Fun?" In: Social Media + Society (July-September), pp. 1–12.

Halvorsen, Sam (2017): "Spatial dialectics and the geography of social movements." In: Transactions of the Institute of British Geographers, pp. 1–13.

Hammond, John L. (2013): "The significance of space in Occupy Wall Street." In: Interface 5/2, pp. 499–524.

Hansen, Derek L./Shneiderman, Ben/Smith, Marc (2011): Analyzing Social Media Networks with NodeXL, NY: Morgan Kaufmann.

Harel, David/Koren, Yehuda (2002): "A Fast Multi-Scale Method for Drawing Large Graphs." In: Journal of Graph Algorithms and Applications 6/3, pp. 179–202.

Harvey, David (2013): Rebel Cities, NY: Verso.

Himelboim, Itai/Smith, Marc A./Rainie, Lee/Shneiderman, Ben/Espina, Camila (2017): "Classifying Twitter Topic Networks Using Social Network Analysis." In: Social Media & Society (January-March), pp. 1–13.

Hjorth, Larissa (2014): "Locating the Social and Mobile." In: Asiascapes 1/1-2, pp. 39–53.

Hollander, Justin B./Graves, Erin/Renski, Henry/Foster-Karim, Cara/Wiley, Andrew/Das, Dibyendu (2016): Urban Social Listening, NY: Palgrave.

Ito, Mizuko/Okabe, Daisuke/Matsuda, Misa (2005): Personal, Portable, Pedestrian, Cambridge, MA: The MIT Press.

Jung, Suk-yee (2015): "Smartphone-based Internet Access Popular in Korea." In: BusinessKorea (businesskorea.co.kr).

Juris, Jeffrey (2008): Networking Futures, Durham, NC: Duke University Press.

Juris, Jeffrey (2012): "Reflections on #Occupy Everywhere: Social Media, Public Space, and Emerging Logics of Aggregation." In: American Ethnologist 39/2, pp. 259–279.

Kim, Eun (2016): "5ho-seon Gwanghwamun-yeok-I 'Park Geun-hye Jeukgakt' oejinyeok'euro? [Is Gwanghwamun Station on Line 5 Changing to Park Geun-hye Resign Station?]. In: Joongang Ilbo 12/2/16 (http://joins.com).

Kim, Moon-Hwan (2009): "The Plaza as Public Art: The Case of Kwanghwamun Plaza in Seoul." In: The Journal of Asian Arts and Aesthetics 3: P21-28.

Kim, Mun-Chu (2004): "Surveillance Technology, Privacy and Social Control." In: International Sociology 19/2, pp. 193–213.

Kitchin, Rob (2014): "The real-time city?" In: Geojournal 79, pp. 1–14.

Lee, Seung-Ook/Kim, Sook-Jin/Wainwright, Joel (2010): "Mad Cow Militancy." In: Political Geography 29/7, pp. 359–369.

Mahmud, Jalal/Nichols, Jeffrey/Drews, Clemens (2014): "Home Location Identification of Twitter Users." In: Transactions on Intelligent Systems and Technology 5/3, Article 47.

Mowbray, Miranda (2014): "Automated Twitter Accounts." In: Katrin Weller/Axel Bruns/Jean Burgess/Merja Mahrt/Cornelius Puschmann (eds.), Twitter and Society, NY: Peter Lang, pp. 184–194.

Neuhaus, Fabian (2011): "New City Landscape – Mapping Twitter Usage." In: Technoetic Arts 9/1, pp. 31–48.

Ozkul, Didem (2013): "'You're virtually there'." In: First Monday 18/11, November 4, (http://firstmonday.org/ojs/index.php/fm/article/view/4950/3781).

Penney, Joel/Dadas, Caroline (2014): "(Re)Tweeting in the service of protest." In: New Media & Society 16/1, pp. 74–90.

Rojo, Luisa Martin (2014): "Occupy: the spatial dynamics of discourse in global protest movements." In: Journal of Language and Politics 13/4, pp. 583–598.

Ryu, Jeh-hong (2004): "Naturalizing Landscapes and the Politics of Hybridity." In: Korea Journal (Autumn), pp. 8–33.

Sharp, Deen/Panetta, Claire (2016): Beyond the Square, NY: Terreform/Urban Research.

Smith, Marc/Rainie, Lee/Himelboim, Itai/Shneiderman, Ben (2014): "Mapping Twitter Topic Networks." January 20, (http://www.pewinternet.org/2014/02/20/mapping-twitter-topic-networks-from-polarized-crowds-to-community-clusters/).

Thelwall, Mike (2014): "Sentiment Analysis and Time Series with Twitter." In: Katrin Weller/Axel Bruns/Jean Burgess/Merja Mahrt/Cornelius Puschmann (eds.), Twitter and Society, NY: Peter Lang, pp. 83–96.

Tremayne, Mark (2014): "Anatomy of Protest in the Digital Era." In: Social Movement Studies 13/1, pp. 110–126.

Vie, Stephanie (2014): "In defense of 'slacktivism'." In: First Monday 19/4, April 7, (http://firstmonday.org/article/view/4961/3868).

Weller, Katrin (2016): "Trying to Understand Social Media Usage." In: Online Information Review 40/2, pp. 256–264.

Wessel, Ginette, Caroline Ziemkiewicz and Eric Sauda (2015): "Reevaluating urban space through tweets." In: New Media & Society 18/8, pp. 1636–1656.

Yoon, Hong-Key (2008): The Culture of Fengshui in Korea, Lanham, MD: Lexington Books.

Screen Screen Tourism

Marion Schulze

Abstract

*In the article, I discuss new forms of mobility allowed by digital prac-
tices, i.e. digital mobilities consisting in visiting geographical places
from and through a screen. This discussion is based on my online ethnographic research on international fans of South Korean television
series, K-Dramas. The international fandom of K-Dramas, and in a
larger sense, South Korean pop cultural products – exemplified by the
success of South Korean rapper Psy's "Gangnam Style" in 2012 –, is a
continually growing global phenomenon that has been observed from
the end of the 2000s on; a fandom that is mainly constituted through
the Internet. However, instead of discussing already thoroughly
researched "classic" participatory digital activities of television series
fans, as blogging or writing fan fiction, I will focus on still overseen
forms of mobility practices engendered by the watching of K-Dramas.
My research shows that international fans of K-Dramas are highly
mobile – but as much digitally as actually. They do not only travel
physically to Korea to visit film locations. They also engage in digital
mobilities to Korea through the mediation of desktop web mapping
services like Google Maps and their South Korean equivalents, Daum
and Naver. This screen screen tourism – as I call it –, then, differs in
many ways from screen tourism how it is discussed in previous research
on media. In describing and discussing these forms of digital mobility,
special attention will be given to two dimensions: (1) the techniques
fans use to find film locations, and (2) fans' "ethno-mapping," i.e. the
methods they have created to map out film locations online.*

Introduction

We are standing in front of a shoe store in Apujeong, a bustling part of Seoul,
when Dia opens a black notebook.[1] I see a long, handwritten list of what she tells
me are film locations for K-Dramas, South Korean television series, that she wants
to visit during her stay in South Korea.[2] She meticulously crosses out one line – the

---

1   I thank both of the anonymous reviewers for their constructive remarks.
2   In the following, "Korea" refers to South Korea.

DOI 10.14361/dcs-2017-0208

shop we are standing in front of. Moments before, she had ventured into the shop to confirm that it really was the film location of one of her favourite K-Dramas. She was doubtful because the interior did not match her memory of its appearance in the K-Drama, but the shop's salesperson confirmed the location, telling her that the interior was filmed at another branch just around the corner. We go to the other location right away and, once inside, Dia recounts the scenes and how and exactly where in the shop they took place while excitedly moving around in this unexpected film location.

In her search for film locations, Dia, a K-Drama fan from the Philippines, is not alone. From the mid-2010s on, international fans' interest in K-Drama film locations has grown rapidly – a trend that is also found among fans of other types of television series, as well as films and novels. Between 2011 and 2014, one blogger in particular, under the alias of Manager-Hyung, developed a reputation among international K-Drama fans for regularly posting film locations to a constantly growing following (1,295,413 visits in total to her blog, June 4, 2017). I was following her blog for my research on the international reception of K-Dramas (Schulze 2013, 2016), and judging from the familiar way she wrote about the locations, I was convinced that she either lived in Korea or visited regularly. But she had never been to Korea – at least in an actual sense.

If Dia's activities represent a type of screen tourism that has been thoroughly researched (see Connell 2012), Manager-Hyung's represent new forms of mobility – digital mobilities, which consist of visiting geographical sites through screens and sharing them via screens. Manager-Hyung is engaged in what I call "screen screen tourism," a phenomenon that, to my knowledge, has not been discussed in the literature, whether as a mobility practice among fans, a contemporary everyday routine or a world-making practice. I examine this phenomenon by focusing on K-Dramas' international fandom, part of the increased worldwide circulation and reception of Korean popular culture, also known as Hallyu or the Korean Wave. Exemplified by the success of Korean rapper Psy's "Gangnam Style" in 2012, in recent years, Korean popular culture has become a growing social, cultural and economic force outside Korea, first in East Asia and then rapidly on all continents. Concert tickets for Korean pop groups touring Europe or the Americas sell out online in minutes, while popular Korean television series can be streamed with English subtitles a few hours after they have been broadcast on Korean national television, and they are translated into up to 70 languages. The major facilitator of this global reception of Hallyu is the Internet, through which international fans watch K-Dramas and connect with each other. As such, Hallyu – exemplified by K-Dramas – is also representative of recent structural changes in the global media landscapes.

Nearly in parallel to these changes, and probably partly in response to them, there has recently been a paradigmatic theoretical turn in media research in which the discussion of media practices was a central concern (see e.g. Couldry (2015[2012]: 33 ff.)). Apart from the well-researched "classic" online activities of television series fans – blogging and writing fan fiction – the observation of actual mobilities engendered by media texts also participated in this turn. Usually referred to as "media tourism" or "screen tourism" – terms that include other closely related phenomena, including cinematic tourism and movie-induced tourism – this literature demonstrates that many people who are seriously engaged with media texts become highly mobile in visiting actual film locations. Not surprisingly, K-Drama fandom figures prominently in this literature (Connell 2012). Since the end of the 1990s, Korea's tourism agency has promoted Korea as a travel destination through media texts, particularly K-Dramas. However, digital or virtual mobilities to film locations have rarely been discussed so far (for an exception, see Tzanelli 2007). But as my research shows, international fans of K-Dramas are highly mobile – as much virtually and digitally as actually. They do not only travel physically to Korea to visit film locations. They also engage in virtual mobility to engage with other fans, and in digital mobilities to Korea through the mediation of the Internet, usually in hopes of eventually visiting the locations physically. Since 2014, the ways in which film locations are visited onscreen and shared via screens have also changed significantly and become increasingly standardised. A considerable rise in digital mobilities related to film locations occurred in 2016, especially in regard to two K-Dramas, *The Goblin* and *Legend of the Blue Sea*, and the practice is now a constitutive element of K-Drama fandom. As such, international fans of K-Dramas are similar to Tzanelli's "virtual flâneurs" (2007: 16), tourists who stroll on travel message boards and institutional and cooperative websites that market travel destinations linked to movies. But international K-Drama fans who engage in screen screen tourism differ from virtual flâneurs in the way they navigate through digital space and in the types of digital spaces they navigate. They do not linger or stroll, but instead move in a highly target-oriented manner, as I will discuss in detail below. Second, they cannot be understood as mere (albeit active) consumers of commodified information. In most cases, in looking for film locations on their screens, they produce their own information on those locations, which they then share with other fans through those same screens. This collaborative (by fans for fans) knowledge production is usually necessary because much of the information on the film locations they look for is not provided elsewhere. While in the 2010s fans would share their actual, offline visits to film locations and depended on institutions like the Korean Tourism Organization to disclose (directed) information on film locations, today they are increasingly generating and sharing their own knowledge. To do so, they rely heavily on digital mapping services such as Google Maps, and especially their Korean equivalents, Daum Maps and Naver Maps. As such, the digital spaces that international fans most commonly frequent are those that allow them to search for film locations themselves, i.e. that allow "geobrowsing," active navigation through geographical space (or its digital representation) (Abend/Harvey 2017).

More fundamentally, however, the international reception of K-Dramas is a telling and timely example through which to understand the multiplication of realities by which modernity is characterised (Esposito 2014[2007]). International fans constantly (and often simultaneously) navigate through different realities or different modes of being (Lévy 1998: 16), each of which has specific characteristics. Apart from their own *actual reality* (roughly their actual[ised], offline existence), international fans navigate daily through the *reality of "realistic fiction"* (Esposito 2014[2007], emphasis added) of K-Dramaland, a fictive world "created through the collective activity of writers, directors, actors and viewers of K-Dramas" (Schulze 2013: 378). In addition, these fans move in and through *virtual, online reality*, where gatherings of international fans take place. And finally, they navigate the reality of digital mapping services, or "navigational platforms" (November/Camacho-Hübner/Latour 2010: 583), to visit locations in Korea, i. e. a *digitalised and mediated geographical reality*. This fourfold distinction relies on a simplified version of more complex definitions of and relations between these realities given elsewhere (see e. g. Deleuze 1996; Lévy 1998; Hine 2015), but I consider it a workable analytical framework through which to demonstrate how international fans navigate through this cartography of realities and how these realities intersect.

Hence, this paper has three goals. First, and most importantly, it offers a systematic and empirically grounded account of a new, so far undiscussed, digital navigation practice: screen screen tourism. To do so, it focuses specifically on the techniques fans use to find film locations; fans' "ethno-mapping," i. e. the methods they have created to map out film locations online; and their creation of digital archives of film locations. The other two arguments are corollaries of the first. First, the paper argues that this on-screen navigation is always intermeshed with navigation through other realities, and it attempts to understand how exactly this seemingly smooth and often simultaneous navigation through multiple realities unfolds. Second, the paper argues that more analytical attention should be paid to the practice of screen screen tourism when addressing world-making (whatever social form the world in question may take) because engagement in these digital mobility practices will only continue to increase.

Methods

The following discussion is based on a larger on-going research project on the international reception of K-Dramas I have been engaged in since 2012 (Schulze 2013; 2016) and for which I follow 40 Anglophone blogs and one message board frequented by international fans on a daily basis. The term "international fans" here refers to all fans who reside outside Korea. As I have discussed elsewhere in detail, it is difficult to determine the socio-demographic composition of these fans (Schulze 2013: 373 ff.). As well, bloggers and commenters usually do not disclose their country of residence, ethnicity or gender. More importantly, attempting to support explanations with such information runs the risk of explaining practices through a (presupposed) national culture, ethnicity or gender and thus stereotyping informants as speaking to and for a specific nation, ethnic group or gender because of their national, ethnic or gendered belonging (which is usually determined by the researcher). This said, it is safe to say that international K-Drama fandom spans the globe, with a little less network density in Africa. From my observation, the closer international fans are to Korea (for instance in the Philippines, Malaysia, Indonesia, Thailand, Singapore or the United States), the more they engage in screen screen tourism. Proximity here is thus not understood as exclusively metric, but also as constituted by a *sensed* socio-cultural proximity fostered by, for example, social (kinship) networks (Mueller 2016), as may be the case with Korean-Americans.

Although the larger research project is informed by offline and online ethnography, for this paper I rely only on data collected online (see e.g. Boellstorff et al. 2012; Hine 2015) between January 2013 and June 2017 from three Anglophone blogs that regularly post film locations. These blogs have been selected because they focus exclusively on K-Dramas and are authored by fans for fans, a focus that excludes, for instance, message boards and websites specialising in Hallyu that also post film locations. In addition, the blogs were chosen not by the blogger's country of residence, for instance, but according to how regularly they post and how active their followers are. I additionally rely on analytic auto-ethnography as defined by Anderson (2006), among others. In relying on this form of auto-ethnography, I aim to highlight not only my own participation in these digital mobilities, but also my *auto*-observation and the constant analytical oscillation between, on the one hand, how international fans *describe* their digital mobilities, i.e. their practices mediated by discourse, and, on the other, my (embodied) experiences. In following international fans' discussions and their descriptions of their practices, I have not always been able to understand the difficulties and emotions they describe. Auto-ethnography has helped me understand practices whose meaning would otherwise have remained opaque to me because they are not accounted for by international fans, as well as corporal practices that are meditated by (and thus often reduced to) language. In other words, I would not have been able to describe screen screen tourism as I do here without engaging in analytic auto-ethnography. Nonetheless, I privilege international fans' descriptions and logics whenever possible.

Starting point: Geographical familiarity

According to international fans, two specific features of Korean television series are that a great number of locations are shown in a very detailed matter, and that the same locations have appeared in different K-Dramas, some for nearly two decades. Consequently, international fans who have watched K-Dramas for an extended period of time state that they have gained a geographical understanding of some of these places. One could also speak, in Kim and Richardson's (2003) terms, of a certain geographical "familiarity" with some Korean sites on the part of international fans. International fans describe places as "awfully familiar" or say that they "recognize the landmarks." One fan half-seriously states: "I'm pretty sure I could navigate through Incheon airport in a blindfold, thanks to all the scenes I've watched that were filmed there" (Amanda 2014).[3] Fans also commonly state that the reappearance of film locations is the reason that they set out to search for their actual, real counterparts. "You know all those places you keep seeing in dramas, and then you see another drama and it's the same damn place?!? Yeah those," begins an article that presents a few film locations: "We've noticed this a while ago, but didn't really care about it. Until ... you know, when someday you ask yourself: 'Are all the schools located in the same neighborhood or what?'" (Twinklelie/SeRose 2013).

However, there is no clear repertoire of must-know film locations. Consequently, the ten must-see locations regularly posted on different websites change constantly – usually as a result of the most popular K-Dramas at the moment. Nor does any website offer a complete overview of film locations, in contrast to websites regarding North American television series. Indeed, it would be impossible to offer an exhaustive list of K-Drama locations. Weekday K-Dramas usually consist of 16 to 20 episodes, and there are roughly ten different film locations per episode and ten K-Dramas per week that are subbed into English (each with two episodes a week). In general, international fans only list film locations for a small number of very popular weekday K-Dramas. The most common pattern is to post film locations of a single K-Drama.

Nonetheless, there is a clear hierarchy of sites, and four types of locations stand out in particular. The first three are locations that recur in a given K-Drama, that are central to the plot of a given drama, or that capture the imagination of an individual blogger because they like their aesthetic. The last consists of specific categories of film locations. International bloggers are most typically interested in cafés, restaurants, parks and residential buildings rather than work places, hospitals, convenience stores or cemeteries – even when the latter also reappear often. This phenomenon may be partly explained by the fact that storylines are often created around a café or restaurant, but a more important reason is that visiting a café, for instance, involves fewer social and physical barriers than visiting an office building, because its function already includes visiting it. Sometimes the search for a given location is additionally driven by other fans' doubts regarding its actual existence. One fan, for example, asks: "By chance, do you two know where they film historical dramas? Do they create a completely new set for it, or do they visit some old villages?" (Animefayinc in: Twinklelie/SeRose 2013).

Some bloggers also consciously exclude some locations from their search. One blogger, for example, states that she does not include some locations "because they seem to be kind of obvious" to people familiar with Seoul (Booksntravel 2016b).

---

3   All quotations from K-Drama blogs are taken verbatim.

Another reason for not posting a location is that it is peripheral to the story or does not appear in any other K-Drama – a highway, for example. Yet another reason is that the blogger believes that another website already offers a comprehensive list of locations: "With regards to Scarlet heart [name of K-Drama], I don't have plans to do up a post on it. Most locations can be found in KTO's [Korean Tourist Organization] article" (Honeystars 2016b).

Measures of verification

Before being able to share a film location, the location has to be found. This is less self-evident that it sounds, considering the way in which K-Dramas are filmed. Signifiers of geographical locations (signposts and street names, for example) are often deliberately excluded or substituted with fictive ones, and the places in question are often purposely changed or digitally rendered. More generally, locations are shot such that their surroundings are framed out, as are the upper parts of buildings, where the names of shops, cafés or restaurants figure. Many locations are also only shot indoors and in close-up. The mise en scène of a café scene, for instance, can consist of only two chairs and a table. As well, buildings such as hospitals, churches, temples and high schools are often architecturally indistinct, which makes it difficult for international fans to identify them, especially with the search techniques they use. Finally, substitute locations are often used. For example, in *The Goblin* (2016–17) a street in Paris was filmed in Quebec, Canada.

To find film locations, therefore, fans use a specific ensemble of techniques. As I will show, all of them employ geobrowsing, which consists of navigating through the digital realities presented by digital mapping services. Through geobrowsing (and in such the mediation of digital maps), fans aim to establish a mimetic correspondence between an on-screen location and an actual place in Korea. Hence, in the territorial logic of international fans, both K-Dramaland – the places (re) presented in K-Dramas – and the corresponding locations on digital maps are understood as models of a "real" material place. In the same vein, geobrowsing is also regularly combined with (mediated) actual mobilities that are considered to strengthen the web of verification. In this variant, international fans compare the fictive reality of K-Dramaland with the actual reality of material surroundings (Boltanski 2009: 48). The actual reality is usually not accessed directly, however, but in its *digitally mediated* form, i. e. through photos uploaded on the Internet and thus, again, through digital mobility. In engaging in these different mobilities, international fans usually rely on three verification techniques.

The statement "I have found the location of this place some time ago on Korean web" (Booksntravel 2017e) offers a good introduction to the first technique. The "Korean web" in this statement refers to websites in Korean. This means, international fans who have little or no knowledge of the language search for film locations in Korean – "[...] searching in korean did not generate any useful results" (Honeystars 2016d) – often by using the Korean name of the K-Drama in question in combination with "드라마촬영지" ("film location") as keywords. Online reporting of film locations and visits to them is well established in Korea, and it became more prevalent in 2016 with *The Goblin* (2016–17) and the increased use of Instagram among Korean fans, actors and the managers or owners of the locations used. The Internet pages international fans land on when searching for film locations are thus usually blogs authored by Korean fans, message boards where Korean fans gather or Instagram posts. But Korean news portals and tourism organisations' websites and offices regularly report on film locations as well, and they also serve as a source for international fans. Korean fans' blogs usually offer the most detailed reports on film locations and are hence the most cited sources by international fans. These blogs contain multiple photos and usually an embedded Naver Map of the location, and in the case of restaurants and cafés also photos of the food and the menu. The photos are usually taken by Korean fans during actual visits to the film locations, as I will explore more in detail below. In other words, this search technique entails both mobility through actual reality on the part of (in most cases) Korean fans and mobility through the virtual reality of (Korean) K-Drama fandom on the part of international fans. International fans usually attempt to verify these film locations by making use of online mapping services and thus engaging in digital mobility. From the perspective of international fans, this research technique remains, however, entirely within the realm of virtual and digital reality, as they do not actually visit the locations, but only access them through digital mediation.

The second technique involves "clues in the drama" (Booksntravel [2016b]). Three types of clues are employed. First, clues can be taken from the list of sponsors (often prominently showcased through their logo) in a K-Drama's end credits. Food and coffee chains usually utilize this sort of product placement. But even if the chain store is known, this does not necessarily make the search easier. For example, Booksntravel explains how she "tried to find [a] place for a few days" (2017d). Because she could not do so, she "decided to go through the street view of every noodle shop in Seoul and Incheon and then search for those that cannot be seen at all/clearly on street view by google" (ibid). This technique thus often yields uncertain results. Booksntravel writes for example: "I think this is the most likely one, 98% similarity with the one in the drama [...]" (2017d). In this case, the uncertainly resulted from the fact that only the interior of the restaurant in question was filmed and the chain requires the interiors of its franchises to look very similar. Verifying film locations digitally in this way thus comes with clear limits, and bloggers usually express their uncertainty or refrain from sharing the location at all. Unusually, Booksntravel finally verified the location through actual mobility: when she visited the restaurant in person, she saw a poster of the K-Drama in question on the wall, and a sales person confirmed that it was the correct location, both testifying to the veracity of the location. Another and more common way in which international fans circumvent this clear limitation of digital mobilities is by writing the potential film location via email or other online message services for verification.

Second, clues can consist of images that contain words, syllabic blocks or letters in the fictive reality of K-Dramaland. These clues are usually things like an advertising sign, a shop logo, a roughly digitally rendered name of the location (often only some words, syllabic blocks or letters are erased) or a street name (if shown and not modified). These words, syllabic blocks or letters are (re)transcribed and searched for with a search engine or directly inserted into a mapping service. If this search does not yield results, especially in the case of English-language words (restaurants and bars often have English names, for instance), possible prefixes or suffices are added. If this research yields results, the name of the location will be looked up via the 3D function of a mapping service, usually Daum or Naver. The next step consists of oscillating between the place in the K-Drama (either in the form of a screenshot or by putting a streaming site on pause) and the place as represented in a digital mapping service. While moving the camera and zooming in and out, the fan compares the shape of the building and the materials it is made of, as well as the distance of lampposts or street signs (if any) with the site as represented in the K-Drama. Are the different clues mirrored in the right proportions and at the right distance? Are the surfaces the same? If this comparison based on visual "material detection" is deemed successful, international fans connect the K-Drama site to its model on a mapping service, and further to a specific territorial location in Korea represented by the map. This navigation through digital maps thus clearly relies upon a mimetic understanding of maps: international fans "rely on a resemblance between two elements (signs on the map and territory [...])" (November/Camacho-Hübner/Latour 2010: 586).

Third, clues can consist of architectural features that appear in the fictive reality. These include buildings that fulfil a specific function, like high schools, theatres, libraries, museums, galleries or hospitals, or specific architectural features that might be documented online, like a landmark building or a sculpture. These architectural clues are then looked up via keywords (in either English or Hangul), usually through Google Images. To verify the results of this search, international fans then compare small details of the representations of the site in question in K-Dramas with photos of the same locations found online. If a search is deemed conclusive, the site will be looked up on mapping services for further verification. In this verification process, international fans will, again, temporally navigate through two different realities; the one of K-Dramaland and the one of a digital map representing Korea for verification. In doing so, floor patterns, lamp posts, the shape of a fence, road marking, stones or, in the case of Honeystars, the clothes worn by the clients, become crucial elements:

I ended up googing suanas [googling saunas] /spa/jjimjilbangs [public bath] in Seoul and looked through the images to find the familiar clothes and surroundings [...]. How did I confirm the location? By looking at the wooden logs and clothes in the photo [...] from their official website! (2016c)

A third technique for finding film locations is to compare the fictive reality of K-Dramaland with virtual images that are "stored" in the form of memories from past mobilities to Korea – a technique that implies human cognition and a technological dispositive simultaneously. Whether those travels were undertaken actually or digitally, reference is usually only made to actual travels, as in the case of Booksntravel: "Maybe I have been to Naksan Park for too many times, so I recognized it immediately." (2017b). Even when the fan recognises the location immediately, they often verify it through digital mobility. In most cases, however, fans recognise an area or a street rather than a precise location: "This is the street where my accommodation was located in my last trip to Seoul, I remember I have walked past this location, but of course I do not remember the shop [...]," Booksntravel (2017a) comments about a specific location. Sometimes locations in the fictive reality of K-Dramaland look familiar because of past actual mobility there. But fans do not always deem their memories sufficient to confirm a location, in which case they draw on online mapping services or compare locations to photos from the Internet for final verification, as Booksntravel indicates: "I thought it looked quite familiar and so I went to search for pics in the web to compare, and it should be the same place" (2017 f.).

But past digital mobilities to Korea can also result in immediate recognition of film locations. International fans who have already looked for specific locations via online mapping services often recognise the location the next time it appears onscreen and will not usually verify it again, as Manager-Hyung explains:

This is by far one of the easiest places to locate. I haven't been to any part of Seoul yet but at first look, I knew immediately [...]. I have ID-ed Katakomb Underground City for quite a few times already so it's not difficult. (2015a)

International fans employ four other techniques in their search for film locations, but because they are less frequent I only mention them briefly. First, fans address other fans who mention having visited film locations through actual mobility without mentioning the exact location and ask them for details, as with Booksntravel: "I saw someone mentioning about going to Bong Soon's [main character in K-Drama] home online, so I went to ask [...]" (2017b). Second, fans submit information to bloggers who list film locations to rectify mistakes or submit a location that has not yet been listed, a technique that is also incited by bloggers. Third, fans directly address staff from the film site in question: "As verified by a Canadian Reader and the Hotel (thanks for replying), the filming is done in Frontenac Suite" (Honeystars 2016d). A final technique that I have not seen mentioned, but which I have used when searching for film locations online, is uploading a screenshot to Google Images. For easily recognisable buildings, this technique usually has positive results.

The untrustworthy digital reality

Although fans now routinely move through space via digital mapping services when searching for film locations, uncertainty is a common trope in all narratives about such mobility. One cause of the uncertainty is the fictive reality of K-Dramas themselves, because their settings can be invented as much as their stories (especially in form of film sets). "Dramas production are seriously not cheap," comments Honeystars, for example, on a film locations and continues: "For this scence, they had to hire so many foreigners and caucasians [...] for it to look like Spain. It kind of got me fooled for quite a while as I did not recall Barcelona having such huge shoping malls" (2016c).

But the main difficulty in finding locations is caused by the nature of digital mobility: online mapping services do not always make it possible to verify film locations because they either do not offer a view of a location or offer only an unclear one (bushes, busses or cars may block the view, or the image is of poor quality – one remedy can be to consult older street views as provided by Daum or Naver, e. g.), or the images shown by the mapping service are dated, i. e. a building in question had not yet been built when the last capture was made. In these scenarios, which reveal the limits of geobrowsing, international fans usually warn their readers of potential inaccuracies or not post their finding. In a similar vein, international fans also voice their uncertainty when they offer directions based on digital mapping services without having been to the locations through actual mobility.

A final difficulty involves the Korean language. As mentioned above, most international fans who share film locations online do not have perfect command of Korean or Hangul. "For episode 1, I believe it is filmed at this place called 경산 반곡지 (Gyeongsan Bangokji) I can't find much information about this place in english that's why I didn't blog about it," states Honeystars (2016a). In addition, English is the lingua franca of international K-Drama fandom, and bloggers are thus often keen to offer a translation for the name of the film location, and they sometimes ask their readers for help in doing so. But they do not always offer an English translation because they prefer to stick with the official translation, which they often cannot find. In referring to "Incheon Songdo Sinhang Seaside Rest Area," a site I have looked up as well, Booksntravel (2017c) writes: "I can't find the official English translation of this place, so the name is translated by me, it might be different from the official translation." This site is not referred to by name on digital maps, nor is it found on official tourist sites. It is only mentioned by name on blogs by hobby fishers, as it appears to be a good fishing spot. Another example of the difficulty of translating names into English is small-town harbors. Maehyangri Pier [매향리선착장], which recently appeared in episode 12 of *Strongest Deliv-*

eryman (2017) and which I found, is named on Naver Map, but not on Daum or Google Maps; otherwise I would have had to make up a name, as there was no difficulty in verifying the site.

Ethno-mapping

An integral part of finding film locations is sharing them with other fans, a practice that fortifies the existence of the world of international K-Drama fandom. Although locations are shared in various ways, these practices became more standardised in 2016, and some transversal conventions of how international fans present the information on their sites can be observed. I will refer to these practices developed by international as a specific form of "ethno-mapping," i.e. methods international fans have created to map out film locations online using specific technologies and devices.

The rapid establishment of conventions can be explained as resulting from a (usually virtual) feedback loop between bloggers and their readers. This feedback loop occurs through the comment function on social media, through which readers ask for specific information (including opening hours, access [private or public], directions and fees), which the blogger may include in subsequent posts. While some bloggers and readers establish codes of co-producing the necessary knowledge, other readers put bloggers in the position of service providers from whom precision can be demanded. In both variants, the feedback loop is mainly informed by actual future mobility to the film locations in question. As in tourism in general, where travel is often planned beforehand by reading about places to visit, international fans of K-Dramas often plan their visit to Korea in advance by looking up film locations online.

Nowadays, three types of reporting about film locations based on digital mobility are conventionally used among international fans. The first consists of proposing a selection of the most important film locations to visit (often reduced to the top ten), and the second of briefly mentioning a single film location during discussions on message boards or blogs. I concentrate on the third, and predomi-nant, type: fans usually concentrate on one currently airing K-Drama that they are watching and that is usually popular among other fans. Apart from giving the name of the K-Drama and the location in question – in addition to, in some cases, the number of the episode and a brief description of the scene in question – this reporting style contains four main textual and image blocks: an image block with photos of the locations juxtaposed with a screenshot of the K-Drama text, a descriptive text block that provides directions, a map and additional descriptive text elements.

The most important building block is a screenshot of a location taken from the K-Drama in question (or, rarely, a short clip of the relevant scene). In most cases, this image is juxtaposed with a photo of the same location taken by someone who visited it through actual mobility. In the logic of international fans, this juxtaposition of a two-dimensional place – with its own meanings and uses in a fictional reality – with the "actual" place is intended to verify the accuracy of the location presented. In other words, the location is relegated to the fictional realm and only becomes real once "proven." The fictional image can thus only be trusted when juxtaposed with the actual. In this sense, in the logic of international fans there is a trustable, real reality and another reality that needs to be proven real. As discussed above, this juxtaposition is also one of the main techniques employed by bloggers to verify locations. In sharing a juxtaposition, bloggers thus make their search transparent, but also allow readers to confirm the veracity of the location by comparing the two images: the photo becomes proof. These photos are usually taken from other Internet pages or were taken by the bloggers themselves on prior actual site visits. The main source, however, is entries by Korean bloggers who have visited the place through actual mobility, uploaded several images of the place and documented it in detail (outdoor and indoor images, including the food and the menu). Wikipedia, the Korean Tourism website and the website or Instagram of the location in question serve as additional photo sources.

Importantly, international fans prefer photos to screenshots from online mapping services. This might be explained as resulting from the long-standing use of photos as documentary proof in Western image traditions (Gunning 2008), but also by the modern view that sight is the most important sense (see e.g. Classen 1997). A photo – even if now a digital one – taken by a "real" person still stands for actual reality through its ascribed mimicry. In other words, the photo is still believed and understood as an icon, a sign that is defined by its mimicry of the subject photographed. As such, it stands in opposition to a screenshot of a street view from an online mapping service, which implies multiple layers of mediation and possible transformations or – in Serres' (2014) terms – parasites and interferences (a digital camera on the top of a car; the rendition of these images on a computer; the device itself, which offers multiple perspectives of the location; and the screen on which the screenshot is taken). In addition, the photo, unlike a screenshot, indirectly also stands in for an actual person (and not a car driving by with a camera with a fixed width and angle) who went to the place and verified the location with their own eyes. Finally, this person is not simply another human, but another fan who went to the location with the same purpose as the person who navigates to their site: this other fan has already verified the site *as a K-Drama fan*. This last point demonstrates the importance in modernity of sight as the most trustworthy sense (also implicit in the homologues "I" and "eye" in the English language). International fans thus prefer to rely on the *actual* seeing – represented through a photograph – to a meditated image. Consequently, a blogger's use of their own photos heightens the credibility of the information in the valuation system of international K-Drama fans, in which information provided by Korean-American fans or fans who have visited Korea are usually held in higher esteem because they are considered more trustworthy (Schulze 2013). Hence an actual visit also increases one's status among international fans.

Photos are also juxtaposed with screenshots from the K-Drama text because they can make it easier for fans to find locations when they engage in actual mobility. As mentioned above, building exteriors are often not shown in the K-Drama's fictive reality. Knowing what the exterior of a location looks like helps international fans find it when they are actually present in Korea. Honeystars is thus addressed by a fan as follows: "Hi, is Riverlang spa easy to find? [...] Do you have a pic of what the front look like so we can find it?" (2016c). This is also the reason a blogger gives for juxtaposing screenshots of the K-Drama text with screenshots of the street view of an online mapping service: "Here's what you guys have been waiting for.. a direct comparison of drama footages vs actual google street view to 'verify' the addresses even if you're not there yourself physically" (Honeystars 2017e).

The second building block in international fans' ethno-mapping is a written text providing directions. In its recent conventionalised form, it is reduced to a minimum. Usually the train or subway station and exit are mentioned (subway stations in Seoul often have more than ten exits, which can be a considerable distance apart), together with their Korean name, and the relevant bus route and stop may also be mentioned: "Transport: Beomil Station Exit 7 or 9 walk for about 1 km" (Honeystars 2017f). The directions usually refer exclusively to public transportation as indicated by digital mapping services. If the route from the station or stop is not easy and requires walking, some international bloggers provide more detailed directions or offer links to webpages where the directions are explained in detail. In some cases, however, international fans explicitly refrain from sharing the directions, particularly when the film location is not open to the public or situated in a residential area and bloggers are concerned with protecting residents from visiting fans, as Booksntravel states: "I guess it is not open for visit, so I am not providing the transport details" (2016c).

Third, these written directions are often combined with a map. This map can either, on the one hand, consist of a screenshot of a mapping service in which the blogger has marked the exact location, or, on the other, be directly embedded in the blog or consist of a link to a mapping service. In the case of the latter, and more common, in this building block, fans usually use Google Maps, possibly because it is easier to embed Google Maps than other mapping services in WordPress, the main content management system used by bloggers. As well, Google Maps' services are available in several languages and mainly English. Their Korean analogues, Daum Maps or Naver Maps, in contrast, are usually only available in Korean and can make navigating difficult even with a translation application. The embedded maps usually show only the immediate surroundings of the location in question, making it impossible for readers to place the location in a larger geographical context. As such, these maps become a "frozen image" (November/Camacho-Hübner/Latour 2010: 583), a visual abstraction of space that will only be concretised once the larger map is accessed digitally or the location is visited through actual mobility.

The fourth building block, which is not yet standardised, consists of some information about the location, derived from various sources, including online sources such as the English-language version of Korean Tourism's website, Wikipedia, information from other (usually Korean) bloggers or comments and reviews from tourists on TripAdvisor. This information is usually cited directly. Fans also sometimes include personal information about their own visit to the location. Such personal information is rare, however, because fans usually only visit these locations through digital mobility. Following Stafford (2016), actual presence at an actual site is required before one can add a more personal layer of information in the form of memories and experiences. When accessed only through digital mobility, the site remains a landscape, i.e. a distant (and often only two-dimensional) view of a place in question. Consequently, personal impressions can only be shared by fans on the basis of actual mobility, as Booksntravel does: "Highly recommend going to Naksan Park at night! Apart from seeing the night view of Seoul, you can see the old city walls at night, which is a really pretty sight." (2017b)

Ethno-archiving

In listing film locations, fans also digitally archive them. The archiving is usually not done consciously, but is instead a result of their search for and sharing of film locations. As mentioned above, two main archiving methods can be distinguished. In the first, locations from one particular K-Drama are posted one at a time. In the second, all locations are collected on one page, which is updated regularly. One blogger, for instance orders the film locations according to two different logics in the same post, geographically (country, region, district) and chronologically (by episode). A very recent development is the use of differently coloured place markers in Google Maps, each colour corresponding to a different K-Drama. When one clicks on the place marker, the actual name of the location appears in English along with the number of the episode in which it appears in the K-Drama in question (see e.g. Honeystars 2017g).

Conclusion

In this article, I have introduced a specific and very recent form of digital mobility, screen screen tourism, to the study of media practices. Based on a case study of international fans of Korean television series, I have described the diverse techniques these fans use to engage in this type of mobility and the conventions they have established to share the results thereof.

Screen screen tourism is distinct from "classic" screen tourism in at least two regards. In descriptions of screen tourism, navigating a digitalised and mediated geographical reality – if it is discussed at all – is usually understood as a transitional phase on the way to actual mobility. Screen screen tourism can serve the same aim, but – and this is a major difference – it is most often the end goal. Consequently, in screen tourism the "destination" or the "place travelled to" is automatically understood as an actual place. The same is not true in the case of screen screen tourism: the final destination of this practice is a digitally mediated "actual" location, even if actual mobility may follow. In most of the literature on screen tourism so far (for an overview, see Connell 2012), the taken-for-granted hypothesis is that watching films and television series will naturally induce *actual* mobility. The practices of international K-Drama fans demonstrate that this is not always so. Another difference is that fans often engage in screen tourism to re-enact scenes from films or television series, while the same is not true in the case of screen screen tourism: when engaging in this type of mobility, fans instead resemble geomatics engineers who collect, monitor and archive data on spaces, because their foremost aim is to determine the actual geographical locations of K-Dramaland locations through correspondence verification. In doing so, they do not stroll online like virtual flâneurs; instead, they meticulously *screen* virtual and digital geographical (and sometimes actual) sites and present their findings for other fans to *screen*. As such, screen screen tourism does not merely consist of tourism done through the screen and induced by a screen. It also consists of, first, the very act of *screening*, of methodologically examining digital and virtual material to determine whether there is a mimetic correspondence to an actual place, and second, the presentation of the location found for other fans to view it on a screen – to *screen* (as in screening a film) locations for other fans.

More fundamentally, the case study presented here is a telling example through which to understand the multiplication of realities characteristic of modernity. In particular, it reveals how we constantly and simultaneously navigate through two or more of these realities through conversions from one reality to another, conversions that usually rely on the mediation of one or more other realities. In the case of international K-Drama fans, I have demonstrated that the conversion from fictive to actual reality is mediated through virtual and digital reality. Navigating multiple realities thus relies on constant mediation and the parasites and interferences it hinges upon (Serres 2014) – for example the bus that blocks the view of a digital site being screened by an international fan. Second, this case study also demonstrates the profound changes that have occurred over the last decade in media landscapes in particular and knowledge production and diffusion in general, including the shift from corporate knowledge creation to many-to-many and participatory knowledge production and the introduction of new (virtual and digital) realities. As such, these new digitalised geographical realities, and particularly those of digital mapping services, should be considered in future research as an important realm of fans' engagement with media texts and as daily routines and practices in world-making processes.

Last but certainly not least, I hope that my ethnographic screening of international fans' activities and my participation in such activities will demonstrate the usefulness of an ethnographic approach to the study of "maps as geomedial action spaces" (Abend/Harvey 2017: 172).

References

Abend, Pablo/Francis Harvey (2017): "Maps as Geomedial Action Spaces: Considering the Shift From Logocentric to Egocentric Engagements." In: GeoJournal 82/1, pp. 171–183.

Amanda (2014) "Navel gazing and sweeping generalizations: Watching drama as an American", July, 2014 (http://outsideseoul.blogspot.ch/2014/07/navel-gazing-and-sweeping.html).

Anderson, Leon (2006): "Analytic Autoethnography." In: Journal of Contemporary Ethnography 35/4, pp. 373–395.

Boellstorff, Tom/Nardi, Bonnie/Pearce, Bonnie/Taylor, T.L. (2012): Ethnography and Virtual Worlds. A Handbook of Method, Princeton, Oxford: Princeton University Press.

Boltanski, Luc (2009): De la critique. Précis de sociologie de l'émancipation, Paris: Gallimard.

Booksntravel (2016a): "鬼怪 第1&2集拍攝地點- 石牆路、光化門 Goblin Episode 1 Filming Locations- Stone Walled Roads & Gwanghwamun", May 10, 2016 (https://koreatravelart.wordpress.com/2016/05/10/secret-love-affair-filming-location-jeonju-restaurant/).

Booksntravel (2016b): "Secret Love Affair Filming Location- Jeonju Restaurant", December 16, 2016 (https://koreatravelart.wordpress.com/2016/12/16/鬼怪-第12集拍攝地點-石牆路、光化門-goblin-episode-1-filming-locations-stone-walled-roads/).

Booksntravel (2016c): "鬼怪 拍攝地點- 恩倬學校及圖書館 Goblin Filming Locations- Eun Tak School and Library", December 23, 2016 (https://koreatravelart.wordpress.com/2016/12/23/鬼怪-拍攝地點-恩倬學校及圖書館-goblin-filming-locations-eun-tak-school-and-library/).

Booksntravel (2017a): "大力女子都奉順拍攝地點- Plate-B Strong Woman Do Bong-soon Filming Location- Plate-B 플레이트 비", March 14, 2017 (https://koreatravelart.wordpress.com/2017/03/14/大力女子都奉順拍攝地點-都奉順父親的店-strong-woman-do-bong-soon-filming-l/).

Booksntravel (2017b): "大力女子都奉順拍攝地點- 駱山公園&梨花洞壁畫村 Strong Woman Do Bong-soon Ep 7 Filming Location- Naksan Park & Ihwa Mural Village", March 23, 2017 (https://koreatravelart.wordpress.com/2017/03/23/大力女子都奉順拍攝地點-駱山公園梨花洞壁畫村-str/).

Booksntravel (2017c): "大力女子都奉順第六集拍攝地點- 仁川松島新港海邊休息場 Strong Woman Do Bong-soon Ep 6 Filming Location- Incheon Songdo Sinhang Seaside Rest Area 송도신항바다쉼터", April 2, 2017 (https://korea

travelart.wordpress.com/2017/04/02/大力女子都奉順第六集拍攝地點-仁川
松島新港海邊).

Booksntravel (2017d): "大力女子都奉順第十二集拍攝地點- Noodles Tree 永登浦
KNK分店 Strong Woman Do Bong-soon Ep 12 Filming Location- Noodles Tree
Yeongdeungpo KNK Branch", April 5, 2007 (https://koreatravelart.wordpress.
com/2017/04/05/大力女子都奉順第十二集拍攝地點-noodles-tree-永登浦knk
分/).

Booksntravel (2017e): "大力女子都奉順拍攝地點- 高陽市自由路廢車產業 Strong
Woman Do Bong-soon Filming Location- Goyang Jayu Road Car Disposal
Place", April 8 2017 (https://koreatravelart.wordpress.com/2017/04/08/大力女
子都奉順拍攝地點-高陽市自由路廢車產業-strong-w/).

Booksntravel (2017f): "大力女子都奉順Ep 15拍攝地點- 雙大炮烤肉店 Strong
Woman Do Bong-soon Ep 15 Filming Location- 쌍대포 BBQ restaurant", April 15,
2017 (https://koreatravelart.wordpress.com/2017/04/15/大力女子都奉順ep-15拍
攝地點-雙大炮烤肉店-strong-woman-do-bong-soon-ep-15-filming/).

Classen, Constance (1997): "Foundations for an Anthropology of The Senses." In:
International Social Science Journal 49/153, pp. 401–412.

Connell, Joanne (2012): "Film Tourism – Evolution, Progess and Prospects." In:
Tourism Management 33, pp. 1007–1029.

Couldry, Nick (2015[2012]): Media, Society, World: Social Theory and Digital
Media Practice, Cambridge, Malden: Polity Press.

Deleuze, Gilles (1996): "L'actuel et le virtuel." In: Gilles Deleuze/Claire Parnet
(eds.), Dialogues, Paris: Flammarion, pp. 179–181.

Esposito, Elena (2014 [2007]): Die Fiktion der wahrscheinlichen Realität, Frankfurt am Main: Suhrkamp.

Gunning, Tom (2008): "What's the Point of an Index? Or, Faking Photographs."
In: Karen Beckman/Jean Ma (eds.), Still Moving: Between Cinema and Photography, Durham and London: Duke University Press, pp. 39–49.

Hine, Christine (2015): Ethnography for the Internet: Embedded, Embodied and
Everyday, London: Bloomsbury Publishing.

Honeystars (2016a): "[Filming Location] Moonlight Drawn by Clouds", Septem-
ber 19, 2016 (http://www.flyhoneystars.com/2016/09/19/filming-location-moon
light-drawn-by-clouds/).

Honeystars (2016b): "[Filming Location] Moonlight Drawn by Clouds – Pink
Flowers Field", October 22 2016 (http://www.flyhoneystars.com/2016/10/22/
filming-location-moonlight-drawn-by-clouds-pink-flowers-field/).

Honeystars (2016c): "[Filming Location] Legend of the Blue Sea", October 22, 2016
(http://www.flyhoneystars.com/2016/10/22/filming-location-moonlight-drawn-
by-clouds-pink-flowers-field/).

Honeystars (2016d): "[Filming Location] Goblin: The Lonely and Great God",
November 25, 2017 (http://www.flyhoneystars.com/2016/11/25/filming-location-
legend-of-the-blue-sea/).

Honeystars (2017e): "Goblin Filming Location in Quebec – The Ultimate Guide", January 23, 2017 (http://www.flyhoneystars.com/2017/01/23/goblin-filming-loc ation-in-quebec-the-ultimate-guide/).

Honeystars (2017f): "三流之路拍攝地點- 釜山凡川洞&水晶洞 Fight My Way Filming Location – Busan Beomcheon-dong & Sujeong-dong", June 1, 2017 (https://koreatravelart.wordpress.com/2017/06/01/三流之路拍攝地點-釜山凡 川洞水晶洞-fight-my-way-filming-location-busan-beomcheon-d/).

Honeystars (2017g): "Filming Locations (Korea)", 2017 (https://www.google.com/ maps/d/viewer?mid=1LiWIsYQ4PB0_DHptyLZoMVFZRGI&ll=37.375205202 325176%2C127.32169109130868&z=10).

Kim, Hyounggon/Richardson, Sarah L. (2003): "Motion Picture Impacts on Desti-nation Images." In: Annals of Tourism Research 30/1, pp. 216–237.

Lévy, Pierre (1998): Becoming Virtual. Reality in the Digital Age, New York et al.: Plenum Press.

Manager-Hyung (2015a): "[Fated to Love You] THERE IS NO WAY I'M NOT GOING TO THIS BAR WHEN I GET TO SEOUL", January 2015 (http://managerhyung. blogspot.ch/2015/01/fated-to-love-you-there-is-no-way-im.html).

Mueller, Alain (2016): "Beyond Ethnographic Scriptocentrism: Modelling Multi-Scalar Processes, Networks, and Relationships." In: Anthropological Theory 16/1, pp. 98–130.

November, Valérie/Eduard Camacho-Hübner/Bruno Latour (2010): "Entering a Risky Territory: Space in the Age of Digital Navigation." In: Environment and Planning D: Society and Space 28/4, pp. 581–599.

Rutledge Shields, Vickie (2003): "The Less Space We Take, the More Powerful We'll Be. How Advertising Uses Gender to Invert Signs of Empowerment and Social Equality." In: Angharad N. Valdivia (ed.), A Companion to Media Studies, Malden, Oxford, Carlton: Blackwell, pp. 247–271.

Schulze, Marion (2013): "Korea vs. K-Dramaland: The Culturalization of K-Dra-mas by International Fans." In: Acta Koreana 16/2, pp. 367–397.

Schulze, Marion (2016): "Manifesting (Inappropriate) Desire: Women Watch-ing Korean Television Dramas Online." In: Andrew Jackson/Colette Balmain (eds.), Korean Screen Culture, New York: Peter Lang, pp. 293–320.

Serres, Michel (2014): Le Parasite, Paris: Les éditions pluriel.

Stafford, Fiona (2016): "It's not easy to make landscape a place: you have to feel it", November 7, 2016 (https://aeon.co/ideas/it-s-not-easy-to-make-landscape-a-place-you-have-to-feel-it).

Twinklelie & SeRose (2013): "A Detective's Corp. Journal in Dramaland", Septem-ber 30, 2013 (http://mydramalist.com/article/2013/09/30/a-detectives-corp.-jour nal-in-dramaland#.UlCI3VCshPk).

Tzanelli, Rodanthi (2007): The Cinematic Tourist: Explorations in Globalization, Culture and Resistance, London and New York: Routledge.

Audiences, Aesthetics and Affordances

Analysing Practices of Visual Communication on Social Media

Maria Schreiber

Abstract

This research investigates how the practices of sharing pictures with specific audiences on social media may be related to aesthetics and affordances. Based on fieldwork (interviews, picture analysis and digital ethnography) with a group of female teenagers in Vienna, Austria, how they visually curate their accounts is mapped and reconstructed. Regarding content and aesthetics, different kinds of pictures are shared using different apps. Snapchat, for example, (for this specific group at the time of the investigation) is the preferred medium for live communication with very close friends using fast, pixelated, "ugly" pictures, while Instagram serves to share polished, conventional, "beautiful" pictures with broader audiences. Based on this case study, three conceptual arguments can be made. First, visual communication is practised in relation to specific social settings or audiences. Social media is part of these practices, and users navigate differences between platforms to manage identities and relationships. Second, the analysis of practices embedded in specific software, therefore, has to be contextualised and related to the structures of these environments. Software co-constructs processes of editing, distribution, sharing and affirmation, and its affordances have to be related to the ways in which users exploit them. Third, as visual communication becomes an intrinsic part of online communication, the exploration of how distinctions between audiences and affordances play out stylistically appears to be of particular interest, which entails calibrated aesthetics; however, this visual layer is seldom investigated closely.

Introduction

In recent years, networked visual communication has become a common everyday practice. Billions of photos and pictures have been shared and shown on a broad variety of apps and platforms in a wide range of contexts. Social media has brought into question the clear distinctions between public and private communi-

DOI 10.14361/dcs-2017-0209
DCS | Digital Culture and Society | Vol. 3, Issue 2 | © transcript 2017

cation and between mass-mediated and interpersonal communication (boyd 2011; Wagner 2014). Users exploit and calibrate differences, not only between apps and platforms, but also within platforms (Gershon 2010; Marwick 2013). By navigating these structures, users "exploit differences between media to express emotions and manage mediated relationships" (Madianou 2014: 667).

Communicative practices always take place in relation to specific social settings or audiences (Goffman 1959) and belonging and distinction constitute groups, relationships and all forms of sociality (Bourdieu 1972; Mannheim 1980). However, over the past 20 years, social media has become intrinsic to these practices, and the technical structures of platforms and apps are now integral to networked interpersonal communication. Based on a dialogue of theoretical concepts and empirical data, this contribution is aimed at investigating how photo-sharing practices constitute and maintain social relations. More specifically, the relevance and role of the visual styles and aesthetics of pictures and the technical affordances of apps as intrinsic characteristics of the visual communicative process are discussed.

Audiences

While earlier research on online identities focused on the elements of self-presentation, recent research has shifted to understanding identity as constituted in relation to sociality and thus highlights *practices of interaction and communication* as practices of doing (social) identities (Baym 2015; Marwick 2013; Papacharissi and Easton 2013). Praxeological approaches have become popular in social-constructivist media research on everyday communicative practices as they place embodied, routinized doings and sayings structured by implicit, habitual knowledge in the foreground of analysis (Bräuchler and Postill 2010; Couldry 2004). Within this framework, identities have long been conceptualised as networked, as they are not fixed, but dynamically constituted in relation to specific social contexts and groups (Bourdieu 1972; Goffman 1959). Within networked social media, the contexts we constantly navigate have become more visible and, therefore, potentially more reflexive. For example, we might designate a person as a close friend on Facebook or share a photo with our partner but not with our extended family on WhatsApp. These *networked* or *intimate publics* (boyd, 2011; Baym, 2015; Hjorth et al. 2012) are co-constituted by the software that is used, usually provided by commercial actors (boyd 2011; van Dijck 2013). Their algorithms, codes and interfaces are an intrinsic part of our communicative practices.

Aesthetics

These communicative practices are multimodal (Baym 2015: 58 ff.; Meißner 2015) and the range of modes of expression is continuously being expanded and refined: from texting *kiss*, to sharing a selfie with puckered lips, to sending a GIF of kissing Minions. Digitally mediated communication has shifted from a primarily text-based practice to a form of multimodal, heavily visual communication – a trend accelerated by the smartphone, its ubiquitous networked camera, and fast, affordable, mobile broadband connections. Identities and socialities are constituted not only by picturing the self(ie)[1] but by communicating in general and by communicating visually through all kinds of images: food pics, memes, business portraits, holiday shots and many more. It is not only language, narratives and discourses, but also visual sense-making and communication that are constitutive elements of sociality. Visual media, therefore, are understood as socially constructed, but at the same time, they co-construct sociality:

It is not just that we see the way we do because we are social animals, but also that our social arrangements take the forms they do because we are seeing animals. (Mitchell 2002: 171)

In this regard, new media seem to amplify and utilise certain potentialities of pictures, enabling a "general aesthesia" (Grace 2014: 14). Grace describes this "increased general sensitivity to the audio-visual space of the everyday" (2014: 14), in which pictures become important means of embodied everyday creativity and communication and a new form of mass expression. Just as when we use language, we express ourselves aesthetically when we communicate in and through pictures (Przyborski 2017) – both regarding *what* we show as content and motifs (explicitly and iconographically) and *how* we show content stylistically and aesthetically (implicitly and iconologically). How pictures are framed and cropped (Kanter 2016), which perspectives and compositions are chosen (Przyborski and Haller 2014), and how close or far away the camera is positioned (Schreiber 2017b) co-constitute visual sense-making. What is perceived as beautiful, interesting and worth photographing, showing and sharing is socially and habitually constituted.

We can also code-switch according to the context. For example, while we might use portraits for both our CV and our Facebook profile, these portraits are probably very different as they are embedded in various contexts with different audiences and communicative practices. Pictures, therefore, are conceptualised as aesthetic products and means of communication which allow explicit and implicit visual sense-making (Bourdieu 1990; Panofsky 1975). On social media, in particular, pictures serve as a means of interpersonal communication, and these communicative practices are entangled with the technical structures of the platforms that are used.

---

1   For research on selfies, see Senft and Baym (2015), Tiidenberg and Gómez-Cruz (2015) and Warfield, Cambre and Abidin (2016).

Affordances

Digital pictures depend on hardware (e. g. displays and screens) and software (e. g. code, apps and programmes) to become visible and perceived as pictures by the human gaze. The conditions of these mediations are relevant in a range of ways: abstract conditions such as digitality, networked mobility and convergence are as constitutive of materiality as pixels, scrollbars and LEDs. The importance of material and technical affordances as components of communication was widely acknowledged in early media and communication studies and is emphasised in recent research (Hand 2012; Lehmuskallio and Gómez-Cruz 2016; Maynard 1997). However, most empirical research in this field has been "strangely without object" (Zillien 2008, 181, translated from German by the author). The concept of *affordances* has been mainly used in analyses of the human perception of artefacts in the fields of perceptional psychology, Human-Computer-Interaction and Science and Technology Studies (Gibson 1977; Norman 1999; Wright und Parchoma 2011). It only recently became popular as a potential solution to the lack of technical materiality in empirical research in Media and Communication Studies (Bucher and Helmond 2017; Hutchby 2014). The actual implementation and uses of the concept are manifold[2], ranging from high-level analysis (boyd 2011; Schrock 2015) to the micro-reading (McVeigh-Schultz and Baym 2015) of material and/or technical characteristics.

Following Hutchby (2001) and McVeigh-Schultz/Baym (2015), affordances are understood as neither deterministic, nor relativistic, but rather as relational. Affordances frame, enable and constrain practices yet are

not things which impose themselves upon humans' actions with, around, or via that artefact. But they do set limits on what it is possible to do with, around, or via the artefact. [...] What is made of them is accomplished in the interface between human aims and the artefact's affordances. (Hutchby 2001: 453)

Affordances are understood as potentiality. The different ways they are actually used have to be analysed in practice (ibid) or, as Vyas/Chisalita (2006) state, as "affordance in interaction" (2006: 92). However, if affordances are integrated empirically, a separate analysis of the artefact has proven to be useful for understanding the "material substratum which underpins the very possibility of different courses of action in relation to an artefact" (Hutchby 2001: 450).

Regarding social media, van Dijck proposes five elements that are required to analyse the technological dimension of platforms and apps: "(meta)data, algorithms, protocols, inter-faces, defaults" (2013a: 30 ff.). To those without any tech-

---

2   This also became clear in a recent online discussion in E-Seminar 60 on "Social Media as Practice" on the popular Media Anthropology Network (http://www.media-anthropology.net/index.php/e-seminars).

nical expertise, metadata, algorithms and protocols are hard to access and under-stand and mostly hidden by the operators and owners. The *interface* and *default settings*, though, are visible and thus analysable by the researcher. Technical features (e. g. the interface, buttons, scroll bars and icons) and regulatory features (e. g. the requirement to register or create a profile to use an app) co-constitute the connections of users with, for example, other users and content. Default settings can be understood as affordances of the app in the sense of habitual characteris-tics.

These elements have proven to be reliable access points, so this study focuses on exploring what structure and dramaturgy the interface and the upload process of an app have in the practice of sharing pictures. These features of three apps are elaborated on in the empirical case study, in which their interfaces and default settings are understood and analysed as affordances on a micro-level. The overall aim of the case study is to relate these affordances to the ways the participants exploit them: how are they interpreted, used and perceived, and how do they become relevant (or not) in the practices of visual communication and photo-sharing[3]?

These theoretical issues are further explored in a qualitative case study of a group of Viennese teenage girls. Visual networked communication can be defined as an interpersonal, mediated communication practice that always takes place in relation to specific audiences through aesthetics and is embedded in the technical affordances of software. The argument that all kinds of picture are filtered – in both the social-cultural and technical senses – is elaborated on based on the case study. First, the research methodology and empirical data are briefly introduced.

Research methodology

The case study is based on materials collected during fieldwork with a group of three teenage girls in Vienna, Austria[4]. The data and materials consist of two in-depth group interviews (conducted in January 2014 and March 2015), several pictures shared by the participants and online ethnographic notes and screen-shots of the participants' social media accounts. Based on these materials, their practices of sharing and showing pictures in diverse smartphone apps are mapped and analysed. At the time of the second set of interviews, Anna, Bele and Clara

---

3   McVeigh-Schultz and Baym (2015) introduce "vernacular affordances" as a specific perspective on the "sense-making involved as people conceptualize the relationship between material structure and practice for the technologies they use" (2015: 10).

4   I conducted the empirical research for my doctoral thesis (Schreiber 2017a). This case study was one of four, and some points discussed in this contribution are pub-lished in German articles (Schreiber 2017b; Schreiber and Kramer 2016).

were between 14 and 15 years old. They went to high school together and spent a lot of time with each other outside school.

Framed by a praxeological understanding of media use, the analysis is informed by flexible, adaptable research strategies (Hine 2015; Hirschauer 2008; Markham 2004) and the documentary method, as elaborated by Bohnsack (2008)[5]. This interpretive approach differentiates between, and systematically relates, two levels of meaning: *what* is said or is visible is separated from *how* it is actually conveyed within language (e. g. interview transcripts), practice (e. g. observation notes) and pictures (e. g. screenshots of Instagram accounts). Through reconstructing the *how*, the documentary method is aimed at reconstructing habitual, implicit patterns of practice, which are understood as tacit knowledge embedded in everyday practices of action and perception (Bourdieu 1972). This approach enables the analysis of structures of social life that goes beyond intentional, instrumental, rational action, without claiming any a priori knowledge of these structures. The in-depth analysis of the material that was collected is intended to promote an understanding of the habitual patterns of picture sharing within networked media environments.

The main objects of analysis are practices as narrated in the interviews and observed online. Specific apps become relevant elements in the narrations and observations but, as mentioned above, technical affordances are also analysed independently. Descriptions and interpretations of the uploading process[6] for WhatsApp, Snapchat and Instagram are briefly summarised in the case study. Pictures are understood as aesthetic documents of visual elements of expression, so they are also analysed according to an iconographic/iconologic approach (Bohnsack 2008), focusing on embodied and aesthetics performances. These different kinds of data provide specific perspectives on the practices of photo sharing and visual communication, which are condensed and related to each other.

The fieldwork was conducted in 2014 and 2015. As in any research on new media, platforms, apps and visual social media seem to be a "moving target" (Hogan and Quan-Haase 2010: 310) for researchers. Technical environments are continuously being changed and transformed, and software is invented and updated over a very short time. Nevertheless, the case study allows for a detailed account of the specific entanglements of audiences, aesthetics and affordances at a specific point in time. This account forms the basis for the subsequent theoretical exploration of the interrelations of these dimensions.

---

5   Based on Mannheim (1980) and Bourdieu (1972).

6   Referring to the versions of the apps available in autumn 2016 for Android phones and analysed on the researcher's smartphone, a Samsung Galaxy S4.

Case study: Anna, Bele and Clara

Beyond photographic practices: "cool stuff? that you see on your phone"

Picture sharing is part of Anna, Bele and Clara's common everyday communicative practices. They take photos with their smartphone cameras and collect pictures and screenshots online. Their sharing practices have a broad range of contexts. For school purposes, for example, taking and sharing pictures is described as highly practical by Anna: *"you do not need to carry books around. You can just take a picture"* to share book pages, blackboard notes and workbooks with peers. In this context, the use of the smartphone camera is more similar to the practices of scanning than personal photography (Lehmuskallio 2016). However, taking photos of things and sharing photos with each other also continue to be crucial components of the girls' practices: friends, faces, toenails, books, mountains and more might become motifs, but also *"cool stuff? that you see on your phone"*. With the same ease, the girls move through the offline and online worlds, collecting and capturing pictures of what they see and like – *"for example, there was something with strawberries that looked so cool, so I made a screenshot and installed it as background picture"*.

In the girls' practices, it does not really matter if a picture is a photo in the sense of an indexical "surface marking created with light" (Maynard 1997: 34) or an accumulation of pixels on a screen. As a digital, networked device, the smartphone allows a range of practices of picture production that goes beyond photographic practices. What is relevant to the girls is not so much who took a picture and how it came to be displayed, but that it appeals to their aesthetic sense. Potential pictures are out there, not only in the world, where they are directly visible to the human eye, but also on the Internet, visible to the eye through screens. Both pictures that are made and pictures that are found can be stored, used, edited and shared as, technically, both consist of code that can appear as pictures on screens through software (Meier 2012). These practices of aesthetic production and curation are closely entangled with what is habitually anchored as "takeable" pictures[7]. Moreover, pictures become a means of interpersonal communication once they are authorised and selected to be shown to and shared with persons in specific contexts and media.

---

7   "[T]he range of that which suggests itself as really photographable for a given social class (that is, the range of 'takeable' photographs or photographs 'to be taken', as opposed to the universe of realities which are objectively photographable given the technical possibilities of the camera) is defined by implicit models which may be understood via photographic practice and its product [...]." (Bourdieu 1990: 6)

Groups as social, technical and conversational structures: "and one with just the three of us"

At the time of enquiry, the girls are mostly using three apps to share pictures: WhatsApp, Instagram and Snapchat. Their politics of showing and sharing pictures are entangled with the functions and settings of these apps. The girls use WhatsApp for a broad variety of different publics that are differentiated very clearly:

Anna: And then, another group with us and Tom, Bele's brother.
Bele: And Lea.
Anna: Yes, and Lea. And Ina. And then another one without Ina. And [laughing] then another one for French? And one with just the three of us. And one for homework and another one with Sarah, Lara and me and a silly group? And then the one where we all are.

The groups on WhatsApp demarcate the social structures that the girls navigate. Each girl has an individual set of groups, and all three girls belong to several groups. Some groups only differ by one person who is included or excluded. WhatsApp allows an elaborate separation of different intimate publics, so the participants view it as a secure, intimate space for communication. It also serves as a backstage space to negotiate which photos are suitable to be uploaded on more frontstage platforms (Goffman 1959). One girl proudly complains that people send her different versions of the same picture and ask her which photo they should post on Instagram. Like offline socialities, WhatsApp groups are dynamic and have different time spans:

Anna: And then you name the group, and you say just for this purpose. And then at some point, you realise it is totally unnecessary, and then everyone leaves.

In these practices of establishing, maintaining and communicating with intimate publics, the differentiation between offline and online spheres dissolves and becomes irrelevant (Markham 2013; Marwick 2013). Physical absence and presence and online and offline communication interlock seamlessly, as shown in the following extract:

Anna: Well, we have a group; we are all in there. And on Thursdays, we watch *Top model* together, and then we meet at someone's place, and then we text to –
Bele: At your place actually always.
Clara: Yes, watching *Top model* at your place.
Anna: Yes: [altering her voice] "Can we come on Thursday? Yes, OK, you can come. I am leaving now. I am already here. Open the door".
[everybody laughing]
Interviewer: Ok, so to meeting up –
Clara: Or, "Guys, entertain me. I'm bored, and the bus hasn't arrived".

Here, the girls enact a typical conversation on WhatsApp that takes place in their "group". The group is not only a social but also a technical and conversational structure embedded within the app's interface – and they are "all in there". The app enables them to establish an ambient intimacy (Hjorth et al. 2012) and presence and to switch from a mediated presence ("entertain me") to a physical presence ("open the door").

As mentioned, the apps' interfaces and default settings are understood as affordances that co-constitute the practices of picture sharing. A close reading of these technical affordances on a micro-level, therefore, can help to more deeply understand the relationship between these affordances and the girls' sharing practices.

Analysing affordances: interfaces and defaults

WhatsApp, Snapchat and Instagram are the apps that are most commonly used by the girls and they are therefore included in the following brief comparative analysis.

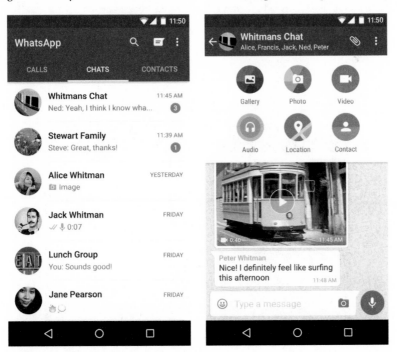

Figure 1: WhatsApp screenshots: chat menu and chat conversation (whatsappbrand.com).

WhatsApp shows all recent conversations in chronological order on the start screen, with the most recent conversation on top. Within a conversation thread, the most recent messages appear at the bottom, similar to an Internet relay-chat interface. Users can send text, images, emojis, voice messages and more. When online, users can converse in real time. In 2014, WhatsApp introduced blue ticks to indicate whether conversation partners had received and read messages. Importantly, the picture-sharing upload dynamics require users to choose with whom they want to share content – which is not mandatory for Instagram, but is for Snapchat.

Once Snapchat is started, the first interface is the camera display of the front camera, which, in default mode, shows the users' face, encouraging them to immediately take selfies. After taking a photo or video through the app, users can choose to whom they want to send it. Unlike most apps, Snapchat's main navigation mode is swiping horizontally from one menu interface to the next. Photos taken with the camera are called Snaps and serve as the canvas for short texts, drawings and a nearly endless choice of emojis – recalling sticker albums or scrapbook aesthetics (Good 2013). In 2015, Snapchat added selfie filters, allowing users to decorate and distort their faces with various masks. A crucial affordance of this app is that shared pictures vanish after a set time, a maximum of 10 seconds, unless they are stored as stories, which stay online for 24 hours and are visible to all of the users' followers. This affordance has been interpreted as an indicator of the emerging visual culture of ephemerality (Chun 2008; Jurgenson 2013; Velez 2014).

Figure 2: Snapchat interfaces: camera display and list of stories (Android Play Store).

Unlike this fleeting visual communication, Instagram remediates characteristics of classic websites. In Instagram's default sharing settings, uploaded pictures are shared with all the followers of users' feeds. Like WhatsApp, Instagram was originally programmed as a mobile app and optimised for use on smartphones. Users need to register with a username and an email address. The user profile is very basic and consists of a profile pic, a short description and the numbers of posts, followers and accounts followed. Earlier versions of Instagram only allowed users to upload pictures. More recently, the app permits sharing videos, stories and more than one picture at a time. The main feed focuses on a vertical, scrollable stream of static pictures.

Figure 3: Instagram screenshots: feed, account, filter and tools (https://en.instagram-brand.com/assets/screenshots).

Based on this comparative analysis, two main modes of picture sharing practices can be categorised following Villi (2013, 2015): *messaging* and *publishing*. These two modes touch upon the various layers of visual networked communication: is the mediation reciprocal and intimate, or is it more one-way and public? How do the platforms afford these modes (or not)? Which kinds of publics are anticipated?

In the interviews, the girls linguistically mark these two modes by using different language to describe what they are doing. They talk about "sending" pictures on WhatsApp and Snapchat but "uploading" or "posting" pictures to Instagram[8]. At the time of investigation, the girls use Instagram for publishing practices and WhatsApp and Snapchat for messaging. These apps' technical affordances and associated communicative modes are closely related to the ways in which the girls establish and maintain different kinds of relationships and audiences. WhatsApp allows the setting up of an unlimited number of groups[9], so a

8   Both apps have since been changed and their interfaces now incorporate stories very similar to those that stay online for 24 hours, as originally introduced by Snapchat. For its part, Snapchat has introduced memories to allow long-term storage of specific pictures. Apps seem to become increasingly similar over time and it will be interesting to track how these trends evolve.

9   A group can contain a maximum of 256 conversation partners (https://www.whats app.com/faq/en/general/21073373).

broad spectrum of different forms of socialities can be generated and thus also a large variety of picture sharing practices. The girls participate in groups for sharing school materials, those for exchanging memes and funny pictures, large groups that resemble Internet relay chats, groups that also allow meta-communication in relation to other groups or public platforms and much more, as already mentioned above. Just as is the case in the offline world, forms of sociality are mainly consti- tuted through inclusion and exclusion (Bourdieu 1972; Goffman 1959). Moreover, the content and tone of visual communication are calibrated for specific platforms and audiences. What has been elaborated on in regard to online communication in general (Gershon 2010; Madianou 2014; Marwick 2013) holds true for practices of visual communication. This is entered into further in the next section.

Calibrated aesthetics: "Bele is the queen of ugly pictures"

Images that the group share on Instagram are rather diffusely textually framed as "beautiful". Looking at Anna's and Bele's accounts, what this might mean (for this group, in this specific context) becomes visible: the pictures they share on this rather public platform are iconographically quite conventional. They are relatable and easy to understand for a broader (Western European, female and teenaged) audience, oriented towards a generalised sense of beauty and established visual repertoires, motifs and styles (portraits, flowers and feet)[10].

The pictures and, especially, the photos that the girls share on WhatsApp and Snapchat have more intimate content and are specifically addressed to more intimate contacts.

Clara: To Bele, I can send anything, any kind of nonsense [laughing]. It wouldn't matter.

As elaborated on by others (Hjorth and Pink 2013; Jurgenson 2013; Velez 2014; Villi 2015), a specific sense of nowness is crucial for real-time pictorial conversa- tions.

Clara: For example, you sit on the toilet and take a picture [laughing] of your feet and write [laughing], "I am on the toilet right now".

Pictures shared in these spaces might be intimate in a sense that they do not necessarily correspond to the general sense of beauty, but to *the girls'* shared sense of what is cool and authentic. The girls themselves textually frame some of these pictures as ugly. When analysing some examples they also shared with me, ugliness seems to imply that the content and/or the aesthetic are rather idiosyn- cratic or make sense only to them. Nevertheless, one can be more or less fluent

---

10   A style or aesthetic identified by some as typical for this platform (Tifentale and Manovich 2016).

within this specific style, as Clara states: *"Bele is the queen of ugly pictures"*. Rather than beautiful/public or ugly/intimate, these two notions can be understood as extreme polarities on a scale, with many possible combinations and modes in between.

Moreover, specific aesthetics emerge that are entangled with the apps' particular technical affordances. For example, Instagram offers various possibilities for editing and modifying pictures after they are taken or uploaded (similar to professional software, see Figure 3), but WhatsApp has only recently integrated some editing features. Furthermore, WhatsApp has long had a function for forwarding pictures to other conversations, but Instagram did not have a save or forwarding feature for years.

In the following final section of the case study, a picture (Figure 4a and 4b) that was visible on Bele's Instagram account and the girls framed as beautiful is analysed to further explore how visual communication with and through photographs is entangled with embodiment.

Photo-sharing as embodied visual communication

Figures 4a and 4b: Pictures shared on Instagram by Bele: faces pixelated by the author; compositional structure sketched by the author.

The picture in Figure 4a shows a group of girls sitting on a wooden structure not originally built to provide seating space. Climbing on trees and buildings is usually perceived as a childlike practice, but hanging around on structures can also be seen an activity of young people, often in connection with first heterosexual encounters and experimentation with cigarettes and alcohol. This group is clearly not playing on a playground in a childlike manner but is also not (yet) engaging in typical teenager practices; they hang out, but in broad daylight and without boys. Two developmental phases seem to overlap in this picture: childlike playfulness and teenage hanging out. The group members are both children and teenagers at the same time, and the picture makes visible both phases, as well as the processuality and in-between-ness of this practice.

This ambivalence also becomes visible in the colours of the picture, which can be seen as girly, candy colours or as a youthful vintage look, especially given the Polaroid-like square format of the grainy picture (Jurgenson 2011). The picture's compositional structure (marked in Figure 4b) clearly shows the group as a collective arrangement; thus, being together and growing together are strongly anchored in the peer group. This important social structure can be protective but also precarious (Autenrieth 2014; boyd 2014; Thiel-Stern 2012). Collective identity is constituted in the picture and amplified through sharing it on Instagram.

Taking a closer look, a certain internal structure of the group also becomes visible, with Bele occupying a clear, central position. In the interview, she also describes the picture similarly:

Bele: This is me with my best friends.
Interviewer: Where are you sitting?
Bele: Well, except for Anna. She took the picture. That's in a park on some kind of roof. We got up there, and Anna took the picture. Or about a thousand.

In this brief quote, another point becomes visible: in digital photography, the human body becomes an easily configurable motif, formed both in front of the screen and on the screen. First, the body is configured by posing and gesturing in a specific way in front of the camera. The girls might have a series of very similar pictures from which to choose ("about a thousand"). Digitalisation has introduced this possibility of selection, as well as the ability to store large amounts of data and to look at pictures on the display, both while and after taking them. The possibilities of playing with identities, poses and gestures through visual media have multiplied and have been simplified through digitalisation (Walker-Rettberg 2014).

Second, once a picture has been authorised as suitable and relevant, it can be further edited, for example, cropped and filtered:

Anna: You can brighten it up, and, and then effects and sometimes retouch something.

The ease of editing is conceptualised as the malleability or the plasticity of the digital picture, when compared to the analogue picture (Hand 2012; Reißmann 2014). If pictures (or media in general) are perceived as more malleable, transformable and processual, are identities and bodies also perceived as more malleable and transformable? The participants clearly develop competences in shaping and modifying their pictures, and cultivating a semi-public persona on Instagram or Facebook is understood as a curating practice.

Yet what they find beautiful, likeable or cool, is subject to change – which could also be typical for the teenage life phase.

Anna: Also when I post ugly – well not ugly but retrospectively ugly pictures [laughing] – super-old pictures that I don't find beautiful anymore, I delete them.

For example, Anna deleted picture in her Instagram feed one year after the first interview. These forms of curating are practised both individually and collaboratively, for example, by asking others for their opinion about various versions of a picture.

Conclusions

Well-established dynamics of interpersonal communication and practices of social inclusion and exclusion are still at play in networked visual communication. Nevertheless, they are remediated (Grusin and Bolter 2000) and "amped up by [the] immediacy and [the] hyper-social nature of digital media" (Thiel-Stern 2012: 100); the practices of making photo albums, creating websites, scanning, messaging, texting, scrapbooking and exhibiting converge in the practices of photo sharing on social media. Networked environments expand and differentiate the ways identity can be performed. While early online research found the lack of social and individual cues to be both liberating and dangerous, the rise of visual communication in social media seems to indicate a (re)embodiment and aestheticisation of networked interpersonal communication.

This implies specific possibilities of aesthetic expression and visual communication, both while producing a picture (e. g. through posing and framing) and while editing a picture (e. g. through filters and cropping). We can quickly tell whether we find a picture beautiful, impressive or authentic, but might experience difficulty verbalising why (Mitchell 2010). We share certain collective aesthetic preferences as taste and (dis)like are socially constituted (Bourdieu 1972). Visual media and aesthetic value and taste, therefore, become means of understanding and affirmation.

Aesthetic differentiation can become even more calibrated in interpersonal visual communication. What is shareable and showable varies by audience and context. These practices of selective sharing have been researched as curation, assemblage and self-presentation (Good 2013; Walker-Rettberg 2014; Whitlock and Poletti 2008). However, how different styles and aesthetics might be means of calibrated visual communication has not been a focus of research. In school, we learn how to use and adapt spoken and written language to be understood in various contexts, but competencies in visual communication are often framed as artsy or unnecessary. Consequently, the elements by which we communicate visually are less reflectively transparent to us, yet are deeply ingrained in our practices of perception and visualisation (Prinz 2014; Przyborski 2017).

With digital photography and networked visual communication, the number of pictures we make and see multiplied, and the range of visual conventions and repertoires we use have become more complex and differentiated. At the same time, digital pictures have developed as common everyday means of communication, elements of aesthetic expression and thus essential parts of the fabric of social life. Whether this democratisation of visual communication and the malleability of the picture open up new possibilities for vision/power regimes (Tiidenberg and Gómez-Cruz 2015: 10), or reproduce normative (beauty) standards and conventional visual cultures, has to be empirically investigated in specific contexts (Müller 2011; Senft and Baym 2015).

Visual communication has become more popular and integrated into all kinds of online communication, so it is especially interesting to investigate how distinction and inclusion play out aesthetically. This visual layer is seldom investigated closely. The separation of mass communication and interpersonal communication is not helpful in these contexts, as briefly mentioned in the introduction. In a canonical work, boyd introduces the concept of *context collapse* as a challenge for communication in networked publics, defined as "the lack of spatial, social, and temporal boundaries makes it difficult to maintain distinct social contexts" (2011: 49). This challenge seems to have transformed as new boundaries have developed: the range of platforms and apps used for networked communication have grown quickly, and the privacy settings on many platforms have become more complex, advanced and/or annoying. Contexts seem to be dynamically constituted in concrete practices in close collaboration with the possibilities and constraints of the respective technical affordances.

Regarding the participants in the case study, it seems that how they practise privacy and visibility is rarely subjected to a strategic decision and reflection but, rather, is entangled with habitual patterns – which are always constituted in relation to specific audiences and affordances. Again, the apps' affordances are essential to this calibrated visual communication. For example, in Snapchat, the girls can select with whom they share pictures, which vanish after a few seconds. Instagram, in contrast, offers a range of standardised filters to enhance pictures with well-established, faux-vintage aesthetics (Jurgenson 2011). Moreover, the different possibilities of the apps' visibility settings show that the technical artefacts afford specific modes of communication – publishing and messaging – that are strongly related to specific levels of privacy or publicness. Whereas the mode of publishing pictures is aimed at a rather more public audience, messaging pictures is practised with different intimate publics.

This fine-grained differentiation of audiences implicitly structures the participants' sharing practices. The girls apparently perceive a certain context collapse in more publicly oriented platforms, such as Instagram, but it does not necessarily have dangerous or negative connotations. They are aware of the public nature and the possible decontextualisation of their pictures, so they use Instagram for "beautiful" pictures which appeal to a general, standardised sense of aesthetics. They do not post pictures there very frequently, but when they do, they carefully select and edit them first. Within this more public (online) sphere, peers continuously affirm each other, for example, through likes and comments (Schreiber and Kramer 2016; Thiel-Stern 2012), and these practices of affirmation are visible to others as well. In contrast, the communicative practices and the established group on

WhatsApp and Snapchat are perceived as clearly contextualised and demarcated. "Ugly" pictures with an idiosyncratic aesthetic are intimate media of communication and trust amongst the girls. These ugly pictures might be dark, full of weird stickers, or blurred, grimacing faces, yet exactly this style indicates an easy playfulness and mutual trust in this sphere of pictorial conversation. Again, a specific *aesthetic* is entangled with both the technical and iconographic *affordances* of the app and also with a specific *audience*. The interrelation of these three dimensions has to be taken into account to understand personal practices of networked visual communication.

Acknowledgements

This research was funded by the Austrian Academy of Sciences (ÖAW). The author thanks the journal editors and the anonymous reviewers of the first version of this article for their helpful, detailed feedback.

References

Autenrieth, Ulla (2014): Die Bilderwelten der Social Network Sites, Baden-Baden: Nomos.

Baym, Nancy K. (2015): Personal connections in the digital age. 2. ed., Cambridge: Polity Press.

Bohnsack, Ralf (2008): "The Interpretation of Pictures and the Documentary Method." In: Forum Qualitative Sozialforschung 9/3, n. p. (http://www.quali tative-research.net/index.php/fqs/article/view/1171/2591)

Bourdieu, Pierre (1972): Outline of Theory of a Theory of Practice, Cambridge: Cambridge University Press.

Bourdieu, Pierre (1990): Photography: A Middle-Brow Art, Cambridge: Polity Press.

boyd, Danah (2011): "Social Network Sites as Networked Publics". In: Zizi Papacharissi (ed.), A Networked Self. Identity, Community, and Culture on Social Network Sites, New York: Routledge. pp. 39–58.

boyd, Danah (2014): It's Complicated: The Social Lives of Networked Teens, New Haven and London: Yale University Press.

Bräuchler, Birgit/Postill, John (2010): Theorising Media and Practice, New York: Berghahn.

Bucher, Taina/Helmond, Anne (2017): "The Affordances of Social Media Platforms." In: Jean Burgess/Thomas Poell/Alice Marwick (eds.), The SAGE Handbook of Social Media, Thousand Oaks: Sage Publications, in print.

Chun, Wendy (2008): "The Enduring Ephemeral, or the Future Is a Memory." In: Critical Inquiry 35/1, pp. 148–171.

Couldry, Nick (2004): "Theorising media as practice." In: Social Semiotics 14/2, pp. 115–32.

van Dijck, José (2013): The culture of connectivity. A critical history of social media, Oxford: Oxford Univ. Press.

Gershon, Ilana (2010): "Breaking Up Is Hard To Do: Media Switching and Media Ideologies." In: Linguistic Anthropology 20/2, pp. 389–405.

Gibson, J. (1977): "The theory of affordances." In: R. Shaw/J. Bransford (eds.), Perceiving, Acting and Knowing, New York: Lawrence Erlbaum Associates, pp. 67–82.

Goffman, Erving (1959): The Presentation of Self in Everyday Life, New York: Doubleday.

Good, K.D. (2013): "From scrapbook to Facebook: A history of personal media assemblage and archives." In: New Media & Society 15/4, pp. 557–73.

Grace, H. (2014): Culture, aesthetics and affect in ubiquitous media; the prosaic image, London: Routledge.

Grusin, Richard/Bolter, Jay David (2000): Remediation. Understanding New Media, Cambridge and London: The MIT Press.

Hand, Martin (2012): Ubiquitous Photography, Cambridge: Polity Press.

Hine, Christine (2015): Ethnography for the Internet. Embedded, embodied and everyday, London: Bloomsbury.

Hirschauer, Stefan (2008): "Die Empiriegeladenheit von Theorien und der Erfindungsreichtum der Praxis." In: Herbert Kalthoff/Stefan Hirschauer/Gesa Lindemann (eds.), Theoretische Empirie. Zur Relevanz qualitativer Forschung, Frankfurt am Main: Suhrkamp, pp. 165–87.

Hjorth, Larissa/Pink, Sarah (2013): "New visualities and the digital wayfarer: Reconceptualizing camera phone photography and locative media." In: Mobile Media & Communication 2/1, pp. 40–57.

Hjorth, Larissa/Wilken, Rowan/Gu, Kay (2012): "Ambient Intimacy. A Case Study of the iPhone, Presence and Location-based Social Media in Shanghai, China." In: Larissa Hjorth/Jean Burgess/Ingrid Richardson (eds.), Studying mobile media: cultural technologies, mobile communication, and the iPhone, London: Routledge.

Hogan, Bernie/Quan-Haase, Anabel (2010): "Persistence and Change in Social Media." In: Bulletin of Science, Technology & Society 30/5, pp. 309–15.

Hutchby, Ian (2001): "Technologies, Texts and Affordances." In: Sociology 35/2, pp. 441–56.

Hutchby, Ian (2014): "Communicative affordances and participation frameworks in mediated interaction." In: Journal of Pragmatics 72, pp. 86–89.

Jurgenson, Nathan (2011): "The Faux-Vintage Photo: Full Essay (Parts I, II and III)." In: Cyborgology, May 14, 2011 (http://thesocietypages.org/cyborgology/2011/05/14/the-faux-vintage-photo-full-essay-parts-i-ii-and-iii/).

Jurgenson, Nathan (2013): "Pics or it Didn't Happen." In: The New Inquiry, February 7, 2013 (http://thenewinquiry.com/essays/pics-and-it-didnt-happen/).

Kanter, Heike (2016): Ikonische Macht. Zur sozialen Gestaltung von Pressebildern, Leverkusen: Budrich.

Lehmuskallio, Asko (2016): "The camera as a sensor. The visualization of everyday digital photography as simulative, heuristic and layered pictures." In: Edgar Gómez-Cruz/Asko Lehmuskallio (eds.), Digital Photography and Everyday Life. Empirical Studies on Material Visual Practices, Oxford: Routledge, pp. 243–66.

Lehmuskallio, Asko/Gómez-Cruz, Edgar (2016): "Why Material Visual Practices?" In: Edgar Gómez-Cruz/Asko Lehmuskallio (eds.), Digital Photography and Everyday Life. Empirical Studies on Material Visual Practices, Oxford: Routledge, pp. 1–16.

Madianou, Mirca (2014): "Smartphones as Polymedia." In: Journal of Computer-Mediated Communication 19/3, pp. 667–80.

Mannheim, Karl (1980): Strukturen des Denkens, Frankfurt am Main: Suhrkamp.

Markham, Annette (2004): "The Internet As Research Context" In: Clive Seale/Jaber Gubrium/David Silverman/Gobo Giampietro (eds.), Qualitative Research Practice, London: Sage, pp. 358–74.

Markham, Annette (2013): "The Dramaturgy of Digital Experience." In: C. Edgley (ed.), The Drama of Social Life: A Dramaturgical Handbook, Farnham: Ashgate Press, pp. 279–94.

Marwick, Alice E. (2013): "Online Identity." In: John Hartley/Jean Burgess/Axel Bruns (eds.), A Companion to New Media Dynamics, Chichester: Wiley-Blackwell, pp. 355–64.

Maynard, Patrick (1997): The engine of visualization. Thinking through photography, Ithaca: Cornell University Press.

McVeigh-Schultz, Joshua/Baym, Nancy K. (2015) "Thinking of You: Vernacular Affordance in the Context of the Microsocial Relationship App, Couple." In: Social Media + Society 1/2, pp. 1–13.

Meier, Stefan (2012): "Die Simulation von Fotografie. Konzeptuelle Überlegungen zum Zusammenhang von Materialität und digitaler Bildlichkeit." In: Marcel Finke/Marc Halawa (eds.), Materialität und Bildlichkeit. Visuelle Artefakte zwischen Aisthesis und Semiosis, Berlin: Kulturverlag Kadmos.

Meißner, Stefan (2015): "Die Medialität und Technizität internetbasierter Daten. Plädoyer für mehr Offenheit der Qualitativen Sozialforschung." In: Dominique Schirmer/Nadine Sander/Andreas Wenninger (eds.), Die qualitative Analyse internetbasierter Daten; Methodische Herausforderungen und Potenziale von Online-Medien, Wiesbaden: Springer, pp. 33–50.

Mitchell, WJT (2002): "Showing seeing: a critique of visual culture." In: Journal of Visual Culture 1/2, pp. 165–81.

Mitchell, WJT (2010): "Image" In: WJT Mitchell/Mark Hansen (eds.), Critical Terms for Media Studies, Chicago: The University of Chicago Press, pp. 35–48.

Müller, Michael R (2011): "Das Körperbild als Selbstbild" In: Michael R. Müller/ Hans-Georg Soeffner/Anne Sonnenmoser (eds.), Körper Haben. Die symbolische Formung der Person, Weilerswist: Velbrück, pp. 87–106.

Norman, D. (1999): "Affordance, conventions, and design." In: Interactions 6/3, pp. 38–43.

Panofsky, Erwin (1975): "Ikonographie und Ikonologie. Eine Einführung in die Kunst der Renaissance." In: Erwin Panofsky (ed.), Sinn und Deutung in der bildenden Kunst, Köln: Dumont, pp. 36–63.

Papacharissi, Zizi/Easton, Emily (2013): "In the Habitus of the New". In: John Hartley/Jean Burgess/Axel Bruns (eds.), A Companion to New Media Dynamics, Chichester: Wiley-Blackwell, pp. 167–84.

Prinz, Sophia (2014): Die Praxis des Sehens; über das Zusammenspiel von Körpern, Artefakten und visueller Ordnung, Bielefeld: transcript.

Przyborski, Aglaja (2017): Bildkommunikation: Qualitative Bild- und Medienforschung, Oldenbourg: DeGruyter.

Przyborski, Aglaja/Haller, Günther (2014): Das politische Bild. Situation Room: ein Foto – vier Analysen, Opladen: Budrich.

Reißmann, Wolfgang (2014): "Bildhandeln und Bildkommunikation in Social Network Sites." In: Kai-Uwe Hugger (ed.), Digitale Jugendkulturen. Digitale Kultur und Kommunikation, Wiesbaden: Springer.

Schreiber, Maria (2017a): "Digitale Bildpraktiken. Handlungsdimensionen visueller vernetzter Kommunikation." Unpublished Doctoral Thesis, University of Vienna.

Schreiber, Maria (2017b): "Körperbilder als medienbiografische Kristallisationspunkte? Eine rekonstruktive Analyse altersspezifischer Bildpraktiken." In: Ralf Vollbrecht/Christina Dallmann (eds.), Körpergeschichten, Baden-Baden: Nomos. In Press.

Schreiber, Maria/Kramer, Michaela (2016): "Verdammt schön. Methodologische und methodische Herausforderungen der Rekonstruktion von Bildpraktiken auf Instagram." In: Zeitschrift für qualitative Sozialforschung 17/1-2, pp. 81–106.

Schrock, Andrew Richard (2015): "Communicative Affordances of Mobile Media : Portability, Availability, Locatability, and Multimediality." In: International Journal of Communication 9, pp. 1229–46.

Senft, Theresa/Baym, Nancy (2015): "What Does the Selfie Say ? Investigating a Global Phenomenon Introduction." In: International Journal of Communication 9, pp. 1588–1606.

Thiel-Stern, Shayla (2012): "Collaborative, Productive, Performative, Templated: Youth, Identity and Breaking the Fourth Wall." In: Rebecca Anne Lind (ed.), Produsing Theory in a Digital World, New York: Peter Lang, pp. 87–103.

Tifentale, Alise/Manovich, Lev (2016): Competitive Photography and the Presentation of the Self (http://lab.softwarestudies.com/2016/02/a-new-article-by-alise-tifentale-and.html).

Tiidenberg, Katrin/Gómez-Cruz, Edgar (2015): "Selfies, Image and the Re-making of the Body." In: Body & Society 1-26.

Velez, Emma (2014): "Intimate Publics and Ephemerality. Snapchat: A Case Study", The Second Shift. Academic Feminism After Hours (http://www.secondshiftblog.com/2014/09/intimate-publics-and-ephemerality-snapchat-a-case-study/).

Villi, Mikko (2013): "Publishing and Messaging Camera Phone Photographs : Patterns of Visual Mobile Communication on the Internet." In: Kathleen Cumiskey/Larissa Hjorth (eds.), Mobile Media Practices, Presence and Politics: The Challenge of Being Seamlessly Mobile, London: Routledge, pp. 214–28.

Villi, Mikko (2015): "'Hey, I'm here Right Now': Camera phone photographs and mediated presence." In: Photographies 8/1, pp. 3–22.

Vyas, D./Chisalita, C.M. (2006): "Affordance in Interaction." In: Proceedings of 13th European Conference on Cognitive Ergonomics, pp. 92–99.

Wagner, Elke (2014): "Intimate Publics 2.0. Zur Transformation des Privaten und des Öffentlichen in Social Network Sites." In: Kornelia Hahn (ed.), E.Motion. Intimität in Medienkulturen, Wiesbaden: Springer, pp. 125–50.

Walker-Rettberg, Jill (2014): Seeing Ourselves Through Technology, New York: Palgrave Macmillan.

Warfield, Katie/Cambre, Maria-Carolina/Abidin, Crystal (2016): "Introduction to the Social Media + Society Special Issue on Selfies: Me-diated Inter-faces." In: Social Media + Society 2/2, pp. 1–5.

Whitlock, Gillian/Poletti, Anna (2008): "Self-Regarding Art." In: Biography 31/1, pp. V-XXXIII.

Wright, S./Parchoma, G. (2011): "Technologies for learning? An actor-network theory critique of 'affordances' in research on mobile learning." In: Research in Learning Technology 19/3, pp. 247–258.

Zillien, Nicole (2008): "Die (Wieder-)Entdeckung der Medien das Affordanzkonzept in der Mediensoziologie." In: Sociologia Internationalis: Internationale Zeitschrift für Soziologie, Kommunikations- und Kulturforschung 46/2, pp. 161–181.

Mobile Mediated Visualities

An Empirical Study of Visual Practices on Instagram

Elisa Serafinelli and Mikko Villi

Abstract

The escalation of photo sharing through social networking sites is one of the most substantial changes in mobile communication practice in recent years. The launch of smart mobile technologies represents a decisive moment in the production and observation of visualities with an elevated characteristic of digital shareability and reproducibility. Considering recent technological advancements and new social media services, this paper aims to study how social platforms and smart mobile devices are affecting individuals' visual, social and digital practices. In particular, this paper examines the social exchange of photographs online in order to advance an in-depth reading of contemporary mobile media. The mobility afforded by smart mobile devices represents a fundamental condition that shapes the human-technology relationship. The paper studies this condition by concentrating on the dynamic mobility of individuals, devices and visual information. Methodologically, the paper employs a case study approach to analyse how Instagram affects individuals' perception of their mediated lives. Qualitative interviews formed the fieldwork and a sample of 44 Instagram users took part in the study. Visual content analysis of participants' photo sharing further contributed to the investigation. Findings from the study show that the use of smart mobile devices constitutes the development of new forms of mobile mediated visualities. The mobility and mediation afforded by smart mobile devices seem to establish new practices for producing and sharing images that push individuals to think visually of events, people and surroundings. These practices lead to the visual dataification of social practices and intensify the quantity and variety of visual data shared online. Within this context, the visual hyper-representation of social practices is exemplified by the current trend of giving to everything a visual justification (e.g. foodporn). In its conclusions, the paper offers a conceptual apparatus that can help to understand contemporary social, digital and visual interactions.

DOI 10.14361/dcs-2017-0210

Introduction

The escalation of photo sharing through social networking sites is one of the most substantial changes in mobile communication practice in recent years. In many daily activities, indeed, it can be observed that a remarkable number of people cannot do without maintaining visual relationships with the events of their lives: from the coffee cup captured during a coffee break to the girls' Friday night out. This rising practice of online photo sharing is enabled by the use of mobile devices. They play a crucial role in providing new opportunities for capturing and sharing photographs, especially online. These two trends intermingle in visual mobile communication (Villi 2010), i.e. the use of smart phones in photography and photographic communication.

A clear example of how these technological advancements draw new assets for contemporary sociality can be observed in the fact that people are not willing to buy a mobile phone without an embedded camera anymore (or that there would be many non-camera models still available). With smart mobile devices photography has become so ubiquitous that the existence of events, people, and objects seems to be directly connected with being photographed (Kember/Zylinska 2012) and shared, we could add. In fact, the passage from physical sharing (face-to-face and through prints) to digital photo sharing (through the mediation of digital technologies) drives a significant increase in the production and the exchange of photographs. In social media, the 'imperative of sharing' (Van Dijck 2013) is in force and plays a central role in shaping the various types of social communication. The mediated exchange of images is an example of how these social connections are built and maintained on a daily basis. As Gómez Cruz (2016) has noted, photography acts pronouncedly as an interface for visual communication, a 'connective interface'.

Considering the progressive alterations in the media environment, in this paper we analyse the practices of photo sharing by taking into account affordances provided by social media and mobile communication. These affordances represent a decisive moment in the production, communication and use of photographs, and therefore this paper corresponds with the necessity to advance a critical understanding around photo sharing as mobile media practice.

Theoretical Background

This paper builds its theoretical framework on the new paradigm advanced by Couldry (2004) that considers media not as text, but first and foremost as *practice*. Couldry emphasises that to understand the effects on people, the attention on media needs to move towards considering what people actually do with media. The notion of practice here offers the possibility to interpret life experiences in a media-saturated world where certain practices, such as posting, tweeting, liking, and photo sharing seem to become part of social norms. The practice-based approach does not intend to deny the interests of previous media research, it rather aims to broaden the focus on media from text to media practices that shape social life in a more general way (Couldry 2004). This continuity is manifested in practice theory: a branch of social theory centred on practices rather than structures, systems, individuals or interactions (Bräuchler/Postill 2010). This approach offers to the investigation of media phenomena a new way to address questions related to the role of social media in everyday life, in particular considering the ubiquitous presence and use of social media platforms.

Another important strand of thought for this paper is mediation and what is defined as 'mediated' phenomena (Parikka 2012). To help understand this approach Parikka (2012) introduces the idea of 'new materialism' that intends to illustrate the way technical media transmit and process cultures in a way that sees mediated processes as embedded in ephemeral, even though real, *things* (authors' emphasis). In other words, this theorisation (as media theory) looks at where the materiality in discussing media actually is, i.e. in practices. From this perspective, the focus moves from understanding media objects (such as user-generated content) to understanding the practices that mediation generates through the use of social media and smart mobile devices. Mediation is a complex and hybrid process that results from the flows of production, circulation, interpretation and recirculation (Couldry 2008) of objects.

Mediation is an everyday condition that defines new social behaviours. To investigate this condition, Kember and Zylinska (2012) challenge the traditional questions about photography (e.g. truth and indexicality of photography) and suggest understanding photography rather as an active practice of cutting through the flow of mediation. This shift can be observed in the intensification of photographs with hashtags such as #selfies, #foodporn, #picoftheday that testify the importance of showing an online presence. The idea of 'being-as-mediated' (Kember/Zylinska 2012: 40) differentiates the understanding of digital practices. Following this approach, the analysis of images (the object) extends toward the analysis of the practices of photo sharing (the process) and the effects of mediation.

To understand photo sharing as online visual practice, taking into account images only would be limitative. Rather, it is important to consider a plurality of agencies, i.e. the interrelations between users, images, practises and socio-cultural influences (Pink 2007). In fact, photo sharing, as digital practice, is shaped by the combination of connectivity and the convergence of media, and this condition plays a crucial role in the development of digital practices. This is the reason why the concept of mediation is of importance in theorising new media phenomena.

In studying digital practices, it is important to keep in mind that mobile devices present an efficient vehicle for interpersonal connections (Serafinelli 2017). They remove social barriers and increase connectivity and access to digital content. Through their use, they also increase the activity of taking photographs, altering the content of images, and the way they are shared and edited (Serafinelli 2017). This shows that advancements in smart mobile technology contribute to the intense circulation of photographs in social media platforms and elsewhere in the digital environment, creating fertile ground for the interconnection between digital technologies and the development of new mediated practices. In these interpersonal connections, reciprocity seems to define the main motivation that shapes sociality online (Granieri 2005). Other motivations that guide people to participate in online communities are enjoyment, commitment to the community, self-development, and reputation gaining (Lakhani/Wolf 2005). Online platforms are environments where users provide content, advice, and services and where collaborative behaviours are awarded.

In the context of mediation, media platforms and mobile devices become part of people's daily social experiences. The convergent environment of 'mobile interfaces' (Farman 2011), where devices intersect with social and spatial spaces, creates new forms of virtual and imaginative travels combined with physical ones (Sheller/ Urry 2006). To explain this change, Sheller and Urry (2006) argue for the turn towards the 'new mobilities paradigm', which does not simply advocate mobility in today's world but rather focuses on the speed and intensity of flows of people, objects and information. This paradigm also explains social interactions between people located in distant physical spaces. This approach considers the concept of portability a central element in the discourse on smart mobile devices (Siapera 2012), emphasising that they allow people to bring their own media everywhere. Both mobile devices and mobile interfaces appear independent of locality, thus determining paradigmatic changes in social habits towards what Farman (2012) would define as reconfiguration of practices in the digital age.

In sum, this paper examines different ways of using smart mobile devices, explaining their ubiquitous use and the role they play in experiencing everyday sociality. An insightful analysis of motivations, organisation, and transformations of the practices of photo sharing is fundamental to understand how social media affects the visual experience of everyday life. Considering the rising dependence on technology, this paper investigates the uses of smart mobile devices and how they affect people's visual experience of their surroundings. To do so, this paper analyses the features of the popular photo sharing platform Instagram – a smart phone app that enables users to capture, edit, and share photos on various social networks – identifying the key elements that shape contemporary mechanisms of visual communication.

Considering the ubiquitous use of smart mobile devices, this paper interrogates *whether and how the co-presence of the mobility of devices and the mediation of platforms changes the way people experience their everyday life*. To answer this research question, we examine the ways the digital practices of photo sharing contribute to these changes. Through an empirical examination of digital practices, this paper delineates the development of new forms of visual communication.

Data and Method

Qualitative computer-mediated interviews formed the fieldwork for this paper. A sample of 44 Instagram users took part in the study. 29 participants were interviewed via Skype and 15 participants responded to open questions that were sent via email[1]. The sampling was accomplished entirely online circumscribing the investigation within Instagram user groups and owners of smart mobile devices. Following the interviews, visual content analysis was implemented to expand the interview data.

Since the goal of data collection was to gather photographs and understand Instagram users' behaviours, Facebook was recognised as the main platform where users converse. After Facebook bought Instagram in 2012 there has been a rise in the number of Instagram users, partly because of the visibility afforded by Facebook. The call for participants was spread out on Instagram communities' Facebook pages. After the first approach through the social network, participants who had responded positively were approached via private email. The email that participants received consisted of a general description of the study and a consent form with the explanation of the treatment of personal data, which gave us permission to follow their Instagram feed and use their photographs for academic purposes. The target population did not have particular restrictions in terms of gender, race and education. The demographic of this study was formed by 29 males and 15 females between 24 and 52 years old. Participants represented a large geographical mix (Italy, United Kingdom, Germany, Poland, USA, Canada, Spain, Finland, Denmark, Sweden, Norway, Argentina, Turkey, and Iran).

The netnographic approach, a qualitative method that is specialised for the unique computer-mediated contingency of today's social world (Kozinets 2015), was adopted to combine together the different data sources (interviews and photographs). Social sciences are increasingly reaching the conclusion that they can no longer adequately understand many of the most important facets of social and cultural life without incorporating computer-mediated communication into their study. We employed netnography in order to go beyond the mere observation of online phenomena and aim to understand online social interactions within the context of analysis. Netnography was used to examine photo sharing following the idea that analysing visual content is almost impossible without taking into account the context in which the visual is produced and finally received (Bock et al. 2011). In addition, we also considered how photographs alone do not represent emotions, social relations, relations of power and exploitation, but they need to be

---

1   This approach was developed to prevent lack of data caused by the potential inability of recruiting participants willing to do an in-depth interview. Thus, it was decided to give participants the opportunity to choose how to conduct the interview.

contextualised with verbal discourses or other knowledge in order to invoke such experiences (Pink 2007).

Through qualitative interviews, it is possible to understand experiences and reconstruct events in which the researcher does not participate (Rubin/Rubin 2005). Through the in-depth description of social processes, interviews allow an additional understanding of ways and reasons why things change. In this study, the main purpose of the use of qualitative interviews was to find out in the context of photo sharing what happened, why and what it meant more broadly (Rubin/ Rubin 2005). To discover causes, explain and understand the digital practices of photo sharing, participants were asked to show, justify, and comment on photographs in relation to their responses. Additional questions were also asked to explore critical themes (such as privacy and ethics). This approach elicited more details without changing the main focus.

The visual analysis of participants' photographs extended the understanding by focusing more on their disclosures and experiences. Participants were asked to provide their Instagram nickname in order to be observed (followed) online by one of the two researchers. The visual data collection was limited to two months for the 29 participants who took part in the Skype interviews. In the case of the 15 participants interviewed by email visual examples were studied only if they were specifically mentioned. The two-month period included different events, such as working days, leisure time, national holidays, and vacations, producing a more complete view of the variety of participants' photo sharing. Their photo sharing was interpreted through the classification of visual materials and the contextualisation of participants' communicative acts (Bowler 2010). Through a qualitative content analysis, the visual data were translated into categories (holiday, landscape, food etc.), identifying themes and common patterns.

This study did not include semiotic visual analysis. It rather identified the correspondence of meanings through the qualitative analysis of both interviews and images. In the analysis, we did not examine photographs as evidence of the 'who', 'where' and 'what' of reality, but rather as interpretations of how their makers perceived and (re-)constructed it. The analysis followed the idea that while images alone reveal nothing, they are given ethnographic meaning when linked to other types of knowledge (Pink 2015).

Motivations, Organisation, and Transformations of Photo Sharing on Instagram

Data analysis is broken down into three sections: motivations, organisation, and transformations in the practices of photo sharing. This subdivision aims to provide a clear exploration of the phases that form the digital practice of photo sharing, highlighting factors that shape Instagram users' approach to visual communication and how previous habits are transformed.

Practices of Photo Sharing on Instagram

The relationship between mobile devices and photography affects the advancement of new photo sharing practices, emphasising the utility of the practice-based approach (Couldry 2004). The example provided by *Participant 13* illustrates well the connection between mobility and photography:

'I have a photo I shot at the train platform in Florence of a guy and a girl where for sure she was leaving for far away. She had suitcases. He was crying like mad […] but this super passionate kiss … I swear! I could snap it at less than a meter away. My mobile was here and they were next to me, and this is something that with the camera it's not possible. […] That is something you say "I put it on Instagram now or never!"' (See fig. 1).

Figure 1: Kiss at the train station.Instagram, 2014.
Source: https://instagram.com/mimicimme

This response shows how the mobility afforded by smart mobile devices organises sociality around devices that enable people to be individually mobile and also create spheres of connection "on the go" (Sheller/Urry 2006). Instagram seems to be enhancing customised networking systems, which empower people's interactions and mobile connectivity (ibid) in a way that diverges from such sociality that is based on close physical relationships. In this, photographs represent in-material and non-solid objects (Parikka 2012) that hold social lives together. The easy access to social media platforms and the portability of devices help people see in daily life opportunities for sharing visual experiences and establishing their presence online.

As discussed in the theoretical background section, being online is an interactive and creative practice formed often by the principle of reciprocity and the philosophy of "give and take", where media representations offer constant mutual recognitions (Couldry 2004). Participants in our study reported that being an active user is 'very rewarding' especially when receiving social interaction such as likes, positive comments, and feedback. This type of interaction is similar to the motivations of self-satisfaction and recognition described by Lakhani and Wolf (2005). It follows that sharing photographs makes sense when there is social interaction and reciprocity (Granieri 2005). Social responses and the creation of social relationships, indeed, support the continuation of the Instagram experience (Serafinelli 2017). This again supports Couldry's (2004) emphasis on media practices as socially-informed activities.

Initially, participants in our study were asked why they chose Instagram rather than another photo sharing platform, and in their responses it is evident that curiosity and friends' suggestions influenced their initial choice for trying the new platform. These responses underline how the spirit of connectivity (Van Dijck 2013) pushes users to follow their peers' behaviours and, consequently, the use of Instagram.

Participant 5 stresses the innovative potential of the Instagram platform. Thanks to the invention of mobile cameras, in fact, individuals are more willing to capture photographs of what happens around them because now they have a place to share them (Cohen 2005). An example of this is explained by *Participant 23*. She describes her engagement with the platform as follows:

There are situations, moments, objects that make me say 'I need to be Instagramming this!' [...]. One of the last photos I took was in Taormina three weeks ago. I went to Taormina when there was the lava rain. Basically, I was seeing pieces of lava. And that was a moment that I must share. Snap and share! (see fig. 2).

Figure 2: Lava rain in Taormina. Instagram, 2014.
Source: https://instagram.com/erikarotella

This response, together with the one provided by *Participant 13*, are only two examples that show a common interest in sharing photos of particular events. From this, it can be seen that situations and events push individuals to consider images in association with the platform. The use of a precise verb 'to Instagram' connected with the practices of sharing photos on Instagram leads to think about the evident change that the platform makes. The notion of mobility here explains how communication technologies increasingly mediate people's life experiences. Indeed, theorising the new mobilities paradigm, Sheller and Urry (2006) suggest paying attention to these processes. In fact, through the responses provided by *Participant 13* and *23* these conditions emerge clearly together with a strong interest in the use of photographs to recreate events and locations.

Many responses stress the importance of the mobility of smart phones also in capturing worthy images. The emphasis on the mobility of devices makes the difference in visual production. Participants experience the mobility offered by smart mobile devices as a crucial element in capturing new scenarios because, as Parikka (2012) emphasises, that they are not limited to locality. The chance of taking photographs at anytime and anywhere enhances the possibilities of capturing situations, objects and moments that 'must' be posted on Instagram. *Participant 2* describes this phenomenon as "a continuous telling in real time what you are doing many times ... [however, photo sharing] makes you miss out maybe some of what you're doing, a bit of the value of the event that you are following". Photo sharing appears here to be a practice that describes sociality online, connecting people and their experiences visually. Social digital practices locate users and connect them to one another (Couldry 2004). In describing digital practices, it is important to comprehend the reasons that motivate users in expressing their digital sociality visually.

Motivations of Photo Sharing

In order to understand the role of Instagram in shaping new digital practices, participants were asked to explain the reasons and describe what drives their online photo sharing, providing, where possible, visual examples. Personal satisfaction, reciprocity, and experiencing new images were recognised as the main reasons. Motivations can be understood with reference to uses and gratifications theory, which is helpful for analysing how specific forms of media use (in this case photo sharing) are connected to 'digital gratifications', such as the adoption of new roles in online communities (Villi/Noguera 2017).

Participants share photos on Instagram aware that their audience is formed by a variety of users, mainly strangers, who share the same passion for photography. Considering the visibility afforded by the platform, they aim to share 'shareable images', i. e. images that the vast majority of users can appreciate. This common approach follows the intent of reaching a high number of followers re-marking the principles of reciprocity (Granieri 2005) and personal satisfaction (Lakhani/Wolf 2005). Users, indeed, enjoy sharing photos online because they feel it is an act of mutual concession and recognition, as Couldry (2004) would argue. In this case, the principle of reciprocity is based on the expectation of seeing photos shared by other users. In other words, what motivates users to share their visual experiences and unconventional scenarios is the fact that consequently other users will share images as well. In this mechanism of "give and take", users experience feelings of personal satisfaction in social interactions, such as likes, comments and followings.

The findings show that the main reason participants share photos on Instagram is to produce photographs that a wide number of users are willing to appreciate, together with the expectation to receive positive comments and feedback. In relation to this the response given by *Participant 22* demonstrates how:

One of the reasons why I started to share more was because other people who were sharing started to inspire me. I could honestly go to Instagram right now and see ... I call them visual dispatches, but I mean, I can see photographs from Africa, Italy, Spain, Russia and others. I can see them from all over the world and see a tiny portal into someone's world. And I thought "well, it's a kind of sharing/social thing you give me, I give something". So, for me this is just what motivated me to share back.

This response summarises well users' general tendency to share their photographs in relation to other users' practices and interactions on the platform. This response demonstrates how the concept of new materialism (Parikka, 2012) can be used to interpret the practice of photo sharing considering the in-materiality of communication when formed by digital content. Smart mobile devices, in fact, do not only show how people can 'do' things and 'talk' to people without being physically in the same place (Sheller/Urry 2006), but demonstrate how the practices of photo sharing are embedded in a more ephemeral world (Parikka 2012).

Again, the principles of reciprocity (Granieri 2005) and self-satisfaction (Lakhani/Wolf 2005) represent here an incentive to share more photographs. Regarding this, *Participant 26* describes his motivation as follows:

People started to notice me. I got very good comments and I spent the first six months trying to make good pictures and good captions. And people started to comment "Your pictures make my day!" or "Your captions are really great!". And all the comments encourage you to keep doing what you are doing.

As can be seen, receiving positive comments seems to foster users' engagement with other users and increases their visibility and activity on the platform. Moreover, participants report that the more they receive positive feedback and comments the more they are motivated to share images, thereby potentially receiving further positive comments.

Additionally, photo sharing can also be motivated by the presence of certain emotions that occur with images. In particular, 'being in a good mood' seems to stimulate users' motivation in sharing photographs. Participants recognise in their photo sharing the intent to share experiences and emotions through images in such a way that is reminiscent of the notion of reverberation as opposed to that of 'representation', 'narration' or 'impact' (Karatzogianni/Kuntsman 2012). Through this, photo sharing appears as a way to convey people's feelings following the intent of sharing 'shareable experiences'. For instance, on pleasing other users, *Participant 17* comments:

On social media people don't care about the photos but they care about the experiences, right? For instance, yesterday I went to a coffee tasting event in a coffee shop. People like things because they see themselves doing the same things. [...] If I am somewhere doing something and I think people like it, I will post it (see fig. 3).

Figure 3: Coffee break photo. Instagram, 2014.
Source: https://instagram.com/inayali

This response shows that there is interest in sharing personal emotions with those who are not physically present. This approach follows the idea of mediated presence (Villi 2015) which considers mediation as the dynamic logic through which to interpret the practices of photo sharing. Participants in our study reported that, in this way, images convey additional messages through the mere information shown. In fact, most of the time photo sharing involves feelings, as *Participant 7* explains: "Photography for me is emotion and passion and so I try to share the same the emotions that I felt in the moment I saw that particular shot. I try to share it with others. My aim is to try to make others empathise with my persona when observing my photo". Through this response it can be said that the intent in sharing shareable images is determined by the personal emotional engagement with the subject (see fig. 4), but also with the practice itself. In this case, it is visible how the changing structures of feelings and emotions within everyday digital culture (Karatzogianni/Kuntsman 2012) appear on Instagram through such images that aim to convey significations going beyond mere visual pleasure.

Figure 4:. Sharing empathy and emotions.
Instagram, 2014. Source: https://instagram.com/
giuliotolli

To fulfil their aims (experiencing personal satisfaction, reciprocity and new images), participants carefully plan their photo sharing in all its stages (i.e. shot, editing, caption and time of photo sharing) following precise guidelines. Regarding this,

Participant 2 comments: "Instagram must be seen as a means of sharing, like a shop window for the work you produce or also for your daily life". Indeed, the motivations of reciprocity (Granieri 2005) and self-satisfaction (Lakhani/Wolf 2005) in combination with the intent of reaching high numbers of followers, as illustrated above, lead towards a careful organisation of photo sharing. The most frequent responses that emerged in relation to the organisational aspect were connected firstly to the frequency of photo sharing and secondly to the personal photographic style. As *Participant 7* explains: "Initially, I was much more active both posting so many photos that at a certain point I said to myself 'Oh my God! I need to stop because if I identify myself with others ...' there could be someone saying, 'this guy is annoying with all these photos!'".

Organisation of Photo Sharing

Participants report careful planning of photo sharing mainly to ensure visibility to their images. To organise effective photo sharing participants adhere three main strategies: following their own personal photographic style, posting at specific times (time bands) and sharing a set number of photographs (precise frequency of sharing). An additional way of organising content is the well-thought choice of hashtags and geo-tags. In fact, careful photo sharing seems often to be more important than the rapidity of photo sharing.

The temporal organisation is showed in the time bands of photo sharing. The frequency of organisation is connected to the number of uploads per day, week, or month. Content organisation, instead, follows an identifiable photographic style, such as themes or styles, storytelling, and particularities. Participants upload and observe photographs during precise moments in their daily routine. Indeed, they combine coffee breaks with Instagram, lunch with Instagram, waiting at the bus stop with Instagram. Their practices of photo sharing seem to be routinised in combination with other activities. This modality creates in the followers a state of expectation and regular habits. Thus, the term 'organisation' is here used to describe the phenomena as all participants do not follow the fundamental principle of *instant* photo sharing, rather they follow precise guidelines that, often, are distributed throughout time and daily rituals.

In relation to temporal organisation, the guideline related to the time band of photo sharing is particularly useful for increasing the number of followers. *Participant 14* described the organisation of his photo sharing as follows:

I post pictures at 12 pm, 2:30 pm and 5 pm, London time. Even when I was in Australia, 12 pm, 2:30 pm, 5 pm, London time. I was in Israel. I was in New York. Anywhere I go it would be the same time. Why? Because I consider as I am doing a magazine, I am sharing the story of my life through a magazine. I am the publisher and I am the editor and I decide what I want to do and I do it at the same time, and I find it amazing.

Considering that the aim of this approach is to collect a high number of followers it is easily understandable that users perceive this guideline to also enhance their personal satisfaction (Lakhani/Wolf 2005) and recognition (Couldry 2004).

Participant 26 highlights the importance of frequency in the following way:

There is not a single picture or a single caption that made me popular. The basic thing that made me popular has been constant posting every day over a year and always trying to keep the quality high. Telling others what they should do and posting pictures every day. That's the main thing.

This response is only one of the examples that confirms how the imperative of sharing (Van Dijck 2011) shapes users' practices on social media platforms. It demonstrates that many mediated practices (constant posting every day) and social interactions (telling other what they should do) have become part of daily routines. This also keeps users motivated to maintain their presence online.

Finally, regarding content organisation we observed that users tend to think of their photo sharing as a 'whole' rather than a sequence of independent pictures. This guideline makes visible a sense of continuity in the entire stream of photos and renders the fruition of the photographic stream fluid and visually pleasant. *Participant 19* firmly believes that for a good experience of the Instagram platform users should identify the objective of their photographic sharing and the type of story they intend to share on the platform. He labels this his 'photographic project', explaining its importance by how

The photographic project is what allows anyone who gets through your profile to under-stand your intent. [...] The principle is pretty easy out there; there are 180 million active users per month. You, with your photographic profile, need to catch the attention of those who like the kind of things you do, but the genre of things you do needs to be very clear on for those who come across you.

This response evidences the importance of telling stories with digital technologies (Alexander 2011; Scolari 2009) in order to engage with other users and establish an effective presence online.

The principle of storytelling figures as one of the most used ways of organ-ising photo sharing, and often takes the form of a personal visual diary. *Partici-pant 14* describes his way of telling stories using a personal account and an addi-tional account that he created for his dog, Izo (called @theizotime). He explains this choice in the following way:

I also know something thanks to the TV that I work for, to tell a story. I think that it is super important that when you are on Instagram you need to tell a story' [...] 'I opened Izo's account and again with Izo I decided to see like "What is Izo's story? What am I trying to say?" [...] So, I tried to make Izo my alter ego [...] so, Izo is basically saying all those things that, maybe, I don't want to say.

This response exemplifies the concept of 'being-as-mediated' (Kember/Zylinska 2012), a combination of users' interest in sharing photos as a way to define their online presence through personal narrative contributions.

Another common way of organising content was identified in the search for visual particularities. Participants report that their Instagram planning includes specifically unconventional imageries. To describe this *Participant 28* comments: "It is boring to see the perfect Eiffel tower or the perfect building in New York. That is not a new photo, it is just a scan". Sharing photos of unordinary situations and particular scenarios comes from the interest in arousing other users' curiosity and making the personal account stand out among the multitude of accounts. A significant number of participants disclose interest in what they are not used to seeing, such as distant places and uncommon scenes. These new visual experiences are facilitated by the mobility and connectivity of the devices. *Participant 29*'s account is an example of this. Fig. 5 also shows how the portability of smart mobile devices allows to capture scenes instantly anywhere, remarking how technological advancements allow new digital practices (Parikka 2012).

Figure 5: London. People under the underground. Instagram, 2014. Source: https://instagram. com/peopleontheunderground

Transformation of Photo Sharing

As discussed in the previous sections, it is possible to observe how smart mobile devices play a crucial role in shaping the digital practices (Couldry 2008) of photo sharing, following the foundation laid by the theories of mediation, new materialism and mobility (Parikka 2012; Sheller/Urry 2006; Kember/Zylinska 2012). Indeed, all participants in our study report in their daily use of Instagram several modifications compared to their earlier photographic practices. These transformations are identifiable in the constant search for photo opportunities, seeing beauty in the surroundings, and framing images as squares. Participants assume that the transformations of the practices of photo sharing are not so much related to the use of the platform. Instead, they believe that real transformations originate from the invention of camera phones and, afterwards, of smart phones.

The participants describe themselves in a constant search of imageries to draw out, highlighting that the use of smart phones shapes the way they think visually. As *Participant 3* comments: "It helps me to see things more as photo opportunities. Above and beyond just looking for Instagram photos. It is a really good medium. The ability to see even more beauty in situations". This response shows arguably that the use of smart phones shapes the way people think visually and the practices that arise from the use of Instagram, demonstrating the changes that devices make in people's behaviours and how, as Couldry (2004) argues, these changes guide people to incorporate the devices and smart phone apps more and more in their daily routines.

This is epitomised in the observation of *Participant 7* on how

it [Instagram] made a change in my way of watching things. I mean, before if I was in a situation thinking "Ok, I am here" and stop. Now, finding myself in the same situation I could make 3,000 more thoughts and seek something to extract from it. Instagram helped me a lot in this precisely because I photograph, even mentally, a place. Before seeking to extract from that place emotions to share with others would never have happened.

In fact, all participants report that their use of Instagram has gradually changed since their first experiences of the platform, and that their daily use has progressed towards new ways of consuming and producing images. This shows also a progressive improvement in users' literacy in photography and social media use in a more general way. For instance, *Participant 10* says about the platform that "at the beginning I didn't know how it was working and I was posting photos without any reason".

The main changes that participants experience through the use of Instagram are related to the way they look at their surroundings and the increased visual attention they invest in observing them. For instance, *Participant 13* mentions how "I have been passing by that [wall] 250 million times because I pass it by every day because going to catch the train. That day, I had never seen it until that moment [of photography and sharing]." (see fig. 6). Users' visual attention towards the surroundings is augmented because of Instagram use, thereby shaping mediated practices (Couldry 2004).

Figure 6: Tuttomondo, murals in Pisa.
#stopthewomenoicide photo campaign.
Instagram, 2014. Source: https://instagram.
com/mimicimme

This mobile augmented visual attention also modifies participants' presence at events. The use of the mobile phone changes incisively people's experiences of the surroundings because the experiences are mediated through the screens of their mobile devices. The device appears to take a middle position between people and objects, giving people a completely different (mediated) experience of events.

Conclusion: The Mediated Practice of Photo Sharing

The aim of this paper was to advance a critical analysis of the mediated practice of photo sharing that is experienced through the use of the smart phone application Instagram. The analysis formed around three elements in the practice of photo sharing: motivations, organisation, and transformations. According to our study, personal satisfaction (Lakhani/Wolf 2005), reciprocity (Granieri 2005) and expansion of visual knowledge are the main reasons that motivate users' activity on the Instagram platform. Users' gratification is recognised as a reason that enhances the digital practice of photo sharing. The second element, organisation of photo sharing, describes the ways and reasons that drive users to plan carefully their mediated practices of photo sharing. Within this, three ways of organisation were identified: styles and themes, storytelling, and search for visual particularities. Discussing the significant transformations in the practice of photo sharing, this paper indicated how the use of Instagram changes users' visual experience of the immediate surroundings that they live and move in (see Sheller/Urry 2006). Mobility, in particular, allows the expansion towards the 'snap, share and move on' culture. This modification discloses also an increased attention toward 'photo opportunities'. Arguably, the fact that Instagram produces an augmented perception of and connection with physical surroundings is derived from the mobility of smart devices. This finding is connected strongly to our research question focusing on how the co-presence of the mobility of devices and the mediation of platforms changes the way people experience their everyday life.

Through the empirical analysis of interview data and photographs, this paper has demonstrated changes in the social practices of photo sharing that are facilitated by the affordances of smart technologies (mediation and mobility). These changes express how digital photography can be rethought as a social practice. In fact, this paper has responded to the necessity to focus on the processes of mediation (Parikka 2012; Kember/Zylinska 2012) rather than studying photographs as objects when interpreting social practices related to photography in the mobile, social media environment. The paradigm of media as practice (Couldry 2004) is most visible in the attention that users invest in photographing for sharing. In this context, Couldry's (2004) theorisation exemplifies what people do with social media (Instagram) and devices (mobile communication) and how their use affects daily digital practices (photo sharing). Overall, this paper has offered a conceptual apparatus – built upon the co-presence of the mobility of smart mobile devices, the mediation of social media platforms, and the practices of photo sharing – that helps to comprehend the development of new digital phenomena.

References

Alexander, B. (2011): The New Digital Storytelling: Creating Narratives with New Media, Santa Barbara, CA: ABC-CLIO.

Bräuchler, B./Postill, J. (eds.) (2010): Theorising Media and Practices, New York/ Oxford: Berghahn Books.

Bock, A./Isermann, H./Knieper, T. (2011): "Quantitative Content Analysis of the Visual." In: The Sage Handbook of Visual Research Methods, London: Sage, pp. 265–282.

Bowler, G. M. (2010): "Netnography: A Method Scientifically Designed to Study Cultures and Communities Online." In: The Qualitative Report 15/5, pp. 1270–1275.

Cohen, K. R. (2005): "What Does the Photo Blog Want?" In: Media, Culture, Society 27/6, pp. 883–901.

Couldry, N. (2004): "Theorising Media as Practice." In: Social Semiotics 14/2, pp. 115–132.

Couldry, N. (2008): "Digital storytelling, media research and democracy: Conceptual choices and alternative futures." In: K. Lundby (ed.), Digital Storytelling, Mediatized Stories: Self-representations in New Media, New York: Peter Lang, pp. 41–60.

Farman, J. (2012): Mobile Interface Theory: Embodies Space and Locative Media, London: Routledge.

Gómez Cruz, E. (2016): "Photo-Genic Assemblages: Photography as a Connective Interface." In: E. Gómez Cruz/A. Lehmuskallio (eds.), Digital Photography and Everyday Life: Empirical Studies on Material Visual Practices, London: Routledge, pp. 228–42.

Granieri, G. (2005): La Società Digitale, Roma-Bari: Laterza.

Karatzogianni, A./Kuntsman, A. (eds.) (2012): Digital Cultures and the Politics of Emotion: Feelings, Affect and Technological Change, Basingstoke: Palgrave MacMillan.

Kember, S./Zylinska, J. (2012): Life After New Media: Mediation as Vital Process, Cambridge, Mass.; London: MIT Press.

Kozinets, R. (2015): Netnography, 2nd edition, London: SAGE.

Lakhani, K./Wolf, R. (2005): "Why Hackers Do What They Do." In: J. Feller/B. Fitzgerald/S. Hissam/K. Lakhani (eds.) Perspectives in Free and Open-Sources Software. Cambridge, MA: MIT Press, 3–22.

Parikka, J. (2012): "Forum: New Materialism. New Materialism as Media Theory: Medianatures and Dirty Matter." In: Communication and Critical/Cultural Studies 9/1, pp. 95–100.

Pink, S. (2007): Doing Visual Ethnography, 2nd edition, London: SAGE.

Pink, S. (2015): Doing Visual Ethnography, 3rd edition, London: SAGE.

Rubin, J.H./Rubin, I.S. (2005): Qualitative Interviewing. The Art of Hearing Data, 2nd edition, London: Sage.

Scolari, C.A. (2009): "Transmedia Storytelling: Implicit Consumers, Narrative Worlds, and Branding in Contemporary Media Production." In: Journal of Communication 3, pp. 586–606.

Serafinelli, E. (2017): "Analysis of Photo Sharing and Visual Social Relationships: Instagram as a Case Study." In: Photographies 10/1, pp. 91–111.

Siapera, E. (2012): Understanding New Media, Los Angeles and London: SAGE.

Sheller, M./Urry, J. (2006): "The New Mobilities Paradigm." In: Environment and Planning 38/2, pp. 207–226.

Van Dijck, J. (2011): "Flickr and the Culture of Connectivity: Sharing Views, Experiences, Memories." In: Memory Studies 4/4, pp. 401–415.

Van Dijck, J. (2013): "'You have one Identity': Performing the Self on Facebook and LinkedIn." In: Media, Culture & Society 35/2, pp. 199–215.

Villi, M. (2010): Visual mobile communication: Camera phone photo messages as ritual communication and mediated presence, Helsinki: Aalto University School of Art and Design.

Villi M. (2015): "'Hey, I'm Here Right Now': Camera Phone Photographs and Mediated Presence." In: Photographies 8/1, pp. 3–21.

Villi, M./Noguera Vivo, J-M. (2017): "Sharing Media Content in Social Media: The Challenges and Opportunities of UDC (User-Distributed Content)." In: Journal of Applied Journalism & Media Studies 6/2, pp. 207–23.

'Re-appropriating' Facebook?

Web API mashups as Collective Cultural Practice

Stefan Werning

Abstract

In contemporary debates about socio-technical implications of software, the platform metaphor, the corresponding notions of architectures and ecosystems as well as the formatting of data to afford 'platformization' play a central role. This approach has certainly proven fruitful to assess the role of companies like Facebook in contemporary society. However, it characteristically overlooks the messiness of actual usage practices and those studies that do acknowledge the internal power struggles that subcutaneously shape platforms often take a top-down perspective, disregarding bottom-up processes of (re-) appropriation. To address this gap, the article outlines a method to study how users and semi-professional developers collectively frame the cultural imaginary of a platform by conducting a thoroughly comparative content analysis of mashups created using the Facebook Web API. The affordances of many individual mashups might be considered marginal; yet, the tool-assistant comparison allows for inferring common patterns of interpretation that characterize mashup creation as a mobile digital practice, which plays a key role in social media platform development.

Introduction

The article at hand investigates how users repurpose data and features of *Facebook* through mashups using the official API as well as the app-remixing service *IFTTT*, and how this collective practice re-situates their perceptions of *Facebook* use in everyday situations.

APIs are the interfaces that provide users structured access to big data sets[1]; apart from commercial APIs (*Twitter, YouTube, Instagram* etc.), which only offer part of their functionality for free, numerous public APIs exist as well. Most APIs require the user to sign up for their own developer key and in exchange provide (limited) access to a platform's methods and data. For instance, the "common

---

1 For a more comprehensive definition cf. e. g. https://www.programmableweb.com/api-university/what-are-apis-and-how-do-they-work.

DOI 10.14361/dcs-2017-0211

scenarios" section on the Facebook API website[2] lists publishing status updates, determining the friendship status between users, and scheduling *Facebook* Page posts as potential activities that can be implemented via a few lines of code using the official API.

As a topic in software studies, APIs are particularly relevant because recent examples not only facilitate implementing technical tasks (such as *Facebook* posts and search queries) but also legal and administrative functions, thereby black-boxing the underlying processes. For instance, the *Betable* API affords incorporating "real-money gambling" into any app or game, including the technical functionality (e. g. moving funds between Betable accounts) but, more importantly, also providing an 'interface' to the legal framework that offering a gambling service requires.

APIs have been tentatively discussed in terms of the political economy of social media platforms or, more specifically, as catalysts of "platformization" (Helmond 2015, 5). Tarleton Gillespie (2017) recently reassessed the platform as a metaphor that strategically frames both corporate and mainstream perceptions of social media technologies and businesses, arguing that the term hides both the hierarchies and corresponding power struggles that are usually invisible to regular users and the fact that these users themselves do not constitute one coherent community but multiple, sometimes contentious groups. This political economy of APIs is relevant for the argument below since APIs can change their modes of governance at any time; for example, in 2016 *Instagram* notably altered the modalities of its API integration with IFTTT and other aggregation services[3]. Yet, while these complex and dynamic negotiation between platform providers, users, brands and not least mashup developers go beyond the scope of this article, the comparative analysis of mashups – each of which might seem hardly relevant in itself – can offer a valuable conceptual frames and material for follow-up research on the politics of API ecosystems. Thus, rather than conceptualizing platforms primarily from the perspective of data or rhetoric, it aims to rethink them in terms of practices or, more specifically, to analyse the products of API remixing and make systematic inferences about common rationales and approaches that inform this practice.

The professional development of mobile applications, which also includes platforms like *Facebook*, has already been the object of previous research, e. g. via semi-structured interviews with developers to investigate the role user participation plays during design and development (Mosemghvdlishvili and Jansz 2013). In contrast, this study foregrounds processes of bottom-up development in the form of (usually non-commercial) API remixing conducted by users with comparatively little technical knowledge. For that purpose, a comparative content analysis

---

2   Cf. https://developers.facebook.com/docs/graph-api/common-scenarios.
3   Cf. e. g. https://ifttt.com/blog/2016/05/a-change-in-how-instagram-works-with-ifttt.

(Rössler 2012) of IFTTT applets[4] as well as API remixes[5] will be conducted to determine how users with lower and higher affinity for "computational thinking" (García-Peñalvo 2016) respectively re-envision *Facebook* use in conjunction with other services. The *Facebook* API was chosen as a case study because the service affords a broad range of possible uses and repurposing, and motivations for using the platform itself can differ from those of using individual functionalities (Smock et al. 2011). In total, the corpus consists of 490 IFTTT applets and 378 mash-ups on ProgrammableWeb using the *Facebook* API, which were scraped using Outwit Hub including basic metadata. Applets are referenced by unique numerical indices – for instance, [206] refers to an applet to automatically "wish Stephen Hawking a happy birthday on Facebook" by displaying a congratulatory message in the user's *Facebook* status on January 8 – and mashups by their names as listed on ProgrammableWeb, both in square brackets. The corresponding information, which also contains the verbatim quotes referenced below, can be found in an online Google Spreadsheet at http://bit.ly/2r8MEXO. In both cases, the data had to be manually cleaned up e.g. by flagging text from dynamically inserted ads since IFTTT applets are free and frictionless to create and the format has e.g. been abused for automated product placement.

Approach

Both *IFTTT* applets and API remixes can be summarized using the term mashups, which has been defined and institutionalized in the mid-2000s. For instance, Merrill (2006) argues that "one of the big catalysts for the advent of mashups was Google's introduction of its Google Maps API" and indeed mapping is one of the more prominent 'themes' in the corpus of API remixes below. Floyd et al. (2007) define (web) mashups as forms of user-driven innovation, which becomes especially visible in the IFTTT applets. These are small conditional statements that were formerly referenced as "recipes"[6] and combine two supported services or devices; this cooking-related metaphor arguably emphasizes qualities like intuition and direct manipulatability, which stand in stark contrast to traditional software development..

Both types of mashups are essentially characterized by principles of bricolage, i.e. "making do" with (re)using and repurposing pre-existing material

---

4   A Google search for "facebook site:https://ifttt.com/applets/" yields almost 500 results, which have been scraped via Outwit Hub.

5   *Programmableweb* lists more than 370 mashups for the *Facebook* API, which have also been scraped via Outwit Hub; cf. https://www.programmableweb.com/category/all/mashups?apis=62918.

6   Cf. e.g. https://www.wired.com/2013/12/with-location-ifttt-links-apps-to-your-real-world-activity/.

(Vallgårda and Fernaeus 2015: 176). Yet, while traditional bricolage practices require "sampl[ing] media work" (Manovich 2013: 122), i.e. a conscious effort to 'appropriate' the material, mashups utilize ready-made components provided either by the APIs themselves or even an intermediary software like *IFTTT* or *Zapier*. Thus, these 'building blocks' (as well as the companies providing them) claim a much higher degree of agency than the materials in traditional bricolage contexts. This type of control can be understood with Galloway and Thacker (2004) as protocological, as APIs provide technical schemata for using features of a digital platform, which over time can contribute to the formation of cognitive schemata. Accordingly, multiple "protocols at play" during any technologically mediated situation such as a telephone call, "some [...] technical, some social" (14). These include the phone number as a technical identifier but also, in case of mobile phones, the social convention to ask where the person called currently is and whether they are free to speak. Similarly, web APIs as 'protocols' exercise indirect control by only exposing certain parameters[7] but also, through repeated use, produce social norms of use. Moreover, they do not prescribe what users should do with them but making certain use cases easier and more appealing. From that angle, they can and will also be understood as conglomerates of 'game rules' that formulate an 'invitation to play' along, as play is characterized by a similar dialectic between imposing order and affording freedom (Huizinga 1949: 7/10).

Academic contextualization

APIs in general and the *Facebook* API in particular (Hogan 2009) have been used as research 'tools' in the digital humanities to investigate. For instance, Berry et al. (2015) use the *Amazon* API to conduct a tentative network analysis of the Digital Humanities discourse.

However, a close reading of one specific API and its impact on the social and technological imaginary of the corresponding platform is still missing in critical scholarship. Bodle (2011) takes a step in this direction by investigating how Open APIs facilitate interoperability and "regimes of sharing" between the major social media platforms (and Facebook in particular). He analyses *Facebook*'s main Open API releases between 2006 and 2011 to determine how they constrain and reframe sharing on the platform. Complementary to this affordance-oriented perspective, this article looks at what users actually do with the API by comparing non-commercial mashups that use it.

---

7   For instance, the 'photo' construct in the Facebook API provides a list of predefined parameters such as width, height, the time of the last update and the location associated with the image; cf. https://developers.facebook.com/docs/graph-api/reference/photo/.

Most conspicuously, though, previous studies have attempted to 'map' the API ecosystem via network analyses (Evans and Basole 2016; Yu and Woodard 2009). The same approach, built on scraping all available connections around one specific platform, has also being applied to *IFTTT* (Ur et al. 2016). However, these mappings are static snapshots of a highly dynamic phenomenon, with constantly changing alliances. Moreover, they only focus on basic patterns in the ecosystem (e.g. the frequency of deliberate or unwitting imitation) rather than actual usage practices, i.e. while they identify relations between APIs they do not further elaborate on the qualities of these relationships. To complement this body of research, the content analysis conducted below does not rely on digital methods but focuses on identifying patterns in the functionality of API mashups as well as the rhetoric employed to describe them.

Remixing web APIs as mobile digital practice and cultural technique

The use of web APIs as analysed below constitutes a mobile digital practice because it organizes the mobility of data between different platforms. This definition requires a broader notion of mobility as proposed e.g. by Jensen (2013), who argues that mobility had been unjustly framed as a 'novel' paradigm in the context of the so-called "mobile media" (27). Instead, Jensen emphasizes the mobility of information, arguing that "for centuries, print media have disseminated information and entertainment within and between countries and across continents" (27).

From that angle, while previously data often constituted a value through controlled scarcity, web APIs constitute a new paradigm in which the mobility of data creates value. For instance, in his analysis of how TV companies can use social media APIs, Lahey (2016) defines the points of access between service that APIs define as a "'sharing' ecology" (431), which helps users (in his case fans) move across platforms without actively switching between apps or web sites. He furthermore points out that "web APIs philosophically are not new" but that "contemporary interest in them is built on a type of structured openness and sharing, where many businesses want to give away access to their data and services but only on their terms" (433). That is, the code a company implements in its API functions and the data that pass through them become valuable primarily through 'movement'.

In line with the theme of this issue, the article at hand thus considers API remixing as a mobile digital practice and, more specifically, as a contemporary cultural technique. Practice-minded books on the subject already intuitively frame API use as "remixing" (Yee 2008). Moreover, as Manovich (2013: 167) notes, remixing is an iterative, self-sustaining practice that constantly forms new combinations, and "parts of these combinations enter into new remixes, ad infinitum".

This self-sustaining quality can be observed in the API remixes but especially the IFTTT applets, e. g. as different variations on popular 'themes' such as automated birthday greetings reappear again and again in slightly different forms.

As will be elaborated below, API remixing should be conceptualized as an emergent cultural technique (Winthrop-Young 2013) because it constitutes a form of self-expression and of interpreting the world. While not yet feasible at scale, tools like IFTTT increasingly makes this practice wide-spread enough to be culturally formative, similar e. g. to how Adobe Flash afforded digital game making as a form of "social comment" (Thompson 2002) in the early 2000s. The concept of cultural techniques originated in post-war German media theory but has been tentatively introduced into Anglo-American media and culture studies discourse as well (Siegert 2013). According to Krämer and Bredekamp (2013), the conceptual relevance of cultural techniques has been to challenge the notion of culture as text and the primacy of "textual analysis and hermeneutics [as] the favorite model for the understanding of cultural orders" (21). Similarly, this article seeks to avoid reducing the cultural dynamics of API use to "monolithic immobility congealed in works" and, through its decidedly comparative approach, considers the individual mashups less as self-contained 'texts' than as manifestations of API remixing as a practice. As such, the patterns inferred from this material can serve as frames of reference for further praxeographic or netnographic studies that focus more on individual users or user communities.

Bogost (2009) addresses a similar ontological distinction regarding digital games, framing them (according to Jesper Juul) as lived experiences, which are shaped by the game as a rule system and can be studied via (digital) artefacts such as gameplay videos created in the process. This article attempts to adapt this ontological perspective to APIs as experienced 'in practice', pursuing the hypothesis that API remixing helps define the contours of *Facebook*'s platform identity by keeping it 'mobile', in flux, through the constant use and repurposing of its core functionality.

More specifically, cultural techniques "also comprise sign systems such as musical notation or arithmetical formulas located outside the domain of the hegemony of alphabetical literacy" (20). In the case at hand, the API with its contingent selection of methods to access and manipulate data from an otherwise proprietary platform like *Facebook* prototypically fits that category. Like a new system of musical notation, e. g. graphical notation schemes introduced in the second half of the 20th century (Evarts 1968), it becomes a gradually naturalized framework for self-expression and, even more importantly, its limitations and constraints appear increasingly 'natural' as well. Musical works that defy traditional notation like John Cage's 4'33" or John Zorn's Game Pieces make this naturalization visible by shaking up the corresponding conventions. Most of the API mashups analysed below suggest that the creators are still familiarizing themselves with these conventions but some uncommon combinations of APIs already suggest the potential to playfully subvert them. For instance, an IFTTT applet dating back to July 10th 2014 [476] creates a "a digital 'Dead Man's Switch'" by repurposing Google's Inactive Account Manager, sending out an automated tweet to officially 'proclaim' the user's death.

Below, the specificity of *IFTTT* mashup creation as opposed to the use of the official *Facebook* API are discussed separately, each with a focus on three characteristic patterns that manifested themselves during the comparison.

Findings

IFTTT Applets

The focus of this analysis lies on establishing and 'validating' a method to critically assess cultural implications of APIs, which would also be applicable similar tools like *Zapier* or *Yahoo Pipes*. Thus, it necessarily pursues an exploratory approach and does not claim the generalizability or statistical validity of instead findings. Instead, the comparative content analysis seeks to identify recurring patterns that characterize API remixing as a cultural technique by exhibiting distinct values and routines.

Werning (2016) points out that mobile applications, both those built into mobile operating systems and third-party apps, often require an inherently diachronic perspective because their affordances characteristically change constantly and often radically. This particularly applies to the APIs they offer, as methods and policies of data access often change over time or even become obsolete when the

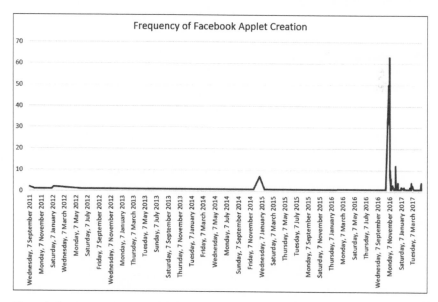

Figure 1: Facebook-themed applets created between 2011 and 2017.

ecosystem around them changes[8]. This analysis does not pursue a decidedly diachronic approach, as the sample size would be too small to meaningfully investigate patterns of change over time, but both this section on applets and the following on mashups begin by contextualizing the corpus, pointing out fundamental changes that already become apparent during a cursory investigation.

The earliest applets that use the *Facebook* API, created between 2011 and 2014, focus a lot on the interoperability of *Facebook* and *Google+*, e.g. by enabling cross-posting or posting via email as in applets [488], [486] and [485]. This suggests that during that time, *Google+* was still interpreted as the most promising future competitor and alternative to *Facebook*. Moreover, the distribution of applets submitted over time shows that the rebranding from 'recipes' to 'applets' as well as the general overhaul of the *IFTTT* platform on November 2, 2016 significantly boosted user activity for a limited amount of time. While before, merely 1–2 recipes using *Facebook* were created per month, the number shot up to 48 on November 2, remained constant for a bit more than a week and dropped again to about three times the previous volume in mid-November.

Self-automation

As they constitute the main value proposition of *IFTTT*, automation practices constitute the bulk of user-created applets. From a media industries standpoint, critical positions on automation primarily focus on top-down production (Napoli 2014), e.g. the algorithmic prediction of demand or even creation of content. When, Lev Manovich referred to automation as a principle of new media (Manovich 2001: 32), he was still referring to algorithmic manipulation of digital content, e.g. a *Photoshop* filter changing colour or transparency values of all pixels in a digital image according to predefined rules. Through tools like *IFTTT*, human users can now apply similar principles to their own (digital) media use, creating 'macros' for their daily habits like recording actions in *Photoshop* "for tasks you perform frequently"[9].

In the early 1980s, the rapid advancement of robotics and microelectronics still prompted critical push-back against the cultural logic of automation. For instance, Sheridan, Vámos, and Aida (1983) posited that "technology should be individually designed to each culture" to ensure a proper match between the user's (mostly a worker's) physiology but also their "psychological and cultural characteristics" (605). In contrast, platforms like *IFTTT* celebrate automation through their curated collections of applets[10] and institutionalize its underlying logic of efficiency and emergent complexity as desirable values through repeated use.

---

8   Major APIs usually offer deprecation schedules to ensure that their own ecosystem can adapt to the changes; cf e.g. https://developers.google.com/adwords/api/docs/sun set-dates.

9   Cf. https://helpx.adobe.com/photoshop/using/creating-actions.html.

10   Cf. https://ifttt.com/collections.

Many applets are rather mundane and appear to be products of users familiarizing themselves with algorithmic logic itself (cf. e.g. applet [108], which allows for cross-posting content on *Instagram* and in a *Facebook* group). However, some culturally significant automation practices also become apparent, most notably updating the user's *Facebook* status message to 'celebrate' birthdays of people in the user's contact list [97, 112, 120]. These applets take up and further expand on an already established use of *Facebook* in popular culture. For instance, Techcrunch argues that "*Facebook* is where people celebrate birthdays online"[11], pointing to recently introduced features such as Birthday Videos, through which *Facebook* attempts to solidify its 'claim' on this constitutive cultural practice. The abundance of birthday-related applet signals that users consolidates this assumption and at the same time suggests that the users' collective imaginary of what *Facebook* can be is notably shaped by the set of affordances currently on offer. Anticipating automation practices like this can also 'lead to' similarly automated follow-up practices. For instance, applet [284] thanks all *Facebook* friends for sending birthday greetings without any manual input required. Thus, while many users may experience social pressure due to Facebook's automated birthday reminders, applets enable them to use automation to 'relieve' themselves of that pressure, thereby leading to a closed loop of purely algorithmic exchange of birthday greetings on the platform. The same applies to other forms of social interaction that are less clearly tied to *Facebook* such as New Year's greetings [422].

These automation attempts occasionally eliminate established practices that had become part of Facebook 'culture', i.e. shared experiences among users of the platform that sometimes become visible because of the 'friction' they incur. For instance, several applets facilitate collecting all *Facebook* photos, in which the user has been tagged (cf. e.g. applets [417] or [429]). The creator of applet [417] demonstrates the habitualization of looking up references to oneself in the profiles of one's peers by claiming that his applet requires "no more scrolling through friends' feeds and albums to find those great pics". A study by Nicolai et al. (2009) indicates that narcissistic forms of web search such as self-googling have become deeply ingrained in many users' online experience. Yet, with the increasing pervasiveness of tools like *IFTTT*, the originally cumbersome processes, which required users to develop their own routines and 'shortcuts' and, thereby, became even more meaningful over time, are more and more discarded or, rather, 'offloaded' to an applet.

In more complex cases, automation manifests itself in the form of a 'communication with oneself', i.e. users explicitly set up algorithmic cues to call themselves to action or reaffirm their own values. For instance, applet [430] enables users to 'manage' their music fandom by uploading the cover art of newly favourited music albums on *Deezer* to a dedicated photo album on *Facebook*. In doing so, they arguably create a socio-technical system for themselves and the technolo-

---

11   Cf. https://techcrunch.com/2016/07/28/facebook-birthday-videos/.

gies (i. e. web platforms) they use. Niederer and van Dijck (2010) use that term e. g. to describe how bots on *Wikipedia* are designed to produce content that is particularly aimed at strengthening the community (1378), i. e. at spurring other users into action. For example, Rambot "pulls content from public databases and feeds it into *Wikipedia*", encouraging (human) users to flesh out the resulting incomplete articles; subsequently, many "bot-generated articles on American cities and counties [are] corrected and complemented by human editors" (1378). The Deezer applet above suggests that individual users employ applets in a similar way to create their own personalized socio-technical systems. The same applies e. g. in the case of applet [372], which emails the user once they have been invited to an event through *Facebook*, thus creating partially redundant content as 'breadcrumbs' for oneself to follow.

Finally, users employ automation practices also to historicize their own *Facebook* activity. For instance, applet [384] creates an automatic backlog of all status messages in a Google spreadsheet, thereby creating a focused form of 'diary' that would not be feasible to maintain by other means. Applets like this reframe *Facebook* as a tool to track one's own emotional development over time independent from factual or even quantified data, as no contextual information is saved alongside the status messages.

'Brand' management

A second recurring pattern is the use of applet for 'self-branding' purposes, i. e. to present oneself according to brand logic. First, this involves maintaining a coherent impression across social platforms. For example, applet [111] automatically synchronizes the user's profile pictures on *Twitter* and *Facebook*.

Second, several applets automatically inform 'followers' of newly created content, e. g. if the user starts a new Twitch stream [113], is currently live-vlogging via *Periscope* [442] or has recently uploaded music on *SoundCloud* [427]. Therefore, applets help user cope with the pressure of having to produce new content on a regular basis; e. g. applet [126] allows for populating one's *Facebook* timeline with blog content via RSS feeds. It is important to note that applets like this re-appropriate the timeline as a key affordance of *Facebook*, turning it from a backlog of events in the user's life[12] to a 'news ticker'. Another technical aspect of *Facebook* that users characteristically re-appropriate via applets is the status message, which has traditionally been used as flexibly as possible e. g. to create "a feeling of connectedness between users" (Köbler et al. 2010) through the topicality of its content. However, algorithmic manipulation takes that flexibility to

---

12   Shortly after its introduction, the feature was summarized as "show[ing] the story of your life, as you choose to tell it or as Facebook has recorded it"; cf. http://uk.pcmag.com/internet-products/66981/feature/12-things-you-should-know-about-facebook-timeline.

unprecedented levels. For instance, applet [343] updates the status with every song a user listens to on *Echo*. Thus, while the status message used to be an asynchronous and quintessentially personal self-assessment of the user's current situation, the aforementioned applets turn it into an affordance that contributes to the specific "realtimeness" (Weltevrede, Helmond, and Gerlitz 2014: 130) of *Facebook* as a platform.

Third, applets allow for rationalizing content posting by using *Facebook* in tandem with a scheduling application to plan one's social media activity. According to brand logic, content should be 'spread out' evenly over time, as this maximizes the recognizability of brand identity and enhances user 'loyalty' by making it easier for them to integrate brand messages into their daily routines (cf. e.g. Broussard 2000). While previously only specialized applications like *Buffer*[13] used to offer that functionality, IFTTT applets make it accessible to anyone. This logic is intuitively applied to individual self-presentation on social media platforms as well. Applications of corporate 'rhetoric' to aspects of private life[14] have already been promoting neoliberal subjectivity (McGuigan 2014) for decades. Yet, applets like these are more influential than language use, allowing users to 'performing' neoliberal rationales online through repeated practice, which makes them 'feel' all the more 'natural' over time.

Finally, the creation and use of IFTTT applets gradually blurs the boundary between private and professional applications. For example, applet [100] targets semi-professional users by implementing "automated Ads reporting into shared Google Drive for marketing teams". More importantly, private and professional entities appear in the same format on the service. For instance, applet [98] "automatically post[s] a celebratory status on Facebook" if the user reaches a set step goal on their pedometer. While this appears like a personal attempt at self-optimizing, the applet was published by the consumer electronics company Withings rather than an individual user to promote their wearable fitness trackers. As applets on IFTTT are curated by the platform according to topic area, this dispositif suggests a kind of ongoing 'conversation' between companies and individual users. Yet, it also requires to be aware of who is 'speaking', as companies use the same format to foster use of their services[15].

---

13   Cf. https://buffer.com/.

14   A 2014 article from *De Groene Amsterdammer* (cf. https://www.groene.nl/artikel/ik-is-een-start-up) aptly summarized the debate by proposing that Foucault's original claim – that people gradually reinvent the "self as enterprise" – may become all the more urgent due to the rise of startups to the status of a social 'role model'.

15   E.g. applet [404] is an applet created by Google that uses its voice recognition capabilities to let users post by 'talking' to *Facebook*.

Filling 'gaps' in affordance networks

Finally, several applets indicate that users become more and more adept at understanding affordance networks[16], i.e. how functionalities between related services overlap, but also which expectable functionalities are 'missing'. For instance, the creator of applet [477] claims that the applet "fixes" the "lack of notifications" on Tinfoil, which they recently switched to because of privacy concerns. Thus, applets are used as workarounds to 'remedy' these omissions. Similarly, applet [470] compensates for the inability of the Xbox One to share screenshots via *Facebook* by posting them first to *Twitter* and then copying them automatically to *Facebook*. This applet illustrates a common principle that users intuitively 'learn' by using applets, namely the need to use a specific nomenclature (in this case for naming the Xbox screenshots posted to *Twitter*) so that they can be reliably detected and manipulated using simple algorithmic means such as the eponymous if-this-then-that logic. For instance, applets [457], [385] and [446] all illustrate the principle using different examples. On a related note, the use of applets 'teaches' users about the kind of structured data that *Facebook* provides. For instance, applet [413] makes *Facebook* notifications available on services that don't usually support them by tapping into the personalized RSS feed that Facebook generates for all users' notifications, but which is not part of the regular interface and, thus, 'invisible' to many users.

Facebook API remixes

Compared to IFTTT applets, remixes using the official *Facebook* API are usually much less focused on one platform but rather combine multiple APIs to reach more freely defined goals. Thus, while applets are often conceived based on technological feasibility, API remixes represent visions of social media use in which any individual API is usually but one building block. Moreover, since API remixes require more active maintenance to develop a stable user base, they are much more volatile than applets. Many mashups in the corpus, still listed on ProgrammableWeb, are already discontinued and the rhetoric employed in some descriptions suggests that longevity is considered a value in itself. For instance, [Noozly] simply claims to provide "social news since 2009", mimicking the same rhetoric that many regional brick-and-mortar businesses have traditionally used to evoke trust and authority. Therefore, considering basic metadata characteristics is a useful step to provide basic orientation for a more interpretive approach.

Upon parsing the API descriptions through Voyant Tools[17], it becomes evident that the most popular terms like 'social' (52) are expectedly rather generic. Similarly, the term 'friends' (43) is used only slightly more often than 'users' (41). The

---

16   Cf. e.g. http://www.normanjackson.co.uk/creativehe/category/affordance.

17   Cf. http://beta.voyant-tools.org/.

most relevant related activities are search (38), photos (21), maps (16) and music (15), i. e. mashups on audiovisual content are particularly appealing. Consequently, the platforms mentioned most prominently in conjunction with *Facebook* are *Google* (27), *Twitter* (21), *YouTube* (15), *Flickr* (10) and *Foursquare* (5). Programmableweb lists 30 API mashups that were already created in 2007, only one year after *Facebook* became publicly available. A few of these mashups anticipate use cases that would only later become billion-dollar industries.

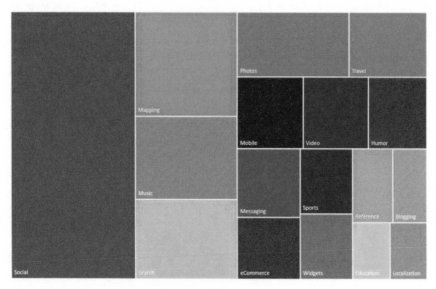

Figure 2: Most popular genres of Facebook API mashups.

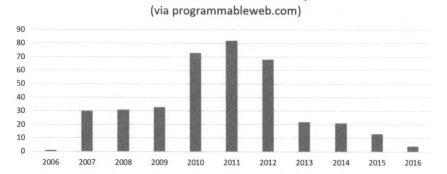

Figure 3: Development of Facebook API mashups between 2006 and 2016.

For instance, [Rendezbook] – the earliest listed mashup from November 2006 – is summarized as "a crush system for Facebook" by enabling users to "tell the system who you would like to become better friends with". While services like OkCupid (2004) and Match.com (1993) had already been established online dating platforms, the format only later, in the early 2010s, became part of mainstream social media use through Tinder (2012) and concurrent offerings. Remixing of the Facebook API appears to have peaked in 2011 with a little more than 80 mashups registered during that year.

While later mashups combine multiple APIs as needed, early examples demonstrate the sometimes-frantic rush to carve out a niche in the Facebook 'economic ecosystem'[18]. For instance, [Mosoto] (Feb. 2007) positioned itself as a new layer "on top of your Facebook account"[19] that characteristically positions filesharing as a quasi-social practice, by integrating it directly into the chat interface. [Facebook Friend Plotter] (Apr. 2007) visualized the location of *Facebook* friends in the UK on a map screen, thereby providing an alternative view on the user's expanding circle of friends. [Facebook Friends Map] (2009) later applied that principle on a global scale. This came at a time when news media began pointing out that *Facebook* users were forming friend relationships "as if they were collecting action figures, stamps or collectables"[20]. Finally, [Zuckerbucks] (Jul. 2007) introduced a points system that could be "use[d] like play money on *Facebook*", years before the platform would officially introduce its own (already discontinued) currency *Facebook* Credits in 2011.

Paul Ricoeur famously referred to literature as "a vast laboratory in which we experiment with estimations, evaluations, and judgments of approval and condemnation", which consequently requires thinking of narrativity as "a propaedeutic to ethics" (Ricoeur 1992: 115). Thus, through literature a society might 'prototype' potential future constellation, which may not yet be feasible at the respective time of writing, and simultaneously constructs a basis for moral judgment. The multiplicity of mashups that (re)interpret the social vision built into *Facebook*'s functionality, especially through redundancies and slightly varying takes on similar themes, arguably performs a similar function. Fluck (1997) makes a similar claim as Ricoeur, arguing that American literature has been producing cultural imaginaries that in some cases later became social reality or paved the way for social changes; by analogy, the process of creating mashups allows for exploring social uses and potential futures of *Facebook* as a platform and the community that emerged around it. For instance, [Two Degrees] (2007) allowed for searching through the *Facebook* friend lists of friends to "find people who should be on your own list", long before algorithmic recommendation of potential

---

18   The term is used following Rachel Rosmarin's definition, who used it to analyze how gaps in the MySpace functionality offered numerous opportunities for small supplementary businesses to fill, which could not exist without the platform's large user base to sustain them; cf. https://www.forbes.com/2006/04/07/myspace-google-murdoch-cx_rr_0410myspace.html.

19   Cf. https://techcrunch.com/2007/02/07/mosoto-share-files-and-chat-on-facebook/.

20   http://www.telegraph.co.uk/news/science/science-news/3306173/Facebook-study-reveals-users-trophy-friends.html.

contacts[21] institutionalized the idea of 'importing' social relations like one would copy and paste digital data from one list into another. Platforms like *Facebook* are constantly in flux, as their underlying algorithms are incessantly tweaked (Bogost 2016) and interface elements added, removed and changed. Therefore, their "technological imaginary" (Lister et al. 2009: 66/67), i.e. the consensual notions of how they will evolve and which role they should play in society, is characteristically blurry. This spectrum of potential interpretations – both on behalf of the users and the designers – is also summarized as the "interpretative flexibility" (Bijker et al. 2012: 34) of technological artefacts in a broader sense. The creation and use of API mashups thus makes this flexibility visible by expressing possible design futures of *Facebook* in the form of discrete, comparable digital objects.

Invitation to play

The corpus of remixes also illustrates that web API use is not purely guided by utilitarian rationales but e.g. also perceived as "fun"[22] or as an invitation to "play"[23]. For instance, the popular online platform *Any API* offers test consoles for about 270 APIs that affords playfully combining data and methods by making the results instantly visible. According to its self-description, *Any API* suggests the cyclical principle "Explore – Discover – Try – Build" as the ideal way to use APIs[24], which also essentially describes the way a player approaches a game. Previous research conducted within the digital media industry, e.g. on the emergence of playful GUIs in the mid-1990s (Yager et al. 1997) or on playful uses of communication technology in the household (Lindley, Harper, and Sellen 2010), shows that playful use can indeed be tapped into as conduit for innovation. While these studies use the notion of play rather intuitively, API remixing exhibits several properties that e.g. Huizinga (1949) considers characteristic of play. It is a "voluntary activity" (7) rather than a task conducted for an external purpose; accordingly, the vast majority of mashups considered in this article have not been created in a commercial context. Furthermore, play is "not 'ordinary' or 'real' life" (8), which is to say it is detached from real-world consequences and allows for practicing specific skills in a safe space. Similarly, mashup creation– especially compared to traditional software development – characteristically affords 'trial and error' because it usually requires no significant investment of time or money and

---

21 For instance, a post on the LinkedIn blog from 2015 argues that all major social networks rely on "their trademark Friend suggestion algorithms"; cf. https://www.linkedin.com/pulse/how-does-linkedin-gives-you-people-may-know-suggestions-atiq.

22 Cf. e.g. https://www.quora.com/What-are-some-cool-fun-APIs.

23 Cf. e.g. https://www.reddit.com/r/webdev/comments/3wrswc/what_are_some_fun_apis_to_play_with/.

24 Cf. https://www.any-api.com/.

because it emphasizes playful bricolage, i.e. 'making do' with ready-made functions created by the API provider, instead of pre-emptive planning. However, while Huizinga argues that technology fosters "commercial competition" and thus arguably diminishes the "immemorial sacred play-forms" (200), API mashups demonstrate that particularly digital technologies not only streamline processes but also create new niches for playfulness (Sicart 2014).

Apart from finding uncommon combinations of APIs, one distinct pattern of play is the application of the 'rules of play' of online social networks to different audiences such as vegan users [VeganHunter], business travelers [Arrivedin.com] or "orchid lovers" [Orcheeder]. Moreover, remixes playfully re-enacting the nomenclature of contemporary mobile applications. These include nonsensical neologisms and misspelling (e.g. [Kiwifruut], a social YouTube discovery service), common morphemes (e.g. [Flixster], imitating iconic names like *Napster* or *Friendster*), active verbs phrased like an appeal (e.g. [ConnectMyRide] or [Stay in Touch]), and vowel omission (as in [NetTickr] or [Listnr]).

Promoting purchasing as quasi-social activity

While the rapid growth of *Groupon* turned social shopping into a dedicated (mainstream) media practice, [fflap] (2010) is but one of many API mashups that contributed to bridge the epistemic gap between ecommerce and online social interaction by combining *eBay* and *Facebook* functionality through their respective APIs. [MyShopping Facebook] (2007) enables users to "to connect with friends, co-workers, or family on your daily shopping activities"; similarly [Mallicious Social Shopping] (2007) "leverages real life relationships on Facebook". Both early mashups reframe shopping as a complementary form of online social interaction by combining the then-newly available *Facebook* API with ecommerce APIs. Other mashups helped discursively stabilize this framing. For instance, [50 Shops] (2011) claimed to enable "buyers to tap into the wisdom of crowds to help with their buying decisions"; that is, it referenced Pierre Levy's dictum, which at that time had trickled down into popular discourse, to make collaborative buying on *Facebook* appear both topical and natural (i.e. 'wise'). Over time, the aforementioned fragmentation of audiences also occured in this mashup 'genre'. For instance, [SuittsMe] (2011) focuses specifically on clothes shopping while [Arms Dealer] (2011) encourages users to frequent and review gun shops and shooting ranges.

While many mashups are evidently designed to boost sales by fostering product-oriented discussions, a few more recent examples also suggest that using the Facebook API in conjunction with ecommerce APIs can also promote 'price literacy', thereby making users potentially more resilient against these very same commercialization attempts. For instance, [GrabEvery] (2012) facilitates the use of coupons and coupon codes by affording price comparison to a previously unprecedented extent; this use of digital technology contributes to an ongoing 'professionalization' of purchasing practices that (Schwartz 2010) calls a subculture of "retail hacking". [PriceZombie] (2015) fulfills a similar purpose as a "price tracker for numerous retail stores and a comparison shopping site".

Providing 'data types' for self-expression

Self-expression on social media platforms is defined by its, more or less visible, constraints such as the 140-character-limit on *Twitter* but also, more recently, *Facebook*'s decision to replace the simple like button with six predefined "Reactions" in early 2016[25]. These 'data types', i.e. structured formats for expressing complex information, directly frame the self-description of those using them. As Drucker and Haas (2017) argue in a broader, almost McLuhanesque sense, "the way in which information is structured is the real information" (119) [translation by the author of this article]. More specifically, (Anderson 1991) shows how the census with its grid-like structure to categorize families has been an actively used tool for colonial governance. Similarly, the six ideal-typical Reactions constrain the spectrum of potential emotional states and thereby narrow down the user's self-description, which made them as well as related 'data types' potential objects of contention and some remixes attempt to expand that focus. For instance, [Expin.me] affords "mid to long format expression", i.e. short story-length user contributions, arguing that *Facebook* posts are not suitable for conveying more idiosyncratic ideas. Moreover, it supports social writing in "Hindi, Marathi, Kannada, Tamil, Bengali or Spanish". [Expressi] (2011) combines providing new categories for self-expression with the aforementioned focus on social shopping. It asks users "which item is the most emotionally and personally relevant for [them]" by combining the Amazon Product Advertising API with sharing capabilities via *Facebook*. This rather unusual combination on the one hand substantiates the common perception that users are supposed to engage in "meaningful interaction with products" (de Medeiros 2014, 16) and that contemporary product design aims for an affective relationship with commodities. However, it also illustrates that these concepts are shaped by technological feasibility as the Amazon Product Advertising API provides ready-made access to products across all the major region-specific Amazon websites as well as discoverability functionality such as "Product Search, Customer Reviews, Similar Products, Accessories, [and] Wish Lists"[26].

Finally, coming back to the initial notion of APIs organizing the mobility of data across platforms, many mashups institutionalize a cross-platform perspective. That is, because multi-API use makes it particularly easy to obtain and compare data from different services, it makes this inherently comparative perspective

---

25   Cf. e.g. https://www.wired.com/2016/02/facebook-reactions-totally-redesigned-like-button/.

26   Cf. https://affiliate-program.amazon.com/gp/advertising/api/detail/main.html.

feel particularly 'natural'. For instance, [Social page authority checker] (2014) aggregates and compares quantitative data for multiple websites from *Facebook* but also *Google+*, *LinkedIn* and *Pinterest* to calculate an overall averaged "social media authority" score. [Rápido] applies the same principle to posting information, enabling users to simultaneously post to *Facebook*, *Twitter*, *Google+*, and *Foursquare*. Through repeated use and incorporation into everyday media routines, these mashups foster a dialectic perspective. On the one hand, online social networks become increasingly fragmented, tailored to increasingly narrow audiences; for instance, Craig (2016) demonstrates the increasing fragmentation of online communities with regard to online dating platforms such as The League, Sparkology, the Dating Lounge, and Luxy. However, the previously mentioned examples at the same time cause the different networks to seemingly 'converge' within the daily practices and, thus, the perception of the users.

Outlook

The comparative content analysis shows that, with a few exceptions, the collective imaginary of what *Facebook* can or should be is still narrowly framed by technical feasibility (e. g. backups and cross-posting) as well as the kind of functionality that *Facebook* 'claims' for itself (e. g. birthday greetings). This is most likely since API mashup creation is still a marginalized practice with comparatively little social interaction between creators and users that would allow for 'refining' the remixes as forms of self-expression. This is relevant because rather than outwardly visible terms of service that would dictate the limits of app remixing, these forms of governance (Light, Burgess, and Duguay 2016: 10) are embedded in the practical affordance of the *Facebook* API (and *IFTTT* as an intermediary). Genuinely playful uses of remixes or even applets, e. g. applet [400] posting a steady stream of martial arts memes to the user's *Facebook* account, are still comparatively rare. While this is plausible in the case of remixes, which are often created by users with 'professional' ambitions, who want to become part of the industry and, thus, expectedly 'play by its rules', it is more surprising in the case of applets. Moreover, most users characteristically direct their mashups at an undefined, inherently global audience, with only few exceptions. For instance, applet [355] was created by a user from the Austrian state of Vorarlberg to monitor speed limit enforcement in his area and share related news with a group of *Facebook* friends.

The results of this exploratory study map out several highly relevant areas for follow-up research. As suggested above, a distinctly diachronic content analysis, potentially including IFTTT applets using all the major online social networks, could be a fruitful direction for follow-up research based on the approach outlined in this chapter. Moreover, as suggested above, applets and API remixes differ in terms of the technical hurdles they impose on the user as remixes require a higher level of both information literacy (Asselin et al. 2011) and algorithmic literacy. While this could not be systematically factored into the analysis above, the notion of literacy is another useful axis in further studies on API use. Finally, investigating different corpora of IFTTT applets can produce interesting results, particularly if not narrowed down by technology (like *Facebook*) but by practice. For instance, IFTTT itself curates selections of applets e. g. by season (Christmas) or theme (e. g. work-outs). APIs as catalysts of mobile digital practices are increasingly incorporated into curricula (Robillard and Deline 2011; Olsen/Moser 2013), which gradually bridges the gap between programmers and non-programmers and helps refine API mashup creation as a genuinely digital cultural technique.

References

Anderson, Benedict (1991): Imagined Communities: Reflections on the Origin and Spread of Nationalism, New York, NY: Verso.

Asselin, Marlene/Dobson, Teresa/Meyers, Eric M./Teixiera, Cristina/Ham, Linda (2011): "Learning from YouTube: An Analysis of Information Literacy in User Discourse." In: Proceedings of the 2011 iConference, Washington: ACM.

Berry, David M./Borra, Erik/Helmond, Anne/Plantin, Jean-Christophe/Rettberg, Jill Walker (2015): "The Data Sprint Approach: Exploring the Field of Digital Humanities through Amazon's Application Programming Interface." In: Digital Humanities Quarterly 9/3, article 222, (http://hdl.handle.net/11245/1.502979).

Bijker, Wiebe E./Hughes, Thomas P./Pinch, Trevor/Douglas, Deborah G. (eds.) (2012): The Social Construction of Technological Systems: New Directions in the Sociology and History of Technology, Cambridge, MA: MIT Press.

Bodle, Robert (2011): "Regimes of Sharing. Open APIs, Interoperability, and Facebook." In: Information, Communication & Society 14/3, pp. 320–37.

Bogost, Ian (2009): "Videogames Are a Mess." Keynote Speech at DiGRA. (http://bogost.com/downloads/Videogames are a Mess slides.pdf).

Bogost, Ian (2016): "Go Tweak Yourself, Facebook." In: The Atlantic, April 28, (http://www.theatlantic.com/technology/archive/2016/04/go-tweak-yourself-facebook/480258/).

Broussard, Gerard (2000): "How Advertising Frequency Can Work to Build Online Advertising Effectiveness." In: International Journal of Market Research 42/4, pp. 439–57.

Craig, Elise (2016): "Niche Dating Apps Like the League Are Icky and Bad for Love." Wired Magazine, June 6, (https://www.wired.com/2016/06/why-tinder-is-bad/).

de Medeiros, Wellington Gomes (2014): "Meaningful Interaction with Products." In: Design Issues 30/3, pp. 16–28.

Drucker, Johanna/Haas, Annika (2017): "Digital Humanities als Epistemische Praxis." In: Zeitschrift Für Medienwissenschaft 16, pp. 114–25.

Evans, Peter C./Basole, Rahul C. (2016): "Revealing the API Ecosystem and Enterprise Strategy via Visual Analytics." In: Communications of the ACM 59/2, pp. 26–28.

Evarts, John (1968): "The New Musical Notation: A Graphic Art?" In: Leonardo 1/4, pp. 405–12.

Floyd, Ingbert/Jones, M. Cameron/Rathi, Dinesh/Twidale, Michael (2007): "Web Mash-Ups and Patchwork Prototyping: User-Driven Technological Innovation with Web 2.0 and Open Source Software." In: Proceedings of the 40th Annual Hawaii International Conference on System Sciences, IEEE Computer Society.

Fluck, Winfried (1997): Das Kulturelle Imaginäre: Funktionsgeschichte Des Amerikanischen Romans, 1790–1900, Frankfurt/Main: Suhrkamp.

Gillespie, Tarleton (2017): "The Platform Metaphor, Revisited" In: HIIG Science Blog, (https://www.hiig.de/en/blog/the-platform-metaphor-revisited/).

Helmond, Anne (2015): "The Platformization of the Web: Making Web Data Platform Ready." In: Social Media + Society 1/2, pp. 1–11.

Hogan, Bernie (2009): "A Comparison of On and Offline Networks through the Facebook API." In: Social Science Research Network Working Paper Series, December 18, doi:10.2139/ssrn.1331029.

Huizinga, Johan (1949): Homo Ludens. A Study of the Play-Element in Culture, London, Boston and Henley: Routledge & Kegan Paul.

Jensen, Klaus Bruhn (2013): "What's Mobile in Mobile Communication?" In: Mobile Media & Communication 1/1, pp. 26–31.

Köbler, Felix/Vetter, Céline/Riedl, Christoph/Leimeister, Jan Marco/Krcmar, Helmut (2010): "Social Connectedness on Facebook – An Explorative Study on Status Message Usage." In: Americas Conference on Information Systems, Lima, Peru. doi:10.2139/ssrn.1953431.

Krämer, Sybille/Bredekamp, Horst (2013): "Culture, Technology, Cultural Techniques – Moving Beyond Text." In: Theory, Culture & Society 30/6, pp. 20–29.

Lahey, Michael (2016): "Invisible Actors: Web Application Programming Interfaces, Television, and Social Media." In: Convergence: The International Journal of Research into New Media Technologies 22/4, pp. 426–39.

Light, Ben/Burgess, Jean/Duguay, Stefanie (2016): "The Walkthrough Method: An Approach to the Study of Apps." In: New Media and Society First published November 11, (http://journals.sagepub.com/doi/abs/10.1177/1461444816675438).

Lindley, Siân E./Harper, Richard/Sellen, Abigail (2010): "Designing a Technological Playground: A Field Study of the Emergence of Play in Household Messaging." In: CHI 2010: We Are Family, Atlanta, GA: ACM, pp. 2351–60.

Lister, Martin/Dovey, Jon/Giddings, Seth/Grant, Iain/Kelly, Kieran (eds.) (2009): New Media: A Critical Introduction, Abingdon: Routledge.

Manovich, Lev (2001): The Language of New Media, Cambridge, MA: MIT Press.

Manovich, Lev (2013): Software Takes Command, New York/London: Bloomsbury.

McGuigan, Jim (2014): "The Neoliberal Self." In: Journal of Current Cultural Research 6/1, pp. 223–40.

Merrill, Duane (2006): "Mashups: The New Breed of Web App." In: IBM Web Architecture Technical Library, (http://www.citeulike.org/user/CEAG/article/7359315).

Mosemghvdlishvili, Lela/Jansz, Jeroen (2013): "Negotiability of Technology and Its Limitations: The Politics of App Development." In: Information, Communication & Society, 16/10, pp. 1596–1618.

Napoli, Philip M. (2014): "On Automation in Media Industries: Integrating Algorithmic Media Production into Media Industries Scholarship." In: Media Industries Journal, 1/1, (http://www.mediaindustriesjournal.org/index.php/mij/article/view/14/60).

Nicolai, Thomas/Kirchhoff, Lars/Bruns, Axel/Wilson, Jason/Saunders, Barry (2009): "Google Yourself! Measuring the Performance of Personalized Information Resources." In: First Monday 14/12, doi:10.5210/fm.v14i12.2683.

Niederer, Sabine/van Dijck, José (2010): "Wisdom of the Crowd or Technicity of Content? Wikipedia as a Sociotechnical System." In: New Media & Society 12/8, pp. 1368–87.

Olsen, Timothy/Moser, Kathleen (2013): "Teaching Web APIs in Introductory and Programming Classes: Why and How." In: Proceedings of the SIG-ED: IAIM Conference. Association for Information Systems (AIS), (http://aisel.aisnet.org/siged2013/16).

Ricoeur, Paul (1992): Oneself as Another, Chicago: University of Chicago Press.

Robillard, Martin P./Deline, Robert (2011): "A Field Study of API Learning Obstacles." In: Empirical Software Engineering 16/6, pp. 703–32.

Schwartz, Matt (2010): "The Coupon Rebellion." In: Wired Magazine 18/12, pp. 188–193 & 224.

Sheridan, Thomas B./Vámos, Tibor/Aida, Shuhei (1983): "Adapting Automation to Man, Culture and Society." In: Automatica 19/6, pp. 605–12.

Sicart, Miguel (2014): Play Matters, Cambridge, MA: The MIT Press.

Siegert, Bernard (2013): "Cultural Techniques: Or the End of the Intellectual Postwar Era in German Media Theory." In: Theory, Cultur & Society 30/6, pp. 48–65.

Smock, Andrew D./Ellison, Nicole B./Lampe, Cliff/Wohn, Donghee Yvette (2011): "Facebook as a Toolkit: A Uses and Gratification Approach to Unbundling Feature Use." In: Computers in Human Behavior 27/6, pp. 2322–29.

Thompson, Clive (2002): "Dot-Columnist. Online Video Games Are the Newest Form of Social Comment." In: Slate, August 29, (http://www.slate.com/articles/technology/webhead/2002/08/dotcolumnist.html).

Ur, Blasé/Ho, Melwyn Pak Yong/Brawner, Stephen/Lee, Jiyun/Mennicken, Sarah/Picard, Noah/Schulze, Diane/Littman, Michael L. (2016): "Trigger-Action Programming in the Wild." In: Proceedings of the 2016 CHI Conference on Human Factors in Computing Systems – CHI '16, New York: ACM Press, pp. 3227–31.

Vallgårda, Anna/Fernaeus, Ylva (2015): "Interaction Design as a Bricolage Practice." In: Proceedings of the Ninth International Conference on Tangible, Embedded, and Embodied Interaction – TEI '14, New York: ACM Press, pp. 173–80.

Weltevrede, Esther/Helmond, Anne/Gerlitz, Carolin (2014): "The Politics of Real-Time: A Device Perspective on Social Media Platforms and Search Engines." Theory, Culture & Society 31/6, pp. 125–50.

Werning, Stefan (2016): "The Home Screen as an Anchor Point for Mobile Media Use – Technologies, Practices, Identities." In: NECSUS European Journal of Media Studies Autumn/Special Issue #Home, (http://necsus-ejms.org/the-home-screen-as-an-anchor-point-for-mobile-media-use-technologies-practices-identities/).

Yager, Susan E./Kappelman, Leon A./Maples, Glenn A./Prybutok, Victor R. (1997): "Microcomputer Playfulness: Stable or Dynamic Trait?" In: The DATA BASE for Advances in Information Systems 28, pp. 43–51.

Yee, Raymond (2008): Pro Web 2.0 Mashups: Remixing Data and Web Services, Berkeley, CA: Apress.

Yu, Shuli/Woodard, C. Jason (2009): "Innovation in the Programmable Web: Characterizing the Mashup Ecosystem." In: Service-Oriented Computing – ICSOC 2008 Workshops, Berlin, Heidelberg: Springer, pp. 136–47.

Entering the Field

Situating Hobby Drone Practices

Julia M. Hildebrand

Abstract

Consumer drones are entering everyday spaces with increasing frequency and impact as more and more hobbyists use the aerial tool for recreational photography and videography. In this article, I seek to expand the common reference to drones as "unmanned aircraft systems" by conceptualising the hobby drone practice more broadly as a heterogeneous, mobile assemblage of virtual and physical practices and human and non-human actors. Drawing on initial ethnographic fieldwork and interviews with drone hobbyists as well as ongoing cyber-ethnographic research on social networking sites, this article gives an overview of how the mobile drone practice needs to be situated alongside people, things, and data in physical and virtual spheres. As drone hobbyists set out to fly their devices at a given time and place, a number of relations reaching across atmospheric (e.g. weather conditions, daylight hours, GPS availability), geographic (e.g. volumetric obstacles), mobile (e.g. flight restrictions, ground traffic), and social (e.g. bystanders) dimensions demand attention. Furthermore, when drone operators share their aerial images online, visual (e.g. live stream) and cyber-social relations (e.g. comments, scrutiny) come into play, which may similarly impact the drone practice in terms of the pilot's performance. While drone hobbyists appear to be interested in keeping a "low profile" in the physical space, many pilots manage a comparatively "high profile" in the virtual sphere with respect to the sharing of their images. Since the recreational trend brings together elements of convergence, location-awareness, and real-time feedback, I suggest approaching consumer drones as, what Scott McQuire (2016) terms, "geomedia." Moreover, consumer drones open up different "cybermobilities" (Adey/Bevan 2006) understood as connected movement that flows through and shapes both physical and virtual spaces simultaneously. The way that many drone hobbyists appear to navigate these different environments, sometimes at the same time, has methodological implications for ethnographic research on consumer drones. Ultimately, the assemblage-perspective brings together aviation-related and socio-cultural concerns relevant in the context of consumer drones as digital communication technology and visual production tool.

DOI 10.14361/dcs-2017-0212
DCS | Digital Culture and Society | Vol. 3, Issue 2 | © transcript 2017

Situating Hobby Drone Practices

Consumer drones and their rapid rise in the domestic sphere over the past few years have been polarising individuals, communities, regulators, and governments by generating "equal parts of excitement, fascination and consternation" (Rabley 2015). Over 670.000 users registered their aerial vehicle in 2016, and the Federal Aviation Administration (FAA) estimates that as many as seven million consumer drones could be sold in the US by 2020 (Huerta 2017). Together, personal and artistic use appear to make up the largest non-violent drone user category in the US (Choi-Fitzpatrick et al. 2016). Popular recreational uses such as aerial photography, videography, and drone racing are predicted to continue to increase significantly over the next few years (Grand View Research, Inc. 2016). While numerous hobbyists feel empowered by this unprecedented access to the skies, skeptics are concerned about potential threats to privacy and physical safety "with the remote 'pilot' controllers having little or no aviation experience or exposure" (Bartsch et al. 2016: 2). The drastic proliferation of the trend and its potential socio-cultural implications suggest a need for a closer look at recreational drone practices.

In this article, I draw on my initial findings from ethnographic fieldwork with hobby drone photographers and videographers in the Philadelphia area, my virtual engagements with hobbyists on social networking sites, and eight interviews with consumer drone pilots based on the US East Coast. The aim is to better situate and interrelate people, things, and data in this mobile practice. Here, I seek to expand on the preferred reference of the FAA to drones as "unmanned aircraft systems." The term "system" encompasses both the unmanned aircraft and "associated elements (including communication links and the components that control the unmanned aircraft) that is required for the pilot in command to operate safely and efficiently in the national airspace system" ("Drone Operation and Certification Regulations – 14 CFR 107" 2016). Moving beyond the aviation lingo and the term "system" suggesting a somewhat static and closed-off network between ground control station, operator, drone, and other equipment, I suggest conceptualising the recreational drone practice more broadly as a mobile assemblage of physical and virtual movements and human and non-human actors. This assemblage-perspective allows for the consideration of many heterogeneous relations and mobile connections between the drone and its surrounding which extends into the digital sphere. Since the aerial device is merged with the communicative affordances of high-definition cameras and streaming capabilities as manifested in the thousands of aerial still and moving images that are regularly uploaded onto the Internet, the recreational trend needs assessment from a social-scientific perspective considering digital visual culture. In the following, I will first discuss what the empirical data have thus far revealed about the spatial situating of the drone practice before moving onto its cyber-spatial situating. While the term "cyberspace" has become somewhat outdated by now, it is helpful for putting the sometimes overlapping physical and virtual activities of hobby pilots into relation, as will be shown.

Spatial Situating of the Drone Practice

Having joined hobby pilots for flight sessions on several occasions now, the complex spatial relations between the "aerial system" and the respective setting become clear. Ranging from atmospheric and geographic to mobile and social relations, all of these conditions play a role in whether and how hobbyists can fly their devices at a given time and place.

The atmospheric relations, for instance, include weather conditions, sunlight hours, and satellite availability. Weather plays a major role in the outdoor drone activity as the equipment is generally not water-proof and thus unsuitable for rain. Moreover, strong winds may overpower the smaller quadcopter models and thus present possibly dangerous flying conditions. More generally, the FAA warns recreational pilots not to fly during times of "reduced visibility" ("Recreational Users | Know Before You Fly" 2017). Another pertinent atmospheric dimension is satellite availability for the GPS signal. The advancement and availability of Global Positioning Systems count as a driving factor for the explosion of drone innovation next to improvements in battery technology, and lightweight cameras, along with the integration of multiple sophisticated sensors (Bartsch et al. 2016). One drone hobbyist shows me his "drone" smartphone folder with five apps that he consults before launching his drone [Figure 1]. Apart from four other drone-specific apps that display weather conditions, sunrise and sunset hours, or no-fly-zones, he uses Solar Sphere to check on the possibility of solar flares having generated geomagnetic storms. Such storms could affect satellites which would then introduce GPS errors for the drone along with other disturbances. The complex and far-reaching interrelations that the consumer drone practice is entangled in come to light.

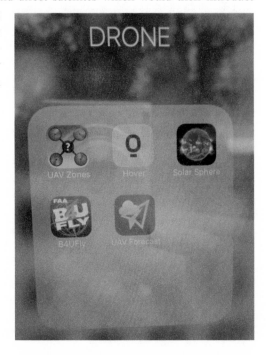

Figure 1: The smartphone folder titled "Drone" of this recreational pilot includes the mobile apps UAV Zones, Hover, Solar Sphere, B4UFLY, and UAV Forecast (foto credit: Julia M. Hildebrand).

By geographic relations I refer to any volumetric obstacle that could potentially interfere in the flight path of the drone along with the texture of the ground suitable for lift-off and landing. The list includes tall architecture, trees, power lines, fences, and so forth. The FAA, furthermore, requires operators to "not fly near or over sensitive infrastructure of property such as power stations, water treatment facilities, correctional facilities, heavily traveled roadways, government facilities, etc." ("Recreational Users | Know Before You Fly" 2017). When I meet Ahmed, a drone hobbyist in his twenties, one Sunday afternoon, the task to find a safe place to fly becomes quite a challenge.[1] An Ultimate Frisbee game is taking place on the open field that we had originally picked, so we continue to search for a suitable space. "Half the time is finding a place to fly," mentions Ahmed as he dismisses another location because of some power lines and a big antenna. While the device's obstacle recognition and collision avoidance systems may prevent crashes into such volumetric obstacles, Ahmed prefers a wide open space with less navigational challenges.

Apart from the atmospheric and geographic relations, the assemblage of the hobby drone practice is deeply embedded in mobile relations. Those relations can be of regulatory or observational nature. Consumer drones cannot fly anywhere at any height. Besides the FAA's rule for consumer drones to operate under 400 feet, the pilots also need to respect controlled airspace and flight restrictions. The FAA adopted classes A, B, C, D, E, and G to its national airspace and requires drone pilots to either stay away from classes B to D or notify Air Traffic Control prior to flight. While class A starts 18.000 feet above Mean Sea Level and is thus prohibited for recreational drone pilots, class G counts as the "good-to-go" uncontrolled airspace. Again several apps, such as Airmap, Skyvector, and the FAA's own B4UFLY can help drone hobbyist determine the respective airspace delineations [images 2 and 3]. Moreover, the apps also inform of any temporary flight restrictions which may be put into effect due to "a temporary hazardous condition, such as a wildfire or chemical spill; a security-related event, [...]; or other special situations" ("Airspace Restrictions" 2017).

Beyond these regulatory relations in the drone practice, several other dimensions potentially restricting mobility that are more of observational nature surface. When tracing Ahmed's DJI Mavic Pro drone in the sky on that partially cloudy afternoon [Figure 4], I am surprised by the amount of 'aerial traffic' occurring throughout the session. Apart from passenger planes visible in the far distance, a news helicopter passes well above us, several other quadcopters fly by, and a handful of model aircrafts close by are ready to take off once Ahmed's last Mavic Pro battery has run out. Moreover, a ball and a Frisbee occasionally enter the lower parts of the aerial space similarly posing a potential crash threat. All the while, Ahmed is cautious of the movements around him and the drone, his gaze moving back and forth between the screen on his controller and the drone in the

---

1   All names have been changed to protect the individuals' identities.

Figure 2: AirMap – an application for planning flight sessions. (screenshot)

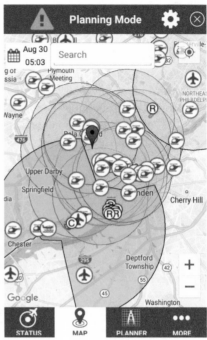

Figure 3: The B4UFLY smartphone app was released by the Federal Aviation Administration. (screenshot)

Figure 4: The DJI Mavic Pro hovering in the sky (foto credit: Julia M. Hildebrand).

sky. On another occasion, Terrence is flying his DJI Mavic Pro quadcopter and a pair of birds starts to circle around the device. "The Mavic has sparked their interest" observes Ahmed standing next to him and recounts how frequently birds get attracted by his own model. Not sure about what the birds will do, Terrence decides to land his drone. These examples illuminate the variety of human and non-human actors necessary to consider in the mobile assemblage of hobby drone practices. Finally, the mobile traffic on the ground needs to be acknowledged. The FAA states, "Do not intentionally fly over unprotected persons or moving vehicles," ("Recreational Users | Know Before You Fly" 2017). Following those guidelines, the pilots I observed made efforts to not fly too close or above busy streets, vehicles, and pedestrians.

Moreover, the photographers and videographers were careful to respect other people's privacy in light of the social relations the drone assemblage includes. While the majority of interviewees thus far reported positive encounters with bystanders who are mainly curious about the trend, a few pilots also mentioned being met with skepticism and distrust as to their intentions. "Peeping Tom"-privacy concerns are brought up in the discourse surrounding the flying camera (Bartsch et al. 2016). Another complaint relates to the drones' noise as a nuisance in public space (Custers 2016). Such perceptions may then shape pilot behaviour regarding flight time, direction, height, distance, speed, and how the camera is operated around bystanders. Ahmed tells me how "people can get really pissed" sometimes about drones. He, consequently, tries to stay out of the way and "keep a low profile" with his flight manoeuvres as much as he can. Besides safety, respect towards others by keeping the small aircraft and camera at a distance is a priority. The position and location of the pilot is relevant, too, as approaching bystanders may pose a distraction to the operation. Hence, several of the pilots I accompanied preferred secluded locations for launching, flying, and landing the drone. The potential agency of others, hence, influences the agency of the pilot. An interviewee in her sixties mentions that she even adjusts her flight times according to the presence of others among other things: "I am a real early-in-the-morning flyer because I don't like to bother people and I like the light in the morning. I am sensitive to people wanting quiet etc., so you have to be a good neighbour. I always talk about the golden rule of droning: Drone unto others as you would want others to drone unto you." The social relations and agency of others are thus another influential component in the assemblage of the hobby drone practice.

Cyber-spatial Situating of the Drone Practice

Next to a spatial situating of the drone practice, a more comprehensive view of the trend also includes its situating in the online environment. In particular, the visual and what I refer to as 'cyber-social' relations on the Internet can be influential in the mobile assemblage when hobbyists choose to showcase their drone-generated imagery online. After the aerial shots have been collected, numerous hobby pilots upload their – frequently edited – creations online. The drastic increase in civilian drone use and the respective image production has resulted in the creation and growth of multiple online archives thematically or geographically organizing thousands of drone-generated photos and videos. Besides Instagram storing several thousand aerial images under hashtags such as #dronevideo or #dronefly and YouTube hosting several drone-specific channels, such as Drone-dOut, Epic Drone Videos, and Drone Compilations, several platforms exists exclusively for sharing amateur and professional still and moving images by consumer drones, such as Dronestagram, Travel By Drone, Skypixel, and Dronetrotter [images 5 and 6].

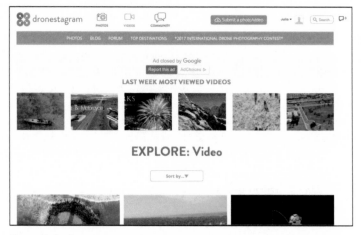

Figure 5: On Dronestagram drone pilots can upload, tag, and share their aerial pictures and videos. (screenshot)

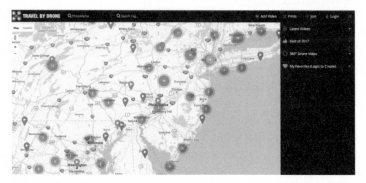

Figure 6: Travel By Drone features drone-generated images based on geo-location. (screenshot)

Next to this 'delayed' sharing of aerial views, some drone pilots have the option to live-stream their footage onto Facebook for instance. The Chinese drone manufacturer and market leader DJI integrated a few live broadcast platforms, such as Facebook Live, into its Go mobile app, which functions as the control interface between device, camera, and controller. This feature allows live-streaming onto Facebook from the DJI Phantom 4 and later models. With the options to share the imagery publicly, to friends only, or privately, the pilot thus provides live footage of the respective time and place. Particularly through this function, I learn that my drone ethnography can and needs to occur both offline and online. One afternoon, one of the drone pilots and I are unable to meet up. By coincidence, I later see that he is live with his drone video on Facebook and I am able to virtually 'participate' in his drone practice. The aerial visuals of suburban rooftops in the soft afternoon sunlight are combined with the sound of breathing and quiet mumbling: The video feed of the drone camera is linked to the audio feed of the smartphone, which he is using as the controller screen. The audio transmission is 'on' by default and allows pilots to communicate directly with their live audience (provided they are aware of this default setting). At least one of my interviewees is making active use of this functionality, creating live drone diaries about what he is recording and why. Moreover, audience members can comment on the feed, which will show on the pilot's screen and allow for reciprocity (Goldman 2016). This virtual interactive component which happens simultaneously to the flying and recording may likewise influence the respective drone practice. When pilot Diego goes live with his drone on Facebook for three minutes, several spectators comment in real-time below the video ("It's cloudy tonight," "That's where I live"). During the footage, Diego is audible saying to his companion "I just went live on Facebook and everyone is lovin' it, bro." His comment indicates his awareness of and even attention to the Facebook audience responses while operating the drone. In another live-stream with seemingly no physical companion, he directly addresses his virtual spectators by explaining "And this is my little town where I live" along with highlighting certain landmarks his drone passes. The drone practice and specifically the pilot's performance thus have the potential to be shaped by the presence of virtual bystanders and their comments. Opportunities for influential interplay of virtual and physical components surface in the consideration of the (audio)-visual and communicative relations in the drone assemblage and its reaching into the digital sphere.

These findings fall under the category of cyber-social relations in the hobby drone assemblage more generally. As aforementioned, when pilots share their aerial images on personal websites, social networking profiles, and drone-specific groups, their creations generate comments, feedback, and scrutiny. Consumer drones have made the sky accessible to hobbyists in new ways. The visuals obtained are insightful and often breathtaking. Sharing those images with the respective cyber-social networks functions as another way to make those vistas available to a wider audience. In the drone-specific groups I follow, members convey respect and admiration to the producers of the shots. Similarly, problematic drone practice is identified and discussed, such as flying too close to architecture, over people or traffic, at night, and so forth. In at least one case, a drone pilot was arrested after Internet users reported serious misconduct in the video of a plane landing (McKirdy/Wang 2017). Two main conclusions can be drawn from those observations: First, next to the suggested "low profile" that operators seek in the physical space of the hobby drone practice, many pilots appear to manage a "high profile" in the virtual sphere with respect to the real-time or delayed sharing of their images. A pilot's desire for the hobby's visibility can thus significantly differ in offline and online environments. This move could also be viewed as a risk-and-return-process towards higher social capital in the larger context of contemporary digital culture. Second, the cyber-social relations, similar to the social relations, can function as a modifying force to the drone practice as the simultaneous or subsequent feedback of others may influence the pilot's conduct.

Geomedia and Cybermobilities

In the endeavour to understand contemporary consumer drone practices as a mobile assemblage of physical and virtual movements and human and non-human actors, two concepts are theoretically relevant: Scott McQuire's (2016) "geomedia" and Peter Adey and Paul Bevan's' (2006) "cybermobilities." The two frameworks help consider the complex workings of consumer drones and their recreational uses in the sense that drone systems function as geomedia and enable different cybermobilities. "Geomedia is a concept that crystallizes at the intersection of four related trajectories: convergence, ubiquity, location-awareness and real-time feedback" (McQuire 2016: 2). The initial findings of the hobby practices bring to light how consumer drones lie at this intersection of the four trajectories. First, convergence applies as different media merge in the drone assemblage (e.g. drone video and pilot audio in the live-stream). Location-awareness is relevant regarding the close attention pilots need to pay to atmospheric, geographic, mobile, and social relations for a safe practice in the physical space. The relevance of real-time feedback surfaces in the multiple signals, sensors, and connections between drone and pilot as well as the Internet. McQuire (2016: 4–5) also speaks of "novel experiences of social simultaneity" and "new forms of recursive communication and coordination between the diverse actors even as events unfold," which suitably describe the interactive drone live-stream. The concept of ubiquity of consumer drones as geomedia, lastly, may become increasingly relevant with the proliferation of consumer drones and the respective analog and digital infrastructures. McQuire clarifies further that "It is this paradoxical conjunction of connection and disconnection – of placement and displacement, of the articulation or jointing of the local and global, of media and immediacy – that I am wanting to grasp with the concept of geomedia" (2016: 6). As consumer drones span spatial and cyber-spatial relations, they exemplify such paradoxical conjunctions in a mobile assemblage.

The concept of "cybermobilities" helps describe the "connected movement that inhabits and inscribes both virtual and physical space simultaneously" (Adey/ Bevan 2006: 57). The hobby drone practice is defined by multiple mobilities and immobilities ranging from the agile flight of the drone and comparative stillness of the pilot, to movement of signals and data between a multitude of human and non-human communicators in physical and virtual spheres. The term "cybermobilities" helps illuminate the multiplicity of spatial and cyber-spatial movements with different atmospheric, geographic, mobile, social, visual, and cyber-social relations which shape the drone assemblage. Physical "low profiles" and virtual "high profiles" of pilots suggest that the "connected movement" that "inhabits and inscribes both virtual and physical space simultaneously" can be influenced by contrasting forces since pilots, physical bystanders, and virtual audiences may have distinct interests regarding the drone practice. The way many drone hobbyists navigate offline and online environments, sometimes simultaneously, also has methodological implications for ethnographic research on the trend. Its study thus far required a similarly mobile assemblage of physical and virtual modes of analysis. Next to the physical "co-present immersion" (Laurier 2002) in which "the researcher moves within modes of movement and employs a range of observation and recording techniques" (Urry 2007: 40), I have been complementing the fieldwork with a virtual, if not 'cyber-mobile' co-presence through what may be termed Facebook-Live drone cyber-ethnography.

Summary

Since the ethnographic work on the practices of drone hobbyists is still in its early stages, this article needs to be viewed as an initial analytical assessment with more research left to be done. The main initial finding is that a more holistic understanding of the "unmanned aircraft system" and its contemporary recreational uses should include the critical consideration of the heterogeneous relations that merge aviation with visual and digital culture. To the ethnographic eye, the hobby drone practice presents itself as a mobile assemblage of physical and virtual movements as well as human and non-human actors. In the spatial situating of the hobby drone practice, I pointed to relevant atmospheric, geographic, mobile, and social relations. In the cyber-spatial situating of the hobby drone practice, I briefly discussed noteworthy (audio)-visual and cyber-social relations. Consumer drones can thus be approached as "geomedia" (McQuire 2016) particularly regarding their convergence with other media formats, location-awareness, and real-time feedback functionalities. Moreover, consumer drones enable "cybermobilities" (Adey/ Bevan 2006) constitutive for the hobby drone practice, with different performative qualities in offline and online environments. These two theoretical frameworks help illuminate the processes of mediation and movement that the physical and virtual consumer drone practice opens up. Ultimately, the assemblage-approach to consumer drones as geomedia affording cybermobilities brings together aviation-related and socio-cultural concerns relevant in the context of consumer drones as digital communication technology and visual production tool.

Acknowledgements

I thank the participants of the Communication, Culture, and Media Graduate Conference 2017 at Drexel University for their helpful comments on a presentation of this work.

References

Adey, Peter/Bevan, Paul (2006): "Between the Physical and the Virtual: Connected Mobilities?" In: John Urry/Mimi Sheller (eds.), Mobile Technologies of the City, London, New York: Routledge, pp. 44–60.

"Airspace Restrictions", (https://www.faa.gov/uas/where_to_fly/airspace_restrictions/).

Bartsch, Ron/Coyne, James/Gray, Katherine (2016): Drones in Society: Exploring the Strange New World of Unmanned Aircraft, London, New York: Routledge.

Choi-Fitzpatrick, Austin/Chavarria, Dana/Cychosz, Elizabeth/Dingens, John Paul/ Duffey, Michael/Koebel, Katherine/Siriphanh, Sirisack/Tulen, Merlyn Yurika/ Watanabe, Heath/Juskauskas, Tautvydas/Holland John/Almquist, Lars (2016): Up in the Air: A Global Estimate of Non-Violent Drone Use 2009–2015 (http:// digital.sandiego.edu/cgi/viewcontent.cgi?article=1000&context=gdl2016report).

Custers, Bart (ed.) (2016): "Drones Here, There and Everywhere Introduction and Overview." In: The Future of Drone Use, The Hague: T.M.C. Asser Press, pp. 3–20.

"Drone Operation and Certification Regulations – 14 CFR 107", June 21, 2016 (http://usdronelaw.com/the-law/operation-and-certification-laws/drone-operation-and-certification-regulations-14-cfr-107/).

Goldman, Joshua (2016): "This Is What It's like to Live Stream from a DJI Drone to Facebook." In: CNET May 24 (https://www.cnet.com/news/dji-drones-now-let-you-facebook-live-from-the-sky/).

Grand View Research, Inc. (2016): "Consumer Drone Market Size to Reach $4.19 Billion by 2024: Grand View Research, Inc." In: PR Newswire May 10 (http:// www.prnewswire.com/news-releases/consumer-drone-market-size-to-reach-419-billion-by-2024-grand-view-research-inc-578762831.html).

Huerta, Michael (2017): "Speech – 'Drones: A Story of Revolution and Evolution'", Federal Aviation Administration (https://www.faa.gov/news/speeches/news_story.cfm?newsId=21316).

Laurier, Eric (2002): "Notes on Dividing the Attention of a Car Driver." In: Team Ethno Online (http://www.teamethno-online.org.uk).

McKirdy, Euan/Wang, Serenitie (2017): "Drone Operator Detained for Flying near Plane in China." In: CNN January 17 (http://www.cnn.com/2017/01/17/asia/china-drone-passenger-plane-near-miss/index.html).

McQuire, Scott (2016): Geomedia: Networked Cities and the Future of Public Space, Cambridge: Polity.

Rabley, Peter (2015): "Foreword." In: Drones and Aerial Observation: New Technologies for Property Rights, Human Rights, and Global Development – A Primer (http://drones.newamerica.org/primer/01-Primer-Foreword.pdf).

"Recreational Users | Know Before You Fly", 2017 (http://knowbeforeyoufly.org/for-recreational-users/).

Urry, John (2007): Mobilities, Malden: Polity.

The Inchoate Field of Digital Offline
A Reflection on Studying Mobile Media Practices of Digital Subalterns in India

Rashmi M.

Abstract

This article reflects on studying mobile phones as digital technologies, while much of the scholarly preoccupation thus far has been to study them as communication technologies. Based on the doctoral study on subaltern users and their mobile media digital practices in India, it discusses some of the theoretical issues and outlines methodological possibilities while entering the field. It makes distinction between the theoretical orientations of techno-sociality and sociality of technology, and highlights the significance of adopting the latter to study new socialities that are emerging due to human interaction with technology. It discusses some challenges of doing qualitative research in new media contexts and suggests measures for overcoming them. In this regard, it reviews the suitability of virtual ethnography and participant observation as methodological approaches to mobile phones. While the popular trend has been to resort to technologised tools of data collection and processing (even within qualitative research in new media and digital technologies) this article suggests and discusses the usefulness of a more basic, yet powerful method of long interview to study users and document their practices. It concludes how such a choice can also be regardful of some ethical issues involved in studying user practices on mobile phones.

Introduction

Mobile phones have become such an integral part of our lives that it is hard to imagine a life without them. Since their inception, mobile phones have not just been phones. Even the most basic feature phones came with options for storing contact numbers, clock, calendar, games, etc. A glimpse at the technological history of mobile phones tells us that they were always modelled along the lines of personal digital assistants and were meant for uses other than communication. Parallel advances in telecommunication technology made it possible to access the Internet through phones. Improvements and innovations in data storage technologies further augmented their capacity. Data sharing protocols such as Bluetooth

DOI 10.14361/dcs-2017-0213

allowed users to transfer files among devices. Most of us remember Nokia phones which created a rage in the market in their heyday by incorporating entertainment features. Phones replaced walkmans as technologies of mobile listening (O'Hara and Brown 2006; Goggin 2006). FM radio was very much part of the basic feature phone even from its very early days. Soon, video technologies were integrated into phones. Simultaneous innovations in the domain of computing united the analogue world through the process of digitisation. Phones today stand for a whole media infrastructure through which the digital (including the virtual) universe on the web can be accessed. Their affordability and slightly easier interface compared to computers make them the most popular among users, especially among the less educated masses who have limited technological access. Smartphone technology has thrived and has seen exuberant growth in the recent years. It is no wonder they are touted as the future of digital technology. One device offering so much makes scholars studying media forms wonder if the term 'phone' is just a misnomer for this technological complex, opening up multiple avenues for theoretical pursuit.

My doctoral study in the city of Bangalore in India starts with such a consideration of mobile phones as a digital media complex and infrastructure that have ushered in not only a communication revolution (Jeffrey and Doron 2013) but also a digital revolution. More than 70 per cent of Indian users have discovered and entered the digital frontier through mobile phone interfaces. The diffusion and spread of this technology has been unprecedented in the Indian media context. Mobile phones have completely changed the socio dynamics of access to digital technologies in India. A majority of users, especially those coming from the marginal sections of the population have not had any exposure to computers and other digital technologies. Feature phones which are available in the range of 1000 to 2000 rupees (approximately twenty dollars) are still popular with users, especially with the less educated and the marginalised sections. The market for used smart phones is also very large and it caters to the marginalised users. This article reflects on studying such mobile phone users and their media practices in Bangalore, outlines methodological challenges, and discusses possibilities for such a study.

Studying mobile media practices of digital subalterns

Of late, mobile phones have received exclusive attention from media scholars. Phone and communication studies (see edited volume by Katz 2008) are slowly gaining traction as a separate branch within media studies. Goggin (2011) suggests that we treat mobile phones as a separate medium altogether. Although I do not entirely subscribe to the notion of mobile phones as a separate medium and only consider them as extensions of "the digital", I acknowledge the importance of noticing the difference between mobile phones and other computing technologies. As scholarship on mobile phones gradually gains prominence, there is more than ever a need to think about methodological strategies that suit phones, not just as communication technologies but also as digital technologies. The available literature does not shed enough light on methodological approaches that can be adopted to study mobile phones and the practices specific to them, especially with regard to qualitative research.

Two distinct trends are noticeable with respect to qualitative research within media studies on digital technologies. The methods scholars adopt are also very predictable following these trends. The studies that focus on people and societal aspects often resort to ethnographic methods, and those which theorise about the medium and its nature take philosophical and interpretative approaches (Hiller 2015). Christine Hine (2000), Wilson and Peterson (2002), Gabriella Coleman (2010) have reviewed the studies that have adopted ethnographic approaches to virtual communities. Studies reviewed by them either look at digital technologies in association with well-defined groups or communities or look at new communities formed around technological use such as geeks, hackers, etc. Even though they address the technological aspects specific to such communities; elaborate on the method of online or virtual ethnography; indicate ways to study technological structures and objects within them, it takes an encounter with the field one wants to study to see how methodologically inadequate one feels to tackle the complexity of the phenomenon of technological use. Often ethnographic methods (even the updated ones that suit new technological environments) are not enough to capture the inchoate, yet patterned practices, especially when they are not contained on an online platform such as Facebook or YouTube. Platforms structure practices in specific ways and the structure itself makes it easier to navigate them during study. However, methods useful on online platforms are not always suitable for offline practices. My research work in Bangalore engages with the much neglected domain of digital offline and the practices that are prevalent there.

I document and study media practices of users I call "digital subalterns" for my doctoral research. My fieldwork in Bangalore involves working with taxi drivers, auto rickshaw drivers, security guards, vegetable vendors and other low end informal sector urban working populations. Many such users are not connected to the Internet all the time. Their phone use is mostly offline.[1] Among

---

1   This is slowly changing due to new schemes introduced by telecom service providers in India. Recently, most telecom service providers have been providing data packages up to a GB per day. Reliance (one of the prominent telecom service providers) introduced Jio, the cheapest telecom network which forced other players in the market to slash down data service charges. Now most service providers offer up to 1 GB data download per day on 3G and 4G network subscriptions. This has automatically increased users' presence online. However, many users consume a lot of already downloaded media content (especially full length regional feature films) due to network interruptions and data download limits on their subscriptions.

many of their activities on phones, multimedia consumption is the most popular. Audio and video consumption via phones is integral to their mode of work which is interspersed with long stretches of waiting and idle time (Rashmi M. 2017). It occupies their empty time. They engage in an entire spectrum of offline practices such as using phones as group devices, sharing media content via Bluetooth and other sharing protocols, exchanging and swapping memory cards loaded with films, procuring media content through small mobile phone shops that offer currency and repair services (unauthorised distribution of media content by side-loading onto memory cards and pen drives etc.). All these practices merit documentation and study as they have a huge influence on both telecommunication and content industries in India. Moreover, the academic discourse is slightly skewed towards those users who are savvy with technology and have means, skills and literacy to participate fully in the new media environment. My research on the digital subalterns in Bangalore is a small attempt to balance this pervasive trend.

Image 1: A typical mobile phones shop frequented by subaltern users for buying currency and media content.

Theoretical and methodological challenges of studying digital offline

A user's interaction with the phone is private and not readily available for observation, especially so when it is offline and steeped in extra legality, as in the case of the subaltern users in India. The interaction is also social in terms of interactivity and commonality among users. The time-tested and classic ethnographic methods, which are otherwise ideal for studying groups and their practices, are not suitable for this context. There is a dearth of studies which look at digital offline, hence very few examples to emulate. Additionally, there is an ethical obligation to respect the privacy of users. The chances for immersive ethnography and observation are very thin in such field contexts. A common strategy (one that is usually practised) to overcome this lack in qualitative methods is to technologise the method itself and resort to computerised tools of data collection and processing. It works if one is working within the framework of a particular platform, governed by algorithmic processes. Coding and designing programmes to extract data may make a researcher's job easier in such instances.[2] However, they may not be of much help if one were to encounter a field of offline technological practices which are so inchoate that they cannot be contained within platforms or algorithmic frames. One has to improvise methods to study practices that are platform independent.

Another aspect that requires attention is the temporality of media practices based on use. Observing the trend within digital media technologies, it is noticeable that the initial adoption and use have received more attention than later uses. It is not just initial use, but also initial users, who thus catch our attention. We often presume that the users and use of the medium will more or less remain the same. We, therefore, give very little attention to what happens to a medium when embraced by larger masses and different kinds of users. The later adoptions of a technology may not be similar to its initial ones. And the use might significantly vary across groups of users, especially so in the case of a versatile medium of digital technologies. Although, there are studies which discuss media use among different groups of users making distinctions based on age, gender and nationality (which are identity based distinctions), the existent literature rarely mentions later uses of the technology as it gets diffused. Such considerations of time will enrich our accounts of media use, and also show how innovations and developments over time are responses to several ways in which different kinds of users adopt the medium to their needs. In this regard, I identify two kinds of approaches within media theory that study technological change – techno-sociality and the sociality of technology.

Techno-sociality

The studies which discuss social change instituted by technological innovation are mostly influenced by the orientation that medium theory propounds. The theoretical focus within medium focused theories has ascribed unbridled power to technology and has made it determine human condition (for example, Kittler 1999). Clearly, technological innovations bring social change. But how we concep-

---

2   Richard Rogers through Digital Methods Initiative (DMI) advocates the need for such tools and programmes to study objects and practices native to digital medium.

tualise this change has a huge impact on the theories we end up with. For instance, if technology is treated as an external force acting upon the social structures and changing it, rather than as a force emerging from within the social, it is likely we end up with a technologically deterministic medium theory. Medium focused theories within media studies have always discussed change from a purely technological point of view, and have mostly neglected the people who define use for those technologies. Nick Couldry (2012) comments on this trend within media theory and advocates a socially oriented theory which will visibilise people behind it, instead of considering a medium as an abstract force acting on a pre-existing social structure.

I understand the early spate of studies as assessing the impact of digital media forms on "the pre-defined social". Such studies highlighted the ruptures caused by the entry of a new technology on community, nation, race, gender, etc. Some of these studies have been compiled in the four volumes edited by David Bell (2006). In an earlier work, Bell (2001) inaugurates the trend of doing cyberculture studies. These studies examine change at the intersection of society and technology. Scholars in this line of research investigated changes which were *caused* by technological innovations.

While it is useful to register these developments, our understanding of change can do better if we were to examine it not in a unidirectional mode of technology acting on social forms, but as change resulting from social use of a particular technology. This, I understand as the major difference between the orientations I differentiate as techno-sociality and sociality of technology. There is a need for a sociological focus which balances out technologisation with the humanisation of media experience. In this article I try to articulate what it is to map the sociality of technology.

Sociality of technology

Working with the awareness that technology, regardless of its novelty, is already embedded within the social helps us see – how at each moment of its life in the world, a media technology gets defined and redefined by uses various users put it into. A medium is thus defined by its use. That use is neither constant nor singular, but always plural and changing. Such an orientation will help us see different kinds of users who define the medium by their use (which does not necessarily match the intended uses at the time of technological innovation). As important as it is to study the use, it is equally essential to study the different kinds of users, know their life contexts and needs and then understand why they use the technologies they chance upon in specific ways. Mapping such diversity across time and groups will help us draw the sociality of a medium. There are no predetermined uses for a technology, neither are there one set of users. It is possible to distinguish users not just based on their social and biological identity, but also by the ways in which they use technology. Such a use-based distinction of users can be one of the important steps towards tracing different and new socialities constituted by the medium.

Recent studies in Science and Technology Studies (STS) and anthropology of science and technology are useful pointers to articulate what a study of sociality of technology would entail. Bruno Latour's idea of actor network theory (2005) provides some useful suggestions in this regard. Following Latour and his proposition of the social as a domain inclusive of the material (the world of objects hitherto classified as non-social), the separate treatment of the technological divorced from the social is very problematic. Such an approach has wide ranging implications for media theory. It becomes possible to conceptualise the social and the technological as co-constitutive domains and not fall into the trap of either kind of over-determinism. Media practices associated with use thus become objects and focus of research, as they are useful entry points to map the sociality instituted by a new technology. Studying practices also serves another purpose – they show how social use shapes the course of technology in concrete ways.

Long-interview method

Keeping in mind the theoretical and methodological issues discussed above, I argue that the method of the long interview (McCracken 1988) is suitable to study mobile media practices of the digital offline. Long interview method as propounded by McCracken (1988) is conceptualised as a substitute to immersive ethnographic interviews. It can generate the rich qualitative data that methods such as participant observation can do. Since it is stretched over time and can be done in multiple sittings, it allows the interviewer to establish a rapport with the interviewee (like in ethnographic interviews), while at the same time being "less intrusive". Through this method, it is possible to construct the life worlds of interviewees and look for categories specific to a culture. In this method, the interviewer lets the interviewee speak at length around the topic of research. It also has advantages over guided questionnaire, as it puts the interviewee at ease and allows the gradual unfolding of narratives on the topic.

I asked users to speak about phones in their lives, the uses they put them into and the activities they engage in while using phones. I analysed the documented narratives to understand the nature and use of the medium. As a method, it was less intrusive, more ethical and transparent than the technologised tools to document and study human interaction, especially with private and personal media technologies such as mobile phones. Users who were uncomfortable sharing details of their activities on phones such as consumption of pornographic material, gradually revealed details when they were generally encouraged to speak on their daily activities. Such details were mentioned casually during conversations, but users I interviewed went quiet if I asked further probing questions. Not asking direct questions about certain questionable practices immensely helped me to understand the private interaction of users with phones and trace the distinct aspects of networks through which they sourced and circulated media content. Knowing about their social situation (extracted from the details they shared about their employment, income, neighbourhoods they lived in, villages and towns they migrated from) helped me construct their life world and situate their media use in the larger urban circumstance.

Long interview method is very conducive to study platform independent offline interaction of users with their phones, as users themselves report what they do. It is important to note that digital traces left offline are not as easily accessible as they are online. The only way to access them is by examining users' phones (which users will be highly uncomfortable sharing) which might sabotage the opportunities for research. In such circumstances, the most ethical way to access this rich pool of offline practices is only when users willingly and consciously part with that information. Although laborious and time consuming, the long interview method is the most effective and ethical of methods to bring out the sociality of technology: as it is easier to cull out the life context, mental universe and specific practices of users from interview narratives.

Conclusion

In this essay, I highlight the importance of studying mobile phones as a digital technology, especially among subaltern users who are not usually the focus of academic discourse on media technologies. I emphasise the importance of inchoate digital offline practices in relation to such users. I argue that the long interview method can be a very effective qualitative research method in capturing the materiality as well as the sociality of user interaction with phones, even though it appears simple. Letting users themselves speak about the technologies they use makes it possible to extract material aspects of the medium in ways that are not possible through a strict technical understanding of the medium or through data extraction tools. In fact, complementing user narratives with technical understanding through secondary sources produces data sets that give unique perspective into media use as practiced on the ground. Market data of media use also can be another valuable resource in this regard. It allows one to historically track the evolution of technology in response to media use.

Acknowledgements

This article is based on my doctoral study at National Institute of Advanced Studies (NIAS), Bangalore. I thank Sarai Programme, CSDS for a generous fieldwork grant and guidance. I am particularly grateful to my advisor Prof. Carol Upadhya for introducing me to the world of Anthropology and teaching me solid fieldwork methods. Many of the ideas in this article are inspired by my conversation with her over the last five years.

References

Bell, David (2001): An Introduction to Cybercultures, London: Routledge.

Bell, David (ed.) (2006): Cybercultures: Critical Concepts in Media and Cultural Studies, Volumes 1–4, London and New York: Routledge.

Coleman, Gabriella (2010): "Ethnographic Approaches to Digital Media." In: Annual Review of Anthropology 39, pp. 1–16.

Couldry, Nick (2012): Media, Society, World: Social Theory and Digital Media Practice, Cambridge: Polity Press.

Goggin, Gerard (2006): Cellphone Culture: Mobile Technology in Everyday Life, London and New York: Routledge.

Goggin, Gerard (2011): Global Mobile Media, New York: Routledge.

Hiller, Moritz (2015): "Signs O' the Times: The Software of Philology and a Philology of Software." In: Digital Culture and Society 1/1, pp. 151–163.

Hine, Christine (2000): Virtual Ethnography, New Delhi: Sage Publications.

Jeffrey, Robin/Doron, Assa (2013): Cell Phone Nation, Delhi: Hachette India.

Katz, James (ed.) (2008): Handbook of Mobile Communication Studies, Cambridge: MIT Press.

Kittler, Friedrich (1999): Gramophone, Film, Typewriter, Stanford: Stanford University Press.

Latour, Bruno (2005): Reassembling the Social: An Introduction to Actor-Network-Theory, Oxford: Oxford University Press.

McCracken, Grant (1988): The Long Interview, New Delhi: Sage Publications.

O'Hara, Kenton/Brown, Barry (eds.) (2006): Consuming Music Together Social and Collaborative Aspects of Music Consumption Technologies, Dordrecht: Springer.

Rashmi M. (2017): "The Digital Others." In: Seminar 694, pp. 40–43.

Wilson, Samuel/Peterson, Leighton (2002): "The Anthropology of Online Communities." In: Annual Review of Anthropology 31, pp. 449–467.

Mad Practices and Mobilities
Bringing Voices to Digital Ethnography

Cherry Baylosis

Abstract

There is a claim that digital media technologies can give voice to the voiceless (Alper 2017). As Couldry (2008) points out it is now commonplace for people – who have never done so before – to tell, share and exchange stories within, and through digital media. Additionally, the affordances of mobile media technologies allow people to speak, virtually anytime and anywhere, while the new internet based media sees that these processes converge to allow stories, information, ideas and discourses to circulate through communicative spaces, and into the daily lives of people (Sheller/Urry 2006). The purpose of this paper is to discuss a methodological framework that can be used to examine the extent that digital media practices can enable voice. My focus is on people ascribed the status of mental illness – people who have had an enduring history of silencing and oppression (Parr 2008). I propose theories of mobilities, and practice, to critically examine voice in practices related to digital media. In doing this, I advocate for digital ethnographic methods to engage these concepts, and to examine the potential of voice in digital mobile media. Specifically, I outline ethnographic methods involving the use of video (re)enactments of digital practices, and the use of reflective interviews to examine every day routines and movements in and around digital media (Pink 2012). I propose that observing and reflecting on such activities can generate insights into the significance these activities have in giving voice to those who are normally unheard.

Introduction

The new digitised media may offer some possibility for people labelled with mental illness to speak out about their experiences. With numerous interactive online spaces dedicated to talking about mental illness (e. g. Baylosis 2015; Boero/Pascoe 2012) people who have not done so before are able to exchange personal stories through digital forms (Couldry 2008). This may offer a correction to what Fraser (2000) calls 'hidden injustices', providing the means to distribute more widely the capacity to tell stories that challenge dominant representations of mental illness.

DOI 10.14361/dcs-2017-0214

As digital media technologies increasingly become interwoven in daily life, so too does our need to develop methodological frameworks that can explore the potential of voice apparently afforded by digital media. By voice, I mean what Couldry (2010) refers to as the capacity to tell one's own story – to self-represent. This does not involve a sonic aspect of voice, but a *process* of meaning making and self-interpretation of experience. Such a capacity is heightened with the ubiquity of digital mobile media, where daily routines revolve in, and around digital media, providing ample possibilities to connect, and circulate stories.

I propose a novel methodological framework to examine the potential of voice in digital media for people living with mental illness. I do this by drawing attention to an emerging field of research where literature on digital practices, mobility and mad studies intersect. Situated at the junction, is a common thread of voice. Specifically, I argue that an examination of this nexus, using digital ethnographic methods, can open up possibilities to explore how, and if, everyday use of digital mobile media technologies can contribute to social change through processes of voice. Though my focus is on mental illness, I suggest that this may be applicable to other fields of research concerning marginalised others who lack voice. To begin, it is first necessary to discuss voice as an analytical focus across these three fields of literature.

Finding mad voices

Mad studies stems from a history of activism that has brought forward the voices of marginalised others in political and social spheres. In particular, mad activists and scholars, decry human rights violations that many people have, and continue to experience under the control of psychiatric care (Lewis 2013). For mad studies, psychiatry is imbued with power relations where those that are labelled as 'mentally ill' are required to *listen* to 'experts' who speak about *their* experiences (Coles 2013). This sets the context for paternalistic relations between health professionals and patients, where the 'mentally ill' are treated as passive recipients of medical attention. This feeds into a history of coercion and harmful treatments, where the voices of the mad have been restricted, or even silenced, in decision-making about how to live their lives. Here, 'expert' voices, are privileged in defining madness and developing treatments (Russo and Beresford 2014)

Thus, for mad studies, voice is crucial to developing counter-narratives that can subvert psychiatric discourses that are privileged in representing realities and 'truths' regarding 'mental illness'. Like Couldry (2008; 2010), mad studies' use of the term voice, refers to the capacity to self-represent, and to self-define (Chamberlin 2005). Here, mad studies problematizes the concept of 'mental illness'. Not only is it predicated on oppressive power relations that exclude the mentally ill from defining their experience, but it also represents a sociopolitical construct that legitimises individualistic medical intervention that largely negates cultural and social factors that contribute to mental health (Cross 2010). Mad studies then, as a way of rebalancing power, bring mad voices to the academic table where experiential knowledge is legitimised in developing a critical discourse on psychiatry (McWade et al. 2015). It strategically reclaims, contests, and negotiates labels and treatments that are imposed on the mad by the psych-sciences (Crossley/Crossley 2001). Hence, the use of the terms 'mad', and 'madness' signifies the reappropriation of language, and an overturning of traditional hierarchies of voice (Lewis 2013).

Mad voices, digital practices, and mobility

Within the new Internet-based media, there has been an emergence of online sites and networks that in a similar vein to mad studies, brings the voices of the mad to the fore. Controversial 'pro-anna' sites, for instance, subvert medicalised conceptions of eating disorders, reframing these experiences as an identity position. Likewise, the Hearing Voices Network (see www.intervoice.org) rejects psychiatric conceptualisation of 'auditory hallucinations', presenting 'hearing voices' as an ordinary and meaningful human experience (Woods 2012). This is not the space here to discuss the potential merits and pitfalls of these online spaces and networks (refer to Dickins et al. 2011; Smith et al. 2013). But I use these examples to demonstrate how voice in new media can work to undermine dominant discourses of mental illness.

It would be technologically deterministic to suggest that such sites and networks are responsible for giving voice in a way that meaningfully destabilises oppressive power relations. Indeed, it might be tempting to praise the new digital media for fostering conditions that enable democratic participation by giving voice to the voiceless (Couldry 2008). But as Carpentier (2011) warns, such celebratory discourses espousing the participatory potential are detached from the political and social context that they are embedded within. Within these contexts, it is important to consider that mad knowledge generated through lived experiences continues to be cast aside in preference for dominant systems of knowledge of mental illness (Coles 2013). Accordingly, there are also numerous online spaces that are dedicated to propagating the medical model of mental illness (Baylosis 2015). And it is precisely this sociocultural context that mad studies and activists must contend with in its work to elevate mad voices. Thus, while new digital media may provide a platform for voice and agency, understanding its potential must take into account the broader sociocultural conditions that can restrict and amplify voices (Couldry 2010).

I propose that digital practices intersect with processes of voice, offering a conceptual tool that can examine the potential of voice in new media. Practices, here, can be defined as routinised and habitual performances based on affective and tacit knowledge and embodied competencies to carry out such actions

(Reckwitz 2002). In terms of *digital* practices I propose that this can involve daily habitual enactments of consuming, producing and sharing online content such as blogs, posts, pictures, music, videos and so on – practices that Lambart (2002) refers to as digital storytelling, and what Couldry (2008) suggests has potential to give voice through enabling self-representation. For digital practices related to madness, I suggest that there is tacit knowledge, and embodied skills that are needed to firstly interact with media devices and interfaces, and secondly to construct and comprehend narratives about madness and/or mental illness.

Here, narratives circulated in digital flows can be understood as forming part of their wider sociocultural conditions, where self-representations of madness are both shaped *by*, and *shape* social and cultural norms. Couldry (2013) explains, that a focus on practices 'decentres' the digital, where practices are viewed as an open range of activities that relate to, or are oriented around digital media. Hence, digital practices are not viewed in isolation, but are seen as forming part of what Fuller (2005: 2) describes as a media ecology, which involves the "dynamic inter-relations of processes and objects, beings and things, patterns and matter". This is important as it allows us to consider how digital practices *related* to madness interact with broader sociocultural contexts, where self-narratives are influenced and are shaped by sociocultural norms.

This allows us to conceptualise how agency and structure can resist and reproduce power through enactments of practices. Pink (2012) points out that De Certeau's (1998) theory of practice celebrates agency, where 'consumers' can negotiate the social world by employing tactics that can resist power within structuring forces in society. In contrast, Pink highlights that Bourdieu's notion of habitus sees that practices are reproduced through unconscious "internalisation of the social order in the human body" (Eriksen/Nielsen 2001: 130). Adopting a Foucauldian view, this can be seen in the internalisation of disciplinary power within 'docile' bodies (Foucault 1975). Although Bourdieu and de Certeau offer diverging perspectives, Pink argues that they reflect a debate regarding whether practices can be understood as resistant or normative. For Pink, practices should not be understood in terms of a maintenance-resistant binary, but as a multiplicity of potential that can reproduce *and* resist power to varying degrees. In term of digital practices, this opens up the scope to examine how differing self-representations can both reproduce and challenge power-laden narratives of mental illness.

The flow and circulation of self-narratives of madness through and within digital spaces can be conceptualised through mobility. This paradigm is concerned with the movement of things, people, and ideas (Sheller 2011). I suggest that there are two core elements of voice here. Firstly, digital practices of voice occur in movement, within and through virtual and physical environments because digital mobile media enables inhabiting and moving through multiple places simultaneously (Pink 2012). Here, the cultural norms of one environment can interact with other contexts. Take for instance, the ethos of the Hearing Voices

Movement, where online representations that normalise hearing voices, can shape daily offline practice related to how one then chooses to respond to auditory hallucinations. The second element of voice is the circulation of self-narratives through digital flows, which allows individuals to not only disseminate stories, but also to encounter the movement of other people, their narratives, information and images, which Urry (2007: 9) explains can "overlap, coincide and converge through digitized flows".

I propose that the mobilities paradigm, similar to practice theory, can offer an analytical tool to understand multiple potentials of voice in new media. Like practice theory, it provides conceptual scope to consider how the movement of mad voices through and within digitised spaces can reproduce and resist power. As Cresswell (2010) explains, mobility intersects with practice theory. Similar to Pink, Cresswell draws on Bourdieu (1990), to argue that movement is experienced, embodied and internalised. Mobility, like practice then, reflects the internalisation and reproduction of social order and power. In terms of madness, it is disciplinary power of psychiatry that is internalised, which regulates behaviour and reproduces normalised mobile subjects (Foucault 1975).

However, movements can also reject social norms and regulatory power. Entangled with Cresswell's (2010) notion of practice, are two further elements of mobility: actual movement and the representation of that movement. Here, physical movements are infused with cultural meaning through their cultural representations. Think representations of the untreated mentally ill free to roam in society as threatening, in need of treatment. Conversely, not all movements adhere to the representations that surround them. Representations can be challenged, and encoded with alternative meanings. For instance, mad activists encode 'mental illness' as an identity position (Graby 2015). These representations resist dominant understandings of mental illness, which leads to circulation of counter-narratives. Like digital practices then, mobility offers an analytical tool that interrogates voice in a manner that is open to multiple potential. In the following section, I outline how these concepts can be engaged methodologically.

Researching voice through digital ethnography

Building on ethnography, digital ethnography provides methodological tools to examine mad voices in digital media through engaging with digital practices and mobility. It employs ethnographic methods to understand culture, while exploiting the interactivity of digital media within research processes (Buccitelli 2016). Following Couldry (2013), researching digital practices involves paying close attention to the enactments of practices, observing what people actually, *do*, *say* and *feel*. Similarly, researching mobility entails what Sheller and Urry (2006: 217) describe as "observing directly or in digitally enhanced forms mobile bodies undergoing various performances" of movement. Digital ethnography as will be described, is particularly useful as it creates a *sense* of being with participants, in a way where it is possible to observe their movements through multiple offline-online spaces. This might otherwise difficult to achieve through direct observations (Pink 2012). Though, there may be variations of such approaches. I outline two methods as an example that can facilitate this, of which reflective interviews forms a basis for both approaches.

The use of reflective interviews, as developed by Pink (2012), builds on traditional interviews adding observations of practice and movement. As Pink argues, standard interviews do not allow actual observations of how a practice is performed; therefore they cannot delve into what is experienced, and the tacit knowledge that is evoked during the performance of practice. The use of reflective interviews through observation, specifically seeks to understand the details of practices, and the collective of the "non-verbalised way of knowing that it entails" (Pink 2012: 41). This is particularly useful for exploring how sociocultural norms interact with self-representations of madness.

Specifically, the use of reflective interviews can be used in conjunction with digital media technologies to observe practices and movement. Firstly, this can involve using participants' digital mobile devices as research probes within interviews. As Gómez Cruz (2016) points out, digital practices performed on personal devices can leave traces of their daily offline-online movements. According to Gómez Cruz, this not only provides representations of a given time, place or event, but they also reveal 'trajectories' of individual's everyday journeys as they move through everyday life. Often overlaid with geo-locative data, these movements can be drawn upon to invite participants to reflect on their digital practices and movements, and the significance these have in exercising voice.

In addition, following Sumartojo (2017) digital technologies can be used to observe practices in motion. This involves inviting participants to film their own digital practices, which can then be viewed with the researcher as part of a reflective interview as described above. Similar, to Gòmez Cruz's (2016), Sumartojo argues that video recordings are not just representations, but a 'visual trace' of individuals' everyday journeys and movements. According to Sumartojo and Pink, these can be viewed with participants, and used as a 'springboard' for reflection, and discussion. Sumartojo and Pink add that viewing these visual traces invites empathetic understandings as it emplaces the researchers in a position that allows a close viewing of the embodied experience of participants. In particular, it allows for a close observation of movements associated with performance of practice. By viewing this footage with participants, it can become possible to not only explore self-representations, but also how differing contexts interact to shape self-narratives.

Conclusion

There is a need to develop methodological frameworks that can interrogate the potential of digital mobile media technologies in giving voice to the mad. As I have proposed in this paper, the intersection of digital practices, mobility, and mad studies can open up research possibilities to examine the potential of voice in the new media. It can bring to light how people carry out their daily lives – as it is lived – to reveal how their everyday engagement with, and around digital media can reproduce and challenge oppressive power structures.

References

Alper M. (2017): Giving Voice: Mobile Communication, Disability, and Inequality, Cambridge, London: The MIT Press.

Baylosis, C. (2015): "Isolated connections: Re-writing the self and social support within online communities." In: Australia Rural and Remote Mental Health Symposium. Australian and New Zealand Mental Health Association.

Boero N./Pascoe C.J. (2012): "Pro-anorexia Communities and Online Interaction: Bringing the Pro-ana Body Online." In: Body & Society 18/2, pp. 27–57.

Carpentier, N. (2011): Media and Participation: A Site of Ideological-Democratic Struggle, Bristol: Intellect.

Chamberlin, J. (2005): "User/consumer Involvement in mental health service delivery." In: Epidemiologia e Psichiatria Sociale 14/1, pp. 10–14.

Coles, S. (2013): "Meaning, Madness and Marginalisation." In: S. Coles/S. Keenan/B. Diamond (eds.), Madness Contests: Power and Practice, Ross-on-Wye: PCCS Books.

Couldry, N. (2008): "Mediatization or mediation? Alternative understandings of the emergent space of digital storytelling." In: New Media & Society 10/3, pp. 373–391.

Couldry, N. (2010): Why Voice Matters, London: Thousand Oaks and New Delhi: SAGE.

Couldry, N. (2013): Media, Society, World, Cambridge, Malden: Polity Press.

Cresswell, T. (2010): "Towards a politics of mobility." In: Environment and Planning D: Society and Space 28/1, pp. 17–31.

Cross, S. (2010): Mediating Madness, Hampshire and New York: Palgrave Macmillan.

Crossley, M./Crossley, N. (2001): "'Patient' Voices, social movements and the habitus; how psychiatric survivors 'speak out'." In: Social Science & Medicine 52/10, pp. 1477–1489.

de Certeau, M./Guard, L./Mayold, P. (1998): The Practice of Everday Life, Volume 2: Living and Cooking, Minneapolis: University of Minnesota Press.

Dickins M./Thomas SL./King B. et al. (2011): "The role of the fatosphere in fat adults' responses to obesity stigma: a model of empowerment without a focus on weight loss." In: Qual Health Res 21/12, pp. 1679–1691.

Eriksen, TH./Nielsen, FS. (2001): A History of Anthropology, London: Pluto Press.

Foucault, M. (1975): Discipline and Punish: The Birth of the Prison, New York: Vintage Books.

Fraser, N. (2000): "Rethinking Recognition." In: New Left Review 3, pp. 107–120.

Fuller, M. (2005): Media Ecologies: Materialist Energies in Art and Technoculture, Cambridge and London: The MIT Press.

Gómez Cruz, E. (2016): "Trajectories: digital/visual data on the move." In: Visual Studies 31/4, pp. 335–343.

Graby, S. (2015): "Neurodiversity: bridging the gap between the disabled people's movement and the mental health survivors' movement." In: H. Spandler/J. Anderson (eds.): Madness, distress and the politics of disablement, Bristol and Chicago: Policy Press, pp. 231–244.

Lambart, J. (2002): Digital Storytelling: Capturing Lives, Creating Community, Berkeley: Digital Dinner Press.

Lewis, B. (2013): "A mad fight: psychiatry and disability activism." In: L. Davis (ed.): The Disability Studies Reader, New York and London: Routledge, pp. 115–131.

McWade B./Milton D./Beresford P. (2015): "Mad studies and neurodiversity: a dialogue." In: Disability & Society 30/2, pp. 305–309.

Parr H. (2008): Mental Health and Social Space: Towards Inclusionary Geographies?, Malden, Oxford: Blackwell

Pink S. (2012): Situating Everday Life: Practices and Places, Los Angeles/London/New Delhi/Sinapore/Washington: SAGE.

Reckwitz A. (2002): "Towards a Theory of Social Practices." In: European Journal of Social Theory 5/2, pp. 243–263.

Russo J./Beresford P. (2014): "Between exclusion and colonisation: seeking a place for mad people's knowledge in academia." In: Disability & Society 30/1, pp. 153–157.

Sheller M. (2011): "Mobility", Sociopedia.isa.

Sheller M./Urry J. (2006): "The New Mobilities Paradigm." In: Environment and Planning A 38, pp. 207–226.

Smith N./Wickes R./Underwood M. (2013): "Managing a marginalised identity in pro-anorexia and fat acceptance cybercommunities." In: Journal of Sociology 51/4, pp. 950–967.

Urry J. (2007): Mobilities, Cambridge and Malden: Polity Press.

An Experimental Autoethnography of Mobile Freelancing

Nadia Hakim Fernández

Abstract

This piece discusses an experimental ongoing research that began with my experience as an academic freelancer. It focuses on my experience of moving frequently within and between cities under specific work/ life conditions. An autoethnography provides insights not observable in quantitative research designs; and allows for access to embodied experience, along with reflections on emerging topics going beyond the purely personal, namely, mobility, advantage, and (work)place-making. This strategy allowed me to delineate the boundaries of the fieldsite across online and offline settings, including the digital technologies I share with other research participants. Personal maps of geolocalised trajectories overlapped with experiential accounts (photos, audio-notes, interviews, and hand-drawn maps) are included. An interpretational thickness emerges from this association of materials. The research process has inspired the development of a smartphone mobile application for documenting such experiences of mobile freelancing, yet to be created with developers, who are, in turn, participants in this research.

Introduction

At the end of my scholarship and university contract, I had to find a new space for continuing my work. At first, the flat I shared with my partner seemed suitable; it had "everything" I needed, and working there would keep my expenses low. My partner had a full-time contract in another university; I would have the required peace at home to develop my work. These conditions would channel all my time in my priority: finishing my thesis.

But I felt increasingly isolated and locked up at home while life continued outside. I began to move through the city everyday to get work done, including meeting with colleagues to learn about funding opportunities and new publications, or to help disentangle my mental processes. This experience made clear to me we are mistaken in believing that with the internet and digital tools, work can be done from anywhere and that reduced commuting times and increased comfort

DOI 10.14361/dcs-2017-0215

DCS | Digital Culture and Society | Vol. 3, Issue 2 | © transcript 2017

in working from home automatically translated into an improvement in one's life conditions.

While I was on scholarship, I could take some days to work away from colleagues, if necessary (e. g., while doing fieldwork or meeting a writing deadline). However, as an academic freelancer, I had no such choice. As isolation became my default, I took any chance to meet with colleagues and supervisors, attend seminars, and visit my research institute. I composed a mental map of "good" public libraries, "good" cafés (i. e., those with vs. without Wi-Fi – the former being useful for obvious reasons, and the latter when I needed to work undistracted). In these places, I noticed I wasn't alone in this situation; many mobile workers seemed to stay at a café for some hours with their laptops and/or having work meetings. I saw this transpiring in Lisbon, Brussels, Madrid, Bogotá, or Aarhus.

While this semi-stationary approach to finding a workspace each day originally felt like a routine adapted to my circumstances, it felt like a burden after some weeks – even physically, as I had to carry all my work equipment along, packing and unpacking each time I settled in to work somewhere else.

In December 2015 I began documenting these movements, taking pictures of my semi-stationary workplaces.

I present a methodology based on an autoethnographical approach (Ellis/ Bochner 2000; Pensoneau-Conway/Toyosaki 2011) applied to the investigation of work/life conditions not bounded to a determined location and happening both online and offline. This approach includes personal circumstances not registered in macro-approaches to contemporary labour conditions. Acknowledging that the "fieldsite" is actively constructed and not just entered (Amit 2000; Burrell 2009), autobiography and embodied first-hand experience are the starting points to this delimitation.

I contextualise this research within social anthropology and mobile methods, I then provide a preliminary analysis of three emerging dimensions of this study: mobility, privilege, and (work)place-making. I finally present materials currently included in this project, with a summary of its potential future development.

1. Autoethnography and Mobile Methods

1.1 Constructing the Fieldsite through First-Hand Experience

The autoethnographic approach (Ellis/Bochner 2000) and, specifically, a reflexive and "complete-member ethnography" (Pensoneau-Conway/Toyosaki 2011: 388) includes self-narratives as a way of turning the analytic lens towards oneself, to connect the researcher's own experiences to wider sociological concerns.

This is the methodology that delimits the boundaries of this research. First, as a reflexive exercise, it foregrounds the material conditions of the researcher with respect to financial and temporal constraints, personal circumstances and social conditionings that might impact her work and experience. Second, academic 'freelancing' has provided me with independence to think about the topics that interest me and apply an experimental methodology, as opposed to the topics and methodologies I would be required to choose within an institutional setting, with its hierarchies and particular cultures. Third, this work/lifestyle has also allowed me to experiment with the divisions between objectivity and subjectivity, and between researcher and participant, in a way not always possible within formal academic settings. Fourth, the fact that I have been self-funding this project also has an impact on its design (Pink, 2000): making my personal life the starting point for the fieldwork allows me to reduce research costs, which makes this project viable.

Detractors of autoethnogaphic methods claim, as Sara Delamont (2007), that autoethnography contradicts the basic principle of the social sciences, which is intended to give a voice to the powerless. However, I find this opportunity relevant for the social sciences. By bringing to light a situation that goes beyond personal circumstances and is, rather, connected to broader societal changes in the meaning and role of work, this project potentially locates a discussion of what 'power' and 'powerlessness' mean in the context of the current precariat (e.g. Standing 2011) – one in which the difference between manual and intellectual labour is not clear-cut.

1.2 A "Fieldsite" encompassing the Online and the Offline

Since the 1990s, discussions in social anthropology about the nature of the fieldsite have prompted going beyond the study of place-bounded cultural units (Gupta/Ferguson 1992; Amit 2000). Empirical works are multi-sited (Marcus 1995; Coleman/von Hellermann 2001) and their boundaries drawn as they develop. Geographical boundaries need not be construed as the natural containers for a project. Place is still important in multi-sited fieldwork, albeit treated from a different perspective, as a product of people's constant movement and connections (Cresswell 2006).

Our lives are interconnected with internet-based digital technologies (IBDTs from now on), and this has pushed this discussion even further (Burrell 2009). In this project I can track not just my own physical mobility – e.g., when I move from workplace A to B – but also my digital mobility, as when I follow a conversation through different digital platforms or follow weblinks. All mobile freelancers in this study use smartphones and laptop computers in their daily life and work, which means my fieldwork must account for their own mobility, both online and offline.

Such digital practices are embedded in everyday work and life along a continuum and should be understood together with the offline (Hine 2009; Miller/Slater, 2000). The result is a "scattered and sporadically connected 'field'"

(Amit 2000: 14). Indeed, my field is multi-sited; I am contacting participants in as many sites as I can, across different cities and events. I am interested in the processes generating a common social condition, that of the "mobile freelancer" in creative/intellectual fields. While united by research interests, we are not a collectivity attached to a physical location.

1.3 Mobile lives and mobile methods

Mobility is at the heart of this project. Devoid of an intrinsic meaning, movement becomes an object of study when associated with the uncertainties of navigating a precarious professional reality. Geographical mobility has traditionally been approached from sociology within the field of migration studies (Sheller 2014). Transnational migration studies are circumscribed by methodological nationalism (Wimmer/Glick-Schiller 2002), in that they construe movement as something happening into or out of nations or as a physical displacement between locations, forgoing what occurs in the in-between (Cresswell 2006). Finally, the field has systematically framed out the researcher's own transnational movements, and their impact in their research (Knowles 2000).

Mobility studies, eminently, is a "transdisciplinary field", which "brings together [...] sociology (inequality, power, hierarchies) [...] geography (territory, borders, scale) and [...] anthropology and media studies (discourses, representations, schemas), while inflecting each with a relational ontology of the co-constitution of subjects, spaces and meanings." (Sheller 20014: 47). The study of movement has evolved, then, from studying simply the displacement from a location to another, to a hybrid approach attentive to the historical, ideological, social constructedness of mobility.

Tim Cresswell distinguishes mobility from movement to highlight the meanings, experiences and practices of and surrounding movement (2006). He mentions three dimensions of mobility: 1) movement, i.e., moving between locations; 2) the meaning and narratives of this movement; and 3) the embodied experience of movement – as a way of being in the world. Mobility is generally conceived as flow, but in highlighting "movement + meaning + power" (Cresswell 2014: 108), Cresswell takes into account the politics of mobility, including questions about choice, rhythm, the experience of mobility as a burden or as a privilege, and friction – what slows or stops flows, and the redirection of these flows as a consequence. Even though power relations are transversal to my object of study, I argue its analysis cannot be simplified with the assumption that one can have more or less "mobility capital" (Kaufmann et al. 2004) or "network capital" (Urry 2007: 197). This hides the increasing degree of life precariousness characterising certain professional fields in specific regions such as academic research in southern Europe.

My aim is to adapt the methodologies to the study of mobility (Büscher/Urry 2009; Büscher et al. 2011). Facilitated by the autoethnographic approach, the researcher's mobility becomes a tool and a way of seeing (e. g. Knowles 2000; Pink 2000; Gómez-Cruz 2015). Annette Markham and Simon Lindgrem (2014) suggest to think creatively the adaption of the methods we apply to our current environment with IBDTs, allowing for constant connections, movement, and information generation. For instance, the photographs in Figure 1 were taken with my smartphone and laptop camera; meanwhile, maps showing trajectories are a feature built in by Google, which, though activated without my consent, I later started to use as well, to generate information for my research (see Map 1, 2, and 3).

2. Emerging questions

FRA-MAD. April 30, 2016.

This is at least the 6th plane I take in 4 months.
I have a horrible headache, and I know it is related to the pace of work this week: teaching a 5-hour class each day, and spending more hours after that preparing specifics for the next day. 4 hour-sleep nights, 2 coffees a day, fast meals. I had to do it, it is only a week, and it depends on my performance that I am called again next year to teach that same class. It does not only depend on that really. There is also the decreasing budgets for education in Denmark, even if these don't get close to the cuts made in Spain. But my performance is the only part I can control. I had to give it all and would do it again.
I'm heading to Madrid for a week to translate for this market research company. I don't like it, but I got some mental peace out of this job as my savings are over. I also have to write my article on young migrants. No idea how I will organise the week after, as my translation job will be finished, I am going to Lisbon Friday to Monday with my partner and I don't know what will the priority be between writing articles, preparing a seminar for my visit to Barcelona, crafting my postdoctoral project, or, if I decide to go to Colombia for a 6-month teaching gig, preparing the trip.

2.1 Mobility and immobility

Technologies relate movement and work. I focus here on semi-stationary work-places (Felstead et al. 2005) (working in places such as cafés or train stations). Though seemingly opposite, mobility and immobility unfold in my everyday life along a continuum.

Frictions, in my experience, slow down or momentarily stop my movement, such as when I must stay at home for several days in a row due to a computer breakdown or when my itinerant workplaces are not suited to the type of work I must do (e. g., a remote meetings while at a café with bad Wi-Fi).

IBDTs allow me to communicate with others, sometimes even in real time; however, the feeling of isolation persists. As noted in the introduction, I have experienced that the tension between isolation and interaction influences the motivations for moving as a freelancer. Also, mobility means instability, both locational and professional.

2.2 Privilege and disadvantage

Most of my family lives in Bogotá, and my partner's family in Brussels, so I make trips to be with them yearly. I enjoy travelling for leisure. Furthermore, the nature of my work as a researcher entails mobility, even for non-freelancing academics (e. g., attending conferences).

High mobility between cities is usually associated with white-collar professions and lifestyle choices, conceptualising such movement as 'privileged'; however, such a generalisation doesn't consider what physically moving implies. While my own frequent mobility is related to lifestyle and circumstances, it is also situated within a broader contemporary process of general precarisation of working conditions.

Even though it has been discussed that privileged workers don't know what real hardship means (Gregg, 2011), I cannot identify as privileged when encountering situations where my worth is not recognised and I experience un- or underemployment. My doctoral degree is not enough to secure a job in Spain. I currently have an income earned along my chosen professional trajectory, but that income is insufficient to cover basic expenses and cobbled together from various teaching gigs and translation jobs. My advantages fall very short of allowing me to reach my own expectations. The sociological question of downward mobility, understood as status loss (Sheller 2014), is a constant threat.

2.3 Workplace-making

Workplace-making encompasses seeking suitable places to work and creating a good environment on that site (in- or outside the home), including the transformation of those places we will occupy for just a few hours, to feel at ease and be productive.

Finding the right place to work – with conditions varying depending on the tasks to get done that day – constitutes part of my work routine, as imperative as any other activities of my job. The collage in Figure 1 llustrates that my frequent mobility is characterised by several semi-stationary workplaces. These photos show how the space is equipped with needed objects – laptop, mobile phone. The experience of constant workplace-making and changing routines implies the multiplication of variables to consider – Depending on the task at hand, where to go? What materials to take? –. My laptop and mobile phone are staple objects that provide me with an illusion of desired stability; meanwhile, the only other consistent feature in my workplace, besides these movable objects, is my own presence.

Figure 1: Mobile phone/laptop computer camera photos, in selected itinerant workplaces in Barcelona, Madrid, Aarhus and Bogotá. 2015–2017.

3. What's been done and future work

To date, the materials gathered include personal objectified geolocalised trajectories maps, overlapped with experiential accounts (e. g., interviews, audio-notes and hand-drawn maps), all of which inform each other and the broader analysis. This approach will be applied to all research participants, including myself.

Geolocalised digital information, gathered through mobile devices, stimulates the process of meaning-making of mobility. Relying on this information has the advantage of collecting materials *while* being produced and then allowing for visualisations. Google's built-in tracker includes timestamps and visualisation tools at different scales (see Map 1, 2 and 3).

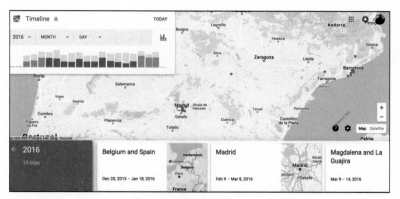

Map 1: Dots representing where I have been ("trips"), Spain. Hotspots: Barcelona – my former city of residence – and Madrid – my current one. 2016.

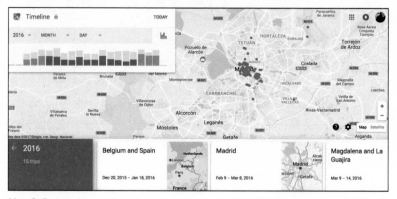

Map 2: Dots representing where I have been, Madrid. Working hotspots. 2017.

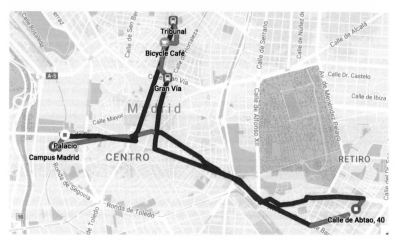

Map 3: Two-coloured line trajectory differentiating means of transport (bus/metro in a darker shade, walking in a lighter shade) linking the workplaces visited. February 20, 2017.

Such static information, however, as interesting as it is, provides no clue as to how to interpret the movement patterns (now) rendered visible, unless a contextual thickness is provided (Ferguson 2011). The same happens for other kinds of materials collected "on the move", such as photographs or audiovisual recordings.

In addition, we don't control the definitions of key concepts in the software gathering this geolocalised information. For instance, only long-distance movement, and not movement within a city, registers in GoogleMaps as "trips." in specific visualisations.

Besides, static information frames out aspects of intimate experience. As a first strategy to "contextually thicken" the subjective experience of my own mobility, I started collecting videos, photos, and texts while moving. It will be interesting to combine this multimedia content within scholarly-acceptable publication formats. For now, let me share 2 screenshots of a video of myself walking home from a public library (Figure 2). I explain that:

Figure 2: "I had to change work locations four times, but I am happy I left the apartment and got things done."

It is desirable to develop a technological application to collect geolocalised information for the participants, anchoring their photos, videos and audio notes on the map with tags produced while in movement. Interestingly, some of these participants are developers; mobile freelancing is common to them. They gave me ideas awaiting further funding for collaborative development. As it is materially impossible to follow the participants physically, I will instead intercept their flows (Burell 2009), wherever I am able, through this anchored information.

Conclusion

An object of study emerged from observing my situation and its similarities to that of many workers in the creative/intellectual fields. Suspecting my personal circumstances reflect a broader phenomenon, I chose to analyse them as part of a study on structural precariousness. Autoethnographic methods have proved powerful in drawing the boundaries of a study that cannot be delimited by geographical locations or place-bounded groups, but rather necessarily combine following connections with the interception of the experience of movement through anchoring personal accounts to geolocalised trajectories. I have suggested a coherent methodology encompassing personal experience, conceptual frameworks and specific techniques. Adding layers for greater contextual thickness is a work in progress, open to creative methods.

This research offers for now more questions than answers, but hopefully productive ones. What is the relationship between mobility and immobility, and between these two, IBDTs and privilege? What are "privilege" and "disadvantage" in our current labour markets? What is the difference between being mobile forcingly vs. willingly? What role mobile workplace-making plays in the search of stability and connection in freelance work?

Acknowledgements

I thank Professor Annette Markham for her support and ideas for this project. I extend my thanks as well to the reviewers who pointed to interesting authors and helped direct my argument.

References

Amit, Vered (2000): Constructing the Field. Ethnographic Fieldwork in the Contemporary World, London: Routledge.

Burrell, Jenna (2009): "The Field Site as a Network: A Strategy for Locating Ethnographic Research." In: Field Methods 21/2, pp. 181–199.

Büscher, Monika/Urry, John (2009): "Mobile Methods and the Empirical." In: European Journal of Social Theory 12/1, pp. 99–116.

Büscher, Monika/Urry, John/Witchger, Katian (eds.) (2011): Mobile Methods, London: Routledge.

Coleman, Simon/Pauline von Hellerman (eds.) (2011): Multi-Sited Ethnography. Problems and Possibilities in the Translocation of Research Methods, Oxon: Routledge.

Cresswell, Tim (2006): On the Move, London: Routledge.

Cresswell, Tim (2014): "Frictions." In: Peter Adey/David Bissell/Kevin Hannam/ Peter Merriman/Mimi Sheller. The Routledge Handbook of Mobilities, Oxon: Routledge, pp. 107–115.

Gómez-Cruz, Edgar (2015): "Trajectories: Digital/visual Data on the Move." In: Visual Studies 1/4, pp. 335–43.

Delamont, Sara (2007): "Arguments against Auto-Ethnography." In: Qualitative Researcher 4, pp. 5–8.

Ellis, Carolyn/Bochner, Arthur P. (2000): Autoethnography, personal narrative, and reflexivity: Researcher as subject. In: Norman K. Denzin/Yvonna S. Lincoln (eds.), Handbook of qualitative research, Thousand Oaks: Sage, pp. 733–768.

Felstead, Alan/Nick Jewson/Sally Walters (2005): Changing Places of Work, New York: Palgrave Macmillan.

Ferguson, James (2011): "Novelty and Method. Reflections on Global Fieldwork." In: Simon Coleman/Pauline von Hellerman (eds.), Multi-Sited Ethnography. Problems and Possibilities in the Translocation of Research Methods, Oxon: Routledge, pp. 194–208.

Gregg, Melissa (2011): Work's Intimacy, Cambridge: Polity.

Gupta, Akhil/Ferguson, James (1992): "Beyond 'Culture': Space, Identity, and the Politics of Difference." In: Cultural Anthropology 7/1, pp. 6–23.

Hine, Christine (2009): "Question One: How Can Internet Researchers De ne the Boundaries of Their Project?" In: Nancy Baym/Annette Markham (eds.), Internet Inquiry, London: Sage, pp. 1–20.

Marcus, George E. (1995): "Ethnography In/of the World System: The Emergence of Multi-Sited Ethnography." In: Annual Review of Anthropology 24, pp. 95–117.

Markham, Annette N/Simon Lindgren (2014): "From Object to Flow: Network Sensibility, Symbolic Interactionism, and Social Media." In: Symbolic Interaction and New Social Media 43, pp. 7–41.

Miller, Daniel/Slater, Don (2000): The Internet. An Ethnographic Approach, Oxford: Berg.

Pensoneau-Conway, Sandra L./Toyosaki, Satoshi (2011): "Automethodology: Tracing a Home for Praxis-Oriented Ethnography." In: International Journal of Qualitative Methods 10/4, pp. 378–400.

Pink, Sarah (2000): "'Informants' who come 'home'". In: Vered Amit (ed.), Constructing the Field. Etnographic Fieldwork in the Contemporary World, London: Routledge, pp. 96–119.

Sheller, Mimi (2014): "Sociology after the mobilities turn". In: Peter Adey/David Bissell/Kevin Hannam/Peter Merriman/Mimi Sheller (eds.), The Routledge Handbook of Mobilities, Oxon: Routledge, pp. 45–54.

Standing, Guy (2011): The Precariat. The New Dangerous Class, London: Bloomsbury Academic.

Urry, John (2007): Mobilities, Cambridge: Polity Press.

Wimmer, Andreas/Nina Glick Schiller (2002): "Methodological Nationalism and beyond: Nation-State Building, Migration and the Social Sciences." In: Global Networks 2/4, pp. 301–34.

In Conversation with ...

Biographical Notes

Pablo Abend is the scientific coordinator of the DFG Research Training Group *Locating Media*, University of Siegen.

Donald N. Anderson teaches at the *Southwest University of Visual Arts* in Tucson, USA, and blogs about the history of technology and urban space at thirdcarriageage.com.

Cherry Baylosis is a PhD candidate at the *Department of Media and Communications*, University of Sydney.

Jamie Coates is a visiting fellow at Sophia University, Tokyo.

Samuel Gerald Collins is Professor of Cultural Anthropology at the *Department of Sociology, Anthropology and Criminal Justice*, Towson University, Baltimore, Maryland.

Nadia Hakim Fernández is part of the *Future Making Space*, University of Aarhus and of the *Catalan Institute of Anthropology*, Barcelona.

Anne Ganzert is research assistant for the project *Media and Participation. Between Demand and Entitlement*, University of Konstanz.

Theresa Gielnik is student assistant for the project *Media and Participation. Between Demand and Entitlement*, University of Konstanz.

Philip Hauser is PhD candidate in *Media Studies* and associated to the project *Media and Participation. Between Demand and Entitlement*, University of Konstanz.

Julia M. Hildebrand is a PhD candidate in *Communication, Culture and Media*, Drexel University, Philadelphia.

Geoffrey Hobbis is an associated postdoctoral fellow at the *Centre de Recherche et de Documentation sur l'Océanie* (Marseille) and a lecturer at the University of British Columbia (Okanagan).

Heather Horst is Professor in the *Department of Media and Communications*, University of Sydney.

Julia Ihls is student assistant for the project *Media and Participation. Between Demand and Entitlement*, University of Konstanz.

Asko Lehmuskallio is Senior Researcher at the *COMET Research Centre* at the Faculty of Communication Sciences, University of Tampere, and Chair of *ECREA TWG Visual Cultures*.

Rashmi M. is a PhD candidate in the *School of Social Sciences* at the National Institute of Advanced Studies, Bangalore.

David Morley is Professor of Communications at *Goldsmiths College*, University of London.

Roger Norum is a postdoc research fellow at the DFG Research Training Group *Locating Media*, University of Siegen.

Isabell Otto is head of the subproject "Smartphone-Communities" of the research group *Media and Participation. Between Demand and Entitlement* and Professor for *Media Studies*, University of Konstanz.

Anna Lisa Ramella is a PhD candidate at the DFG Research Training Group *Locating Media*, University of Siegen.

Noel B. Salazar is Research Professor in the *Social and Cultural Anthropology Department*, University of Leuven.

Maria Schreiber is a postdoc researcher at the *Department of Sociology*, University of Vienna.

Marion Schulze is a senior lecturer in gender studies at the *Center for the Understanding of Social Processes (MAPS)*, University of Neuchâtel, Switzerland.

Elisa Serafinelli is research associate at the *Information School*, University of Sheffield, United Kingdom.

Tristan Thielmann is professor for *Science, Technology and Media Studies*, University of Siegen.

Mikko Villi is Professor of Journalism in the *Department of Language and Communication Studies* at the University of Jyväskylä, Finland.

Stefan Werning is Associate Professor for *New Media and Game Studies*, Faculty of Humanities, Utrecht University.

[transcript]

Gesellschaft für Medienwissenschaft (Hg.)
Zeitschrift für Medienwissenschaft 17
Jg. 9, Heft 2/2017: Psychische Apparate

Oktober 2017, 216 Seiten, kart., zahlr. z.T. farb. Abb., 24,99 €,
ISBN 978-3-8376-4083-0, Open Access

■ Die Zeitschrift für Medienwissenschaft steht für eine kulturwissenschaftlich orientierte Medienwissenschaft, die Untersuchungen zu Einzelmedien aufgreift und durchquert, um nach politischen Kräften und epistemischen Konstellationen zu fragen. Sie stellt Verbindungen zu internationaler Forschung ebenso her wie zu verschiedenen Disziplinen und bringt unterschiedliche Schreibweisen und Textformate, Bilder und Gespräche zusammen, um der Vielfalt, mit der geschrieben, nachgedacht und experimentiert werden kann, Raum zu geben.

Heft 17, Psychische Apparate, hg. von Kathrin Peters und Stephan Trinkaus, geht den Verbindungen zwischen Medienwissenschaft und Theorien des Psychischen nach. Es fragt, ob sich Psychoanalyse als eine Theorie der Medialität verstehen lässt, der Verschränktheit von Innen und Außen, von Eros und Thanatos, Symbolischem und Imaginärem, Ab- und Anwesenheit, Individuellem und Sozialem.

Die Beiträge zeigen: Wo Theorien des Psychischen nicht lediglich als narratologische oder als Figuren-Analyse betrieben werden, tritt anderes hervor: eine grundlegend relationale Perspektive, die nicht nur Verhältnisse zwischen Menschen, sondern auch ihre Beziehung zu Apparaten, ja das Psychische selbst als Apparat oder Maschine beschreibbar macht.